Lincoln

and

Oregon Country Politics

in the

Civil War Era

Also by Richard W. Etulain—A Selective List

Author

Owen Wister

Ernest Haycox

Re-imagining the Modern American West: A Century of Fiction, History, and Art

Telling Western Stories: From Buffalo Bill to Larry McMurtry

Beyond the Missouri: The Story of the American West

Seeking First the Kingdom: Northwest Nazarene University, A Centennial History

Coauthor

Conversations with Wallace Stegner on Western History and Literature

The American West: A Twentieth-Century History

Editor

Writing Western History: Essays on Major Western Historians

Does the Frontier Experience Make America Exceptional?

César Chávez: A Brief Biography with Documents

New Mexican Lives: Profiles and Historical Stories

Western Lives: A Biographical History of the American West

Lincoln Looks West: From the Mississippi to the Pacific

Coeditor

Basque Americans

Fifty Western Writers: A Bio-Bibliographical Guide

A Bibliographical Guide to the Study of Western American Literature

Faith and Imagination: Essays on Evangelicals and Literature

The Twentieth-Century West: Historical Interpretations

Religion and Culture

The American West in the Twentieth Century: A Bibliography

Religion in Modern New Mexico

By Grit and Grace: Eleven Women Who Shaped the American West

Portraits of Basques in the New World

With Badges and Bullets: Lawmen and Outlaws in the Old West

The Hollywood West

Wild Women of the Old West

Chiefs and Generals

Lincoln

and

Oregon Country Politics

in the

Civil War Era

Richard W. Etulain

Oregon State University Press ••• Corvallis

The paper in this book meets the guidelines for permanence and durability of the Committee on Production Guidelines for Book Longevity of the Council on Library Resources and the minimum requirements of the American National Standard for Permanence of Paper for Printed Library Materials Z39.48-1984.

Library of Congress Cataloging-in-Publication Data
Etulain, Richard W.
  Lincoln and Oregon country politics in the Civil War era / Richard W. Etulain.
    pages cm
  Includes bibliographical references and index.
  ISBN 978-0-87071-702-4 (pbk. : alk. paper) -- ISBN 978-0-87071-703-1 (e-book)
1. Oregon--History--Civil War, 1861-1865. 2. Oregon--Politics and government--1859-1950. 3. Lincoln, Abraham, 1809-1865. I. Title.
  E526.E88 2012
  979.5'041--dc23

                              2012043540

First published in 2013 by Oregon State University Press
Printed in the United States of America

Oregon State University Press
121 The Valley Library
Corvallis OR 97331-4501
541-737-3166 • fax 541-737-3170
http://osupress.oregonstate.edu

For the Partch Family

• • •

Three Oregonians

David Scofield Partch: son-in-law—caring, dependable PA
Jackie Etulain Partch: daughter—librarian extraordinaire
Adam Scofield Partch: grandson—much-beloved young Lincoln

Contents

Preface

One day after the presidential elections in November 1864 Abraham Lincoln telegraphed the tentative results to his wonderfully opinionated but supportive old friend from Springfield, Dr. Anson G. Henry, in faraway Washington Territory. Lincoln told the political doctor that it looked increasingly likely he had been reelected to a second term. Lincoln's strong connection to Dr. Henry personalizes the president's persisting political links to the Oregon Country, stretching back nearly two decades to the mid-1840s. Although Lincoln spent but a few days west of the Mississippi River and never traveled farther west than eastern Kansas, he had a demonstrable impact on the politics of the American West, his influences radiating out even to the most distant of the western subregions, the Oregon Country, or the Pacific Northwest.

This brief volume traces these increasingly strong political bonds between Abraham Lincoln and the Oregon Country. It is primarily a study of political history, although discussions sometimes spill over, in abbreviated form, into other areas such as Indian relations, military policies, and North-South ideological conflicts. Lincoln's fingerprints on the Oregon Country appear clearly in his political connections with the region. In fact, no national figure did more than Abraham Lincoln to shape regional politics in the Oregon Country in the 1860s.

The story moves chronologically from the 1840s to the mid-1860s—and then beyond. The first chapter traces Lincoln's and Oregon's pre-1850 experiences and the Illinois politician's contacts with the Far Corner. Chapter 2 treats Lincoln's connections with the Oregon Country in the 1850s, especially through his friendships with Illinoisans who had moved to Oregon: David Logan, Dr. Henry, Simeon Francis, and Edward D. Baker. The crucial election of 1860 and Lincoln's roles nationally and in the Pacific Northwest are the subject of Chapter 3. The book's longest section, Chapter 4, deals with Lincoln and the Oregon Country in the Civil War years, from 1861 to 1864. Chapter 5 discusses Lincoln's actions and successes in his reelection of 1864. The final section, Chapter 6, focuses on Lincoln's last months and more extensively on the Oregon Country's reactions to his tragic assassination and the region's gradual memorializing of Lincoln, especially in the Lincoln centennial and bicentennial celebrations. The concluding bibliographical section features extensive discussions of the major sources for this study and includes a thorough listing of these books and essays.

This short study advances a central thesis about Abraham Lincoln, the Oregon Country, and the Civil War. For well over a century, historians have portrayed most westerners, and nearly all inhabitants of the Oregon Country, as distant spectators, uninvolved in the events and discussions that divided the United States leading to and within its most fractious years of conflict. That view no longer serves well in understanding the ties between Abraham Lincoln and the Oregon Country during the Civil War era. Instead, the Pacific Northwest tied itself to the nation, including links to politics, Indian relations, military policies, civil and legal rights, and northern and southern sociocultural conflicts. This volume attempts to illuminate the clear connections between the East and West by focusing on Lincoln's political connections to the Oregon Country. Rather than uninvolved spectators, residents of the Pacific Northwest reacted strongly to national ideas and events of the Civil War years. Their political bonds with Lincoln are but one clear indication of their participation in national happenings in the Civil War era.

This book also serves as an exemplar of what historian Elliott West terms the Greater Reconstruction. West contends that we need to rethink and rewrite mid-nineteenth-century American history in order to demonstrate that the two most important events of the time—the expansion of the American West and the Civil War—were not separate, isolated events. Instead they were joined experiences, mutually shaping one another from the 1840s to about 1880. This examination of Lincoln's political connections with the Oregon Country provides one example of how studies of the Greater Reconstruction illuminate the interrelations of East and West through notably significant cross-continental influences. Tracing these lines of influence stretching from Washington, D.C., to the Far Northwest illuminates both Civil War era politics as well as the political development of the Oregon Country.

• • •

I am much indebted to several persons and institutions for their help in preparing this study of cross-continental politics. Staff members at the Abraham Lincoln Presidential Library (Springfield, Illinois), the Oregon Historical Society (Portland), the University of Oregon Library (Eugene), the Washington State Library (Olympia), the State of Washington Archives (Olympia), the University of Washington (Seattle), the Idaho State Historical Society (Boise), and the Montana Historical Society (Helena) have been particularly helpful. I am also grateful to Tom Booth of the Oregon State University Press for encouragement and to Sylvia Frank Rodrigue and Sara Vaughn Gabbard, two superb Lincoln ladies, for delightful email exchanges on these topics. At the OSU Press, I also wish to thank Jo Alexander, Micki Reaman, Judy Radovsky, and Mary Braun for their aid and encouragement. I am indebted, too, to Tom Lapsley, enthusiastic Lincoln collector, for information concerning burial sites of Lincoln's friends, the locations of Lincoln sculptures, and other useful material about Lincoln in the Pacific Northwest.

Since this is my fiftieth book, I also wish to mention here those who have especially influenced my career. Bob Woodward, Edwin R. Bingham, and Earl Pomeroy were superb undergraduate and graduate mentors. Bob Swanson and Ron Hatzenbuehler at Idaho State and Frank Szasz of the University of New Mexico were encouraging colleagues. Editors David Holtby, Chuck Rankin, Joanne O'Hare, and Sylvia Frank Rodrigue have also been generous with their time and help. More generally, I owe an intellectual debt to Earl Pomeroy. He urged his students to think continentally, to see continuities as well as discontinuities between the East and the American West. Without abandoning the path-breaking earlier contentions of Frederick Jackson Turner, Pomeroy, by example, showed fellow historians how to understand the shaping eastern influences on the trans-Mississippi West. This study follows Pomeroy's point of view.

I'm also indebted to several editors and publishers for permitting me to draw on without merely repeating my previous writings on Abraham Lincoln and the trans-Mississippi American West. They are Sylvia Frank Rodrigue at the Southern Illinois University Press for allowing use of information in my *Lincoln Looks West: From the Mississippi to the Pacific* (2010); Gregory Lalire at *Wild West*, "Lincoln Looks

West" (April 2009); Molly Holz at *Montana: The Magazine of Western History*, "Abraham Lincoln: Political Founding Father of the American West" (summer 2009); and Sara Vaughn Gabbard at *Lincoln Lore*, "Lincoln and the Oregon Country" (spring 2012). These permissions are greatly appreciated.

And most of all, I am indebted to Joyce—for fifty years of support and encouragement.

Chapter 1: Lincoln Looks Toward Oregon

The unexpected telegram from Washington, D. C., arrived in Springfield, Illinois, in mid-August 1849. Its message was direct and requested a quick answer: would the Honorable Abraham Lincoln, recently retired U.S. Congressman from Illinois, accept appointment as secretary of the new Oregon Territory? With little deliberation, the tall, gaunt politician from the Prairie State rejected the offer. One month later another surprising message carried a second offer: would Mr. Lincoln take the governor's chair of Oregon? After a few days of deliberation and mixed-up, delayed messages, Lincoln also turned down the second overture.[1]

So, in late summer and early fall of 1849 Abraham Lincoln chose not to become an Oregonian. But despite his rejection of these two offers, Lincoln forged several links with the Oregon Country. In fact, even before 1849, Lincoln had connected with Oregon, and after several of his Illinois friends immigrated to the Pacific Northwest in the 1850s, those connections became much stronger. Later, as president, Lincoln tied himself to the Far Corner by appointing dozens of officials in the new state of Oregon, the territory of Washington, and the new territories of Idaho and Montana, the latter two of which began during his administration. He also supported railroad, land, and agricultural and education measures that had a lasting impact on the Oregon Country. During his presidency, letters from his friends and political appointees kept Lincoln abreast of political, economic, military, and ideological clashes and combinations that characterized the region during his years in the White House.[2]

An understanding of Abraham Lincoln's expanding links with the Oregon Country broadens our perception of our greatest president. Those connections also enlarge the meaning and significance of the Far Northwest as part of the Civil War era. Seen whole, Lincoln's links with the Pacific Northwest are moments of illumination for understanding his notable leadership roles as well as for comprehending the expansion and development of the Oregon Country. Together, these Lincoln links and Oregon Country advancements add another layer of meaning and significance to the history of the mid-nineteenth-century United States, particularly its political history.

• • •

Before Abraham Lincoln connected with the Oregon Country, he and that region, separately, stumbled through a series of stuttering steps. In Lincoln's case, his insular family experiences, his inadequate education, and his initial political allegiances circumscribed his earliest acquaintance with the trans-Mississippi American West. Although his three states of residence in his early years (1809-1831)—Kentucky, Indiana, and Illinois—were part of "the West," he knew little about the region beyond the Mississippi. His less than one year of formal schooling also limited his geographical knowledge. In the early 1830s, when Lincoln became a member of the Whigs, both that political party and Lincoln exhibited much less interest in the American West than did the expansionist Democrats.[3]

During the 1830s Lincoln was finding his way as a Whig politician in Illinois. Elected to the state legislature in 1834, he gradually assumed a leading role in his party during the eight years he served in the Illinois legislature. Revealingly, Lincoln avoided the Jeffersonian-Jacksonian Democratic political tradition that won over so many frontier areas like those of Lincoln's earliest residences. Instead, he joined the Whigs, declaring Henry Clay his "beau ideal" as a political leader. Like most other Whigs, Lincoln supported Clay's program of internal improvements: banks, tariffs, roads (and later railroads), expansive land policies for settlers, canals, and improved educational programs. Whigs like Lincoln were convinced that these steps were the best route for individual improvement as well as national economic expansion. Lincoln's affinity for these economic plans, which had begun with Federalist Alexander Hamilton and expanded as the American System under John Quincy Adams, remained centrally important to Lincoln after he switched to the Republican Party in the mid-1850s. He spoke for internal improvements as part of the Republican platforms in the elections of 1856 and 1860, and they became, as well, parts of his presidential policies from 1861 to 1865.[4]

Although internal improvements were notably important for westerners from the early 1840s onward, Lincoln remained relatively silent on other political issues significant to residents west of the Mississippi. Conversely, Lincoln's long-time political rival in Illinois, Stephen A. Douglas, emerged as an enthusiastic cheerleader for western expansion, much earlier than Lincoln. As a Democratic legislator in Illinois (1836-1837), a member of the U. S. House of Representatives (1843-1847), and a U. S. senator (1847-1861), Douglas often stood in the vanguard of political leaders calling for the development of the trans-Mississippi American West. Serving as chair of the territorial committees in both the House and Senate, Douglas formulated and led expansionistic policies. But, like most of the leading Whigs, Lincoln was slower to sense the growing importance of the West in America's future.[5]

Even in the early to mid-1840s, as controversies swirled around the annexation of Texas, the settlement of the Joint Occupation of Oregon, and the outbreak of the Mexican-American War, Lincoln was tardy in his reactions. That would change when he became a member of Congress (1847-1849), where he was forced to become involved in the verbal battles over the Mexican-American War. He also took part in the increasingly complex and volatile congressional debates about Oregon's becoming a territory.

A few minor documents from the beginning of the 1840s mention Lincoln's links with Oregon. As early as 1843, he is cited as attending meetings in Illinois concerning the "Oregon question."[6] During the election of 1844, news of settlers heading up the Oregon Trail rang across the Illinois prairies and filled the columns of the state's newspapers, setting off verbal jousts over expansion. The Joint Occupation of Oregon moved to the arena center, and Lincoln, at least, cast a half glance toward Oregon. In a speech in July 1846, he dealt with "the Oregon Question," the Mexican-American War and the annexation of Texas, the latter of which had occurred the previous year.[7]

Lincoln's position on Oregon was not clear, however. One Illinois newspaper urged him to be more forthright on the British-American competition for the Oregon Country, especially after it became obvious that he planned to run for U. S. Congress. Was he "for 54 4[0], or [was he] for 'compromising' away our Oregon territory to England." The newsman added: "This, the People ought to know before they vote next August. No shiffling, Mr. Lincoln. Come out, square."[8]

Lincoln did not respond to the issue, keeping silent on Oregon until its possible territorial organization forced itself on him in 1848, during his time in Congress.

•••

Meanwhile, Oregon transitioned from its first stages of exploration and settlement to new cultural and economic developments in the 1830s and 1840s as Lincoln emerged as an Illinois and national politician. By the mid-1840s two spheres of influence had gradually evolved in the Oregon Country. The more powerful and longer-lasting of the two, the Hudson's Bay Company (HBC) of England, dominated much of the region for two decades, especially after Dr. John McLoughlin, the towering, imperial, and indefatigable HBC leader, arrived at Ft. Vancouver in 1824. For twenty-one years, spinning out his influence like an unbreakable web, the lordly McLoughlin controlled much of the economy and development of the Pacific Northwest.

The other sphere of influence, commencing with the arrival of American missionaries in the mid-1830s, promised much but eventually proved to be a rather weak competitor to the powerful HBC. In 1834, Jason Lee founded a Methodist mission in the Willamette Valley, near present-day Salem. Two years later, Marcus and Narcissa Whitman and Henry and Eliza Spalding, sponsored by a combined Protestant group, arrived in the Northwest to begin missions at Waiilatpu (close to Walla Walla, Washington) and Lapwai (near Lewiston, Idaho), respectively. Although the missionaries came to convert and "civilize" Indian tribes of the Northwest, conversions were few and problems numerous, and mounting. By 1843, Lee had been recalled from Oregon, and the

Dr. John McLoughlin (left), chief factor of the Hudson's Bay Company, and Jason Lee (right), leader of the Oregon Methodist Mission, competed for dominance in the Oregon Country in the 1830s and 1840s. (Oregon Historical Society Research Library, McLoughlin, carte de visite 707; Lee, image 8342.)

Whitmans and Spaldings faced increased opposition from their Native charges and from Catholic priests, who were often more successful in converting Indians than the Protestants.

Just as the missions were in increasingly shaky circumstances, farmers began to dream of Oregon. They were forced to ponder a move west by the tough economic times invading the Ohio and Mississippi river valleys, particularly following the Panic of 1837. Travelers, congressmen, and other cheerleaders trumpeted the rich, available lands in the coastal Pacific Northwest, a region of mild climate, few troublesome Indians, and agricultural riches.[9]

And the emigrants came. The first group traveled the Oregon Trail in 1841. By the mid-1840s, roughly another four thousand had come, adding up to more than five thousand Americans in the Oregon Country.

The mounting numbers of newcomers traversing the Oregon Trail called for new decisions. In 1846, the Joint Occupation agreement signed in 1818 between the British and the Americans ended; the Hudson's Bay Company retreated from Fort Vancouver to Fort Victoria, just north of what eventually became the American-Canadian border. In the same year, British and American diplomats hammered out a series of agreements that set the boundary between Canada and U. S. at the 49th parallel.[10]

These events on the north Pacific coast demanded attention, first within the territory and then on the national scene. Before long, the controversies swirling about the present and future of the Oregon Country came within the purview of Abraham Lincoln. By the mid-1840s the U. S. was pulsating with conflicts rolling out of the American West, especially from Texas and Oregon. When the Democratic candidate, James K. Polk, asserted that as president he would "re-annex" Texas and "re-occupy" Oregon, expansion was in the air. Texas, Oregon, and, soon, the Southwest in the Mexican-American War, were front-page news. And even a reluctant, non-expansionist Whig like Abraham Lincoln would be forced to take more explicit stances. These controversies led Lincoln into his first contacts with the Oregon Country.

• • •

As these events were sweeping up to a peak of national controversy, Oregonians were trying to deal with a series of vexing problems. Even before the Oregon Country became legal U. S. territory, residents were organizing politically. A number of pressing needs converged to impel them to form what would become the Provisional Government of Oregon. When Ewing Young, a former fur trader, died without a proper will in 1841, when increasing numbers of emigrants came on the Oregon Trail after 1841, and when marauding wolves endangered the Willamette Valley's growing herds of livestock, residents organized a series of meetings to deal with these perplexing issues. In 1843, building on the momentum of previous gatherings to establish a court to probate Young's will and to deal with land and other topics bothering incoming immigrants, the so-called "Wolf Meetings" moved steadily toward a tentative regional government. Then, on 2 May 1843, at Champoeg, former mountain man and now Oregon resident Joseph L. Meek called for a dramatic vote for or against organizing a new government. Folklore, exaggeration, and controversy blanket and complicate what is known about these important decisions at Champoeg. But a majority of attendees—either by a close vote or by "a large majority"—supported the American settlers' organizational efforts. A Provisional Government of Oregon was soon on the books. In continually revised form it served Oregon until March 1849. It would "govern," however tentatively, a wide swath of present-day areas, including Oregon, Washington, Idaho, portions of Montana and Wyoming, and western Canada.[11]

Some of the issues the Provisional Government discussed were similar to those facing Lincoln when he became president in 1861 and had to appoint territorial officials in several areas of the American West. How would the new government be organized politically? Who would hold the reins of power? How would a balance of leadership be achieved between elected and appointed office holders? And of central importance to the mounting numbers of immigrants: what was to be done about land ownership, military organization, and dealings with Indians?

In its half-dozen years of existence, the Provisional Government inched forward by slow accretion. After trying out an elected three-person executive, the government moved to a single governor, George Abernethy, who served from 1845 to 1848. The legislature, first a small committee, evolved into the Oregon House of Representatives, also in effect from 1845 to 1848. Similarly, launched with one supreme judge and lower courts, the judiciary branch expanded into a Supreme Court, with other lower courts dealing with probate and other legal matters. All these moves toward organization began while the Oregon Country was under Joint Occupation; once that competitive international agreement ended in 1846, the Provisional Government took on more significance.

The major challenge facing the Provisional Government was two-pronged. Officials wanted to adopt a land policy that drew new settlers to Oregon but one that also satisfied them once they arrived. Heeding these growing needs, the government generously provided land for new residents in 1843. Claimants could hold 640 acres of land if they improved on it. (Subsequent federal legislation allowed for 320 acres for each adult man and another 320 for his wife.) Here was a forerunner of the famous Homestead Act that Lincoln touted as an ambitious Republican politician in the 1850s and that he signed as president in 1862. These generous grants of land in the fertile Willamette Valley were a huge magnet in drawing land-hungry and ambitious farmers to the Oregon Country. But how to gain the land from Indian tribes and to secure land titles recognized in an established court of law were particularly difficult because the Provisional Government was extra-legal, not recognized by either the British or American governments before 1846, nor by the U. S. government after the areas became American territory in 1846.[12]

Oregon's sociocultural profile rapidly changed in the later 1840s and early 1850s as a result of the pipeline of emigrants continuing to pour into the region. The competition between the HBC and the missions, which had dominated the Oregon Country from the mid-1830s to the mid-1840s, also transitioned in a new direction. The region was evolving into a family farm society. Year after year hundreds of emigrants, especially from the midwestern river valleys, flooded into Oregon, bringing with them occupational, political, and economic experiences that would reshape Oregon cultural landscapes.

The emigrants were, most of all, people of the land. The land donated to the earliest arrivals under the Provisional Government allowed the incoming families to begin afresh in a new country. When Congress passed the Donation Land Act of 1850, accepting much of what had occurred under the Provisional Government and extending its coverage for several years, the act greatly expanded the draw to Oregon. The farm families came with a decided cast of mind; they were not yet market farmers, and they did not exhibit the speculative and transitory tendencies of so many single men who flocked to California after the discovery of gold in 1848-49. Oregon became increasingly the home of farm families bent on living comfortable and satisfied lives in the fertile lands, mild climate, and relatively safe Eden they had chosen.[13]

The conduit of land-hungry emigrants continued to flow. At the end of 1850, the population of the Oregon Country stood at about fifteen thousand. Even though the California Gold Rush dramatically redirected the emigration route to the West Coast in the early 1850s, immigrant agriculturists and their families continued to roll into Oregon. Indeed, Oregonians came to accept a story, undoubtedly apocryphal, that defined their differences from Californians. In southern Idaho, where the Oregon

Trail forked, a two-part sign is said to have pointed immigrants toward California or Oregon. The sign pointing to California featured a gold nugget, that to the north the word Oregon. Those after the almighty dollar, said the Oregonians, went to California; those who could read came on to Oregon.

If the newcomers transported their attachments to the land into Oregon, they also imported their political enthusiasms to the new country. One observer succinctly summed up these predilections. In Oregon, he reported, "there are but two occupations … farming and politics."[14] Most of the new arrivals came as Democrats or as persons tied to the platform ideas of the Democrats. Like Thomas Jefferson and Andrew Jackson, they preferred federal governments that ruled least, leaving more legislative and administrative power at state and local levels. Just as President Jackson had taken on and defeated the U. S. Bank, which he viewed as the symbol of bloated capitalism, centralism, and monopoly, Democrats who came to and resided in Oregon wanted to make their own decisions, keeping choices out of the hands of those they considered arrogant and octopus-like monopolists. Gradually in the 1850s, Oregon Democrats spoke increasingly for popular sovereignty, which meant more than Senator Stephen Douglas's idea of allowing people to decide on slavery issues in his notorious Kansas-Nebraska Bill of 1854. In the Oregon Country, Democrats—and some of their opponents as well—wanted federal government clutches off their affairs and local, democratic control as their *modus operandi*. These ideas—the opposite of those Lincoln would espouse in the 1850s—won over the Oregon Country by the early 1850s and held sway in that decade.

• • •

As early as the 1820s, well before settlement by American farmers had begun, some Oregon enthusiasts had called for organization of the joint-occupation area as a new U. S. territory and begun to introduce bills to that effect in the U. S. Congress. The proposals for territorial status for Oregon continued in the 1830s and 1840s, with many thinking this development would win the area for the United States. News of the massacre of Marcus and Narcissa Whitman and others at their mission in November 1847 and the resultant Cayuse War the following year provided additional emotional support for organizing Oregon as a territory. The people of the area needed aid from the federal government to protect them from Indian attacks. Driven by the urgency of these dramatic events, the legislature of Oregon's Provisional Government hurried a petition to the U.S. Congress, again calling for territorial status for the region.

By time the petition reached Congress, the initial steps toward Oregon territorial organization had already begun. Buoyed by President James K. Polk's call for the "re-annexation of Oregon" and the compromise border agreement in 1846, Stephen A. Douglas, now in the Senate after several years in the House, had pushed for Oregon as a new territory. When representatives from Oregon arrived in the nation's capital with memorials for territorial organization, they found that Douglas, chair of the Senate's Committee on Territories, had already introduced such legislation. But the issue quickly became enmeshed in much larger controversies.

During the first months of 1848, previously contested debates in Congress about Oregon's status gained new intensity. The nation's victory in the Mexican-American War turned the controversy red hot. The Treaty of Guadalupe Hidalgo in February 1848 included the cession of California and New Mexico (comprising those two present states and portions of Utah, Nevada, Arizona, and Colorado). Congress and the rest of the country wanted to know what would happen to these new areas: would slavery be allowed? would the areas be free of slavery? or what other compromises could be worked out? The question of Oregon becoming a new territory quickly became part of the verbal conflicts threatening to rip apart the country. By early summer 1848, one Lincoln scholar writes, "the debate over slavery in the territories grew intense, posing the gravest threat to national unity since the South Carolina nullification crisis of 1832-33."[15]

• • •

Abraham Lincoln, although not a leading figure in the fiery debates over Oregon's possible territorial status, was intensely involved in these issues. Indeed, even though Lincoln had been only tangentially tied to Oregon until his congressional years, for the period stretching from early summer 1848 to late summer and early fall 1849 Lincoln was linked to Oregon by two major decisions. These two events were among the most significant of Lincoln's political connections with Oregon before he entered the White House nearly a dozen years later.

Soon after Lincoln came to Washington in December 1847 to take his seat in the House of Representatives he became embroiled in partisan politics. By this time, the Mexican-American War had been underway for nineteen months, with the bloody military engagements already in the past. As a loyal Whig, Lincoln strongly opposed the war, and his surprising attacks on Democratic President Polk in December 1847-January 1848 stirred up Whigs in Illinois. These political controversies came back to haunt Lincoln in later political contests, especially in the Lincoln-Douglas debates in 1858 and even into the presidency.[16]

Other events were more important, however, in forging Lincoln's links with the Oregon Country. In late summer 1846, looking ahead to what might occur at the close of the Mexican-American War, Pennsylvania Congressman David Wilmot and several other colleagues had introduced legislation to amend a war appropriation bill. The amendment called for

Congressman-elect Abraham Lincoln paid little attention to the Oregon Country in the early 1840s. Later in the decade, he supported territorial status for Oregon without slavery and was offered, but rejected, positions as secretary and then governor of the new territory. (Library of Congress, Prints & Photographic Division, LC-USZC4-2439.)

prohibiting slavery in any territory the U. S. might win from Mexico. The Wilmot Proviso, as it came to be called, passed the House but not the Senate. Although that notable amendment died in Congress, it became the rallying cry—the no-expansion principle—that many northern antislavery Whigs and Democrats supported. The proviso also became the strongly held position of Abraham Lincoln, a stance he resolutely stuck to for the next fifteen years and carried into the White House. It was also the political position that shaped Lincoln's actions toward Oregon in late summer 1848.

One other happening illuminates Lincoln's attitudes toward issues involving the Oregon Country. In the first session of the 30th Congress, convening from December 1847 until August 1848, Lincoln made no notable comments on slavery. But in the second session, Lincoln revealed, for the first time on a national stage, his attitudes about the peculiar institution. In January 1849, after several other Whig politicians had attempted similar measures, Lincoln announced his intention to introduce a bill to end slavery and the slave trade in Washington, D. C. Lincoln's bill, if it received the support of white male voters in the District of Columbia, would gradually end slavery in the nation's capital.[17] Although his views were quite conservative and much less controversial than parallel legislation that abolitionist legislators promoted, Lincoln could not gather the needed support and never introduced the legislation. Perhaps his ideas on compensation for slave owners—and most certainly his proposal to support fugitive slave retrievals—alienated some potential supporters. Much later, Lincoln explained his actions: "finding that I was abandoned by my former backers and having little personal influence, I *dropped* the matter knowing that it was useless to prosecute the business at that time." These attitudes surfaced after his votes on the establishment of the Oregon Territory but likely represent his thinking about slavery as he voted on the Oregon measure. He retained his support for the idea and probably relished signing a bill to end slavery in Washington, D. C., when in the White House in 1862-63.[18]

These ideas on slavery, its possible extension westward, and the Wilmot Proviso, as well as controversies over partisan politics, came together in Lincoln's links vis-à-vis Oregon in the late spring and summer of 1848. The bitter debates and emotionally contested votes in Congress in the first months of 1848 dragged out and then ended quickly. When the year began, champions of antislavery and proslavery measures were already advancing their intense opinions. Most northern antislavery advocates (but not the most radical abolitionists) reluctantly accepted the constitution's protection of slavery where it already existed, but they wanted to stop its spread, especially in any new western areas added to the republic. Conversely, proslavery forces were convinced they must not only protect the institution where it was but also find ways to foster its extension into new frontier regions. Those conflicting viewpoints stoked many fiery congressional debates in early 1848 and thereafter.

The mounting conflicts in Congress in 1847-48 surrounding Oregon's run toward territorial status touched clearly and extensively on Lincoln's political stances. But he did not speak out publicly and enter the fray. Although Lincoln's votes on the House floor revealed his forcefully felt positions on matters increasingly dividing his country, he made no major speeches on these issues as a U. S. Congressman. On one occasion he threatened to speak out on the proposed territories, but under the pressures of time and the discouragement of some of his House colleagues he decided not to.[19]

Nor did he write to friends or political cronies about Oregon and the slavery debates delaying its territorial organization. True, he voted on the measures dealing with Oregon's possible territorial status, but these issues had not yet become the central planks of his political platform, as they later did, beginning with the Kansas-Nebraska imbroglio of 1854.

Other politicians, Democrats especially, were more publicly involved than Lincoln with the debate over Oregon. President Polk pushed hard for organizing Oregon as a territory, particularly after he received news of the Whitman Massacre and subsequent Cayuse War in 1847-48. The president, realizing the divisive issues surrounding the slavery conflict and their increasing linkage with Oregon, called for extending the Missouri Compromise line, which had been hammered out in 1820-21, all the way to the Pacific Coast. Douglas, Lincoln's long-time rival and the new chairman of the Senate Committee on Territories, also championed using the Missouri Compromise line of 36° 30' as a way to close the Oregon debates and move on. Douglas repeatedly tried to keep the compromise at the forefront in the organization of Oregon, but without success.

Northern Whigs and other antislavery supporters would have none of this. In the closing years of Polk's presidency, Whigs preferred delaying tactics. If a Whig won the White House in fall 1848, they reasoned, the newly elected president could appoint party warhorses or other regulars to territorial offices. Polk understood these politically motivated actions. As he recorded in his diary, his Whig opponents wanted "to leave the Territories of Oregon, California and New Mexico without Territorial Governments ... [because] they may stand some chance to elect a Whig President."[20]

Lincoln's votes on Oregon beginning in spring and extending into August 1848 revealed his growing support for the Wilmot Proviso or for similar legislation keeping slavery from expanding farther into the trans-Mississippi West. Lincoln voted against an Oregon territorial bill that would have extended the Missouri Compromise to the Pacific. The vote was 82 (yes) to 121 (no) against the bill in the House. He probably voted with the nays because he did not want to allow the possibility of slavery in the West below the 36° 30' line. Conversely, when an Oregon bill was introduced adopting phrasing from the Northwest Ordinance of 1787 that disallowed slavery in the Old Northwest (the present midwestern states), Lincoln supported that legislation, evidently thinking this was a surer path to keeping slavery out of the trans-Mississippi West.

One scholar studying congressional voting in summer 1848 mistakenly argues that Lincoln "was obstructive with reference to Oregon." To the contrary, he rather consistently followed the Whig Party line in his voting pattern on Oregon,[21] supporting Oregon bills that utilized statements from the Northwest Ordinance or the Wilmot Proviso. Indeed, several years later he exaggerated the number of his votes but correctly identified his stance when he asserted to his friend Joshua Speed, "When I was in Washington I voted for the Wilmot Proviso as good as forty times. ... I now do no more than oppose the *extension* of slavery." And in one case, very briefly, Lincoln made clear his general views. In reference to the Wilmot Proviso, he told his House colleagues, "I am a Northern man, or rather, a Western free state man, with a constituency I believe to be, and with personal feelings I know to be, against the extension of slavery."[22] While not yet closely linked to Oregon in late summer 1848, Abraham

Lincoln was beginning to formulate his stance on the slavery issue: he would accept slavery where the constitution protected it in established states, but he would oppose all possible expansions of slavery into new territories, including Oregon.

Revealingly, roughly one hundred and fifty years later, as the United States began to ponder anew the complicated meanings of a fractious Civil War, the nation still did not comprehend the full meaning of these events beginning to unfold in the late 1840s. Nor have many American historians. True, more and more Americans were coming to realize that slavery and controversies over it were the major reason a civil war erupted in 1861, but very few understood that the conflict also involved a deadly competition for the trans-Mississippi West. Both sides—North and South—were beginning to see that the section that won the West would most likely win the race for power and dominance in the United States. Clearly, the controversies stretching from 1848 to secession and the attack on Fort Sumter were as much about the West as about slavery. In 1848, in his new connection with Oregon and its attempts to become a new western territory, Lincoln was beginning to realize the regional as well as the slavery issues swirling through the country.[23]

As Lincoln ended his two years in Congress in March 1849, he became embroiled in a sticky competition for a federal position before being offered two different appointments in Oregon. After a slow start in spring 1849 in the race for the commissioner of the U.S. General Land Office, Lincoln threw himself whole-heartedly into the contest. Stiff and acrimonious rivalry ensued, with Lincoln losing out to Justin Butterfield, an Illinois lawyer less involved than Lincoln in the election of 1848 that brought Whig Zachary Taylor into the White House. Lincoln was deeply—if not bitterly—disappointed with the outcome.

On the heels of Lincoln's loss the entirely unexpected telegram arrived from Washington offering him the secretaryship of the new Oregon Territory. The tendered position came nearly one year after Lincoln had supported the legislation organizing the new territory. The surprising offer begs for explanation. The constitution gave Congress the right to organize territories after the original states were established on the East Coast. Over time presidents had assumed the duty of appointing a governor, secretary, three judges, and other officials in each newly minted territory. This power to appoint territorial officials became an important part of an expanding presidential patronage in the nineteenth century.[24]

The telegram from Secretary of State John M. Clayton naming Lincoln the Oregon Territorial secretary at a salary of $1,500 was particularly unusual because Lincoln had not been nominated for the post, nor had he expected it. Perhaps the Taylor administration was compensating Lincoln, offering him a consolation prize, after his loss in the bitter battle for commissioner of the General Land Office. Clayton sent his letter appointing Lincoln on 10 August 1849. Eleven days later Lincoln answered the secretary of state "respectfully declin[ing] the office." Without explaining his reasons for rejecting the offer, Lincoln reiterated at length his desire for Simeon Francis, his journalist friend in Springfield, to be given the position. There is no evidence that Lincoln gave the offer serious consideration even though he had vigorously supported Taylor's run for the presidency and, according to the political customs of the time, deserved some kind of reward for his political activities.[25]

One month later, on 20 September, the second message from Washington arrived in Springfield. This time the invitation, coming from Secretary of Interior Thomas Ewing, was for governor of the Oregon Territory at a salary of $3,000. This offer, with added prestige and remuneration, caused Lincoln more pause. Should he accept? What would be the impact on his political career should he take this position in far-off Oregon?

The available details behind the gubernatorial offer and Lincoln's reactions to it, although not fully in view, nonetheless provide tantalizing hints of what might have happened. First, the chronology of the second offer overlaps the first. Were the two cabinet members confused in their offers of Oregon leadership since a second offer came before Lincoln had fully rejected the first? On 21 August, the very day Lincoln wrote to Secretary Clayton declining the position of territorial secretary, his fellow Whig and his doctor in Springfield, Anson G. Henry, wrote to Secretary Ewing that Lincoln "has declined the office of Governor of Oregon, and for reasons I presume entirely personal to himself and *certain friends* whose claims he early pressed upon Gen. Taylor for appointments to office." But Dr. Henry wanted to assure President Taylor and his cabinet secretary that Lincoln was "disposed to yield the administration his most cordial support notwithstanding his refusal to take the office for *himself* so long as his friends are unprovided for."[26] Another Illinois acquaintance telegraphed Secretary Ewing to promise that Lincoln, now out of Springfield, would return home soon and reply to Washington.

But Lincoln was delayed in returning home, and a bit of impatience surfaced in Washington. Even though Lincoln continued to recommend Simeon Francis for the territory's secretarial position and although Lincoln's appointment to Oregon's governorship had been announced in several newspapers, the president and his cabinet had not received an official response from Lincoln—so they thought. On 25 September, Ewing, evidently feeling pressure from Taylor, telegraphed Illinois, asking "Is Mr. Lincoln in Springfield? The President wishes to hear from him immediately." Meanwhile, Lincoln had received the offer and had answered Ewing on 23 September, but that letter had not arrived before Ewing sent his telegram. So, wanting to make certain his position was clear, Lincoln sent a telegram to Ewing on 27 September: "I respectfully decline Governorship of Oregon; I am still anxious that, Simeon Francis shall be secretary."[27] One scholar has posited that Lincoln chose not to take the position because he was embarrassed to do so when others he had recommended for positions had not gained them, and now he had received, unrequested, two offers.[28] And to eliminate any other unanswered questions, Lincoln also wrote Ewing a letter on the same day. Evidently, according to Lincoln, some of his Springfield friends, thinking he had acted too quickly in rejecting the governorship, had delayed sending his answer, hoping to change his mind. But Lincoln settled the question explicitly with his telegram and explanatory letter to Ewing on 27 September.[29]

Clearly, some of Lincoln's closest friends and political advisors wanted him to think long and hard about the Oregon offer, but he took a different route. Why was that? What were the major reasons Lincoln rejected a position that promised political attention when doors for political advancement seemed closed in Illinois after his two-year stint in Congress? The salary for the Oregon governorship would be the same as if he had been named commissioner in the Land Office. At the time and in later years, contemporaries and historians cited family and political reasons as explanations.

Considerable disagreement surfaces, however, among those commenting on Lincoln's decisions concerning Oregon. William Herndon, Lincoln's third and final law partner, pointed his opinionated finger of decision making at Lincoln's wife, Mary. Herndon asserted that "Lincoln himself had some inclination to accept" the governorship offer, but "when he brought the proposition home to his fireside, his wife put her foot squarely down on it with a firm and emphatic NO. That always ended it with Lincoln." Another of Lincoln's law partners, John T. Stuart, told Herndon a similar story in an early interview. When Lincoln's political colleagues urged him to take the governorship, he "[s]aid he would if his wife would consent. [She] Refused to do So."[30] Undoubtedly Mary would have fretted much about all the separations, dangers, and isolations a removal to Oregon would entail. She worried too about her sickly three-year-old son Eddie (he died the following February), and she may have believed rumors of threatening Indians in Oregon.[31] (One modern wag, playing on stereotypes, observed that Mary Lincoln did not want to come to Oregon once she learned it was without a Macy's or Nordstroms.) Realizing Mary's hesitations, Lincoln may even have contacted his best friend, Joshua Speed, then in Kentucky, requesting that he and his wife accompany the Lincolns to Oregon so they could enjoy one another's company and support in the faraway West.

But politics and Lincoln's possible political advancement may have been an equally important determining factor in his decision. Oregon was clearly a Democratic territory, so what political future, as a very loyal Whig, would Lincoln have there? Responses from Lincoln's political acquaintances help to answer these questions as well as to explain the political machinations going on behind the scene of the offers. A group of Lincoln's political friends then in Washington, D. C., including former Illinois editor George T. M. Davis, John Addison, an official in the interior department, and others, "united in an effort to have [Lincoln] appointed governor of the territory of Oregon. Those efforts were so far crowned with success as to be dependent only upon the willingness of Mr. Lincoln to accept the position to secure his appointment."[32] Addison wrote to Lincoln apprising him of what his political supporters in the nation's capital had done. Later, after Lincoln had decided not to take the position, he wrote to Addison, thanking him and "all other friends who have interested themselves in having the governorship of Oregon offered to me; but on as much reflection as I have had time to give the subject, I cannot consent to accept it." Lincoln also asked Addison to thank Davis, "especially, for his kindness in the Oregon matter."[33]

If these were the actions in the East initiating Lincoln's nomination for the governorship, others at the western end helped shape his response. Former law partner John Todd Stuart provided the fullest account of the actions that led to Lincoln's uncertain steps toward rejection. Stuart and Lincoln were in court together in Bloomington, Illinois, when the offer from Secretary Ewing arrived, via a message from a friend in Springfield. Lincoln asked Stuart what he thought, and Stuart replied: "I told him I thought it was a good thing; that he could go out there and in all likelihood come back from there as a Senator when the State was admitted. Mr. Lincoln finally made up his mind that he would accept the place if Mary would consent to go." Then Stuart added the story about Lincoln's contacting Joshua Speed, but he concluded the deciding factor was Mary. She "would not consent to go out there," Stuart noted; "Mary had a very violent temper, but she had more intellectual power than she has generally be[en] given credit for."[34]

Other Lincoln biographers are convinced that Lincoln decided against going to Oregon primarily because of its obvious Democratic cast in politics. True, he might have a run at a senatorial seat if Oregon quickly became a state, but how long would that take in an area safely in the Democratic camp? If that indeed was Lincoln's thinking, the arguments make sense—with one major and significant exception. A decade later Edward D. Baker, Lincoln's Whig friend in Illinois and now a very recent Republican in Oregon, by careful and wise compromises, captured one of Oregon's first senatorial seats.

Whatever the deciding reasons, Lincoln nearly always remained silent afterwards about his decision. However, Lincoln's political friend and supporter from Illinois, Isaac Arnold, does mention one later Lincoln reference to the Oregon governorship, without providing a source. When visitors to the White House asked Lincoln for an army commission for the son of Justin Butterfield, to whom he had lost the disappointing race for commissioner of the General Land Office, Lincoln "then spoke of the offer made to him of the governorship of Oregon. To which the reply was made: 'How fortunate that you declined. If you had gone to Oregon, you might have come back as senator, but you would never have been President.' 'Yes, you are probably right,' he said." Mary also recalled the decisions. Once the Lincolns were safely ensconced in the presidency, she reminded her husband that she had saved him from becoming isolated and forgotten out in the territories. What might have happened to Lincoln—and to Oregon—if Lincoln accepted the governorship? As one scholar rightly notes, "In retrospect, Oregon's loss became the nation's gain."[35]

● ● ●

After his two years in Congress, the disappointment of the Land Office commissionership, and his rejection of the Oregon offers, Lincoln claimed that he lost interest in politics. He exaggerated his political inactivity, however. He remained involved in several ways, regularly reading political news stories, delivering memorial addresses of politicians (including those for Henry Clay and Zachary Taylor), and continuing his political correspondence with dozens of friends and political cronies. Perhaps Lincoln's political fires were banked some between 1849 and 1854, but the live coals remained, needing only a fresh breeze of new controversies to reignite the political embers. The winds of conflict came in 1854, in the Kansas-Nebraska controversy, and they remained, eventually sending Lincoln into the White House in 1861.

Meanwhile, several of Lincoln's closest friends had moved to Oregon. In his continuing connections with them and in his mounting interest in slavery and its dramatic impact on American politics, Lincoln moved into a second and new stage of his links with the Oregon Country.

Chapter 2: The 1850s and Lincoln's Friends in Oregon

Abraham Lincoln wobbled between satisfaction and disappointment. In the midst of his uncertainty, he wrote on 19 November 1858 to Dr. Anson Henry, his former personal physician and Whig crony, now living in Oregon. In referring to his just completed tangle with Stephen Douglas for his senate seat, Lincoln indicated that he was "glad" he had "made the late race" against Illinois's senior senator. The dramatic contest, including the thunderous Lincoln-Douglas debates, allowed Lincoln "a hearing on the great and durable question of the age, which I could have had in no other way." Further, Lincoln was convinced that he had "made some marks which will tell for the cause of civil liberty long after I am gone."[1]

But in the aftermath of his recent loss to Douglas, as revealed in the informal returns early in November, Lincoln also had to admit defeat to his political doctor in Oregon. Lincoln thought he would probably "sink out of view, and shall be forgotten." Lincoln had "*wished*" for "but did not much *expect* a better result."[2]

A few weeks later Henry replied, disagreeing with Lincoln's gloomy prediction. "You have not 'sunk out of sight' as you seem to anticipate, no[r] will you be forgotten," Lincoln's supportive friend in Oregon told him. In fact, the doctor prophesied, "the people—the great & glorious People, will bear you on their memories until the time comes for putting you in possession of their House at Washington."[3]

After attempting to dissuade Lincoln of his defeated spirit, Dr. Henry turned to Oregon politics. As Oregon was officially becoming a state (February-March 1859), its political parties were in disarray. Henry admitted his inclination to sublimate his Republican loyalties so as to bundle with the free-state Democrats, "who are right on the question of Slavery and the Dred Scott discussion." Such a pragmatic union, Henry told Lincoln, "will secure a free constitution for Oregon beyond all question." Rather than push for the narrowest of Republican stances, the good doctor was willing to work with Democratic leaders like Asahel Bush, the energetic editor of the *Oregon Statesman*, to secure a "free Constitution." To do otherwise, Henry continued, would be to "give hope & encouragement to an unscrupulous Pro Slavery Organization, where all former party distinctions & principles are made to yield to the great [']Alpha and Omega' of slavery."[4] (The willingness of other Republicans to "fuse" with antislavery Democrats worried Lincoln in the run-up to the presidency in 1860.)

The contents of these exchanged letters between Lincoln and Dr. Henry in 1858-59 illustrate how much national political issues involving Lincoln had rolled into the distant Oregon Country. Lincoln was gratified that, even though he had lost his bid for Douglas's seat in the Senate, he had been able, in the Lincoln-Douglas debates, to show his clear, unending opposition to the extension of slavery into the West. His position would provide an important rallying point against his better-known opponent's willingness, through popular sovereignty, to allow the serpent of slavery to wriggle into and poison the West. The growing slavery controversy, with fiery emotional support and criticism of the peculiar institution, rearranged politics nationally in the 1850s, destroying much of the political turf on which Lincoln had stood for more than twenty years. He was forced, reluctantly, to join the Republican Party in the 1850s because the brouhaha over slavery had destroyed his Whig Party. In Illinois, Lincoln, a devout former Whig, had to find new political bedfellows to help him increasingly oppose slavery.

Similar disruptions roiled Oregon politics in the 1850s. The Democrats clearly ruled, but controversies over slavery—and political stances about it—were beginning to divide the party and open space for an expanding slavery contingent, including the Republicans. Like Lincoln, Oregonians could not avoid the divisive issue of slavery and the contingent issue of race, even though both were hesitant to deal with racial politics.

Lincoln and the Oregon Country wrestled with several similar issues in the 1850s. These parallels were magnified as four of Lincoln's close friends moved to Oregon between 1849 and 1860. David Logan, Dr. Anson G. Henry, Simeon Francis, and Edward D. Baker all left Illinois and eventually made their way to Oregon. During the decade of the 1850s they wrote to Lincoln about their new homes, often commenting on the fresh settings, far-western politics, and sometimes suggesting what Lincoln ought to do as he climbed the national political ladder. Through these friendships, as well as by way of connections with other Illinois acquaintances now residing in Oregon, Lincoln's links with the North Pacific were enlarged and strengthened.

• • •

Lincoln's career during the next dozen years (1849-61) and his political and personal connections with Oregon and the American West conveniently divide into two periods. In the first five years, following his two-year stint in Congress, the disappointment over the commissionership in the land office, and his rejection of the two Oregon appointments, Lincoln returned to his law office and diligently expanded his Illinois legal practice. Although Lincoln claimed later that he "was losing interest in politics" in these years,[5] he remained involved in both local and national political activities, reacting to important decisions such as the Compromise of 1850, and participating in Whig politics nationally and in Illinois.

An even more important transition was gradually taking place in Lincoln's thinking. For nearly a full generation he placed high value on the idea of an internal improvements system he inherited from Hamilton and John Quincy Adams, as well as from Henry Clay and other Whigs. He spoke often for federal and local support for the improvement and expansion of transportation grids, including roads, canals, and railroads. He was a loyal Whig, too, in plumping for banks, protective tariffs, and improved school systems. These emphases continued through Lincoln's congressional years.

But the dramatic issue of slavery drove Lincoln and most other political leaders (including those in Oregon) in new directions during the 1850s. Although compromises Clay engineered in 1820-21 and 1832-33 and that Stephen A. Douglas led in 1850 helped keep the nation from fracturing itself over slavery and attendant issues, the dam of compromise began to fail in the 1850s and increasingly broke apart from 1854 onward. The Whig Party foundered and divided on the slavery controversy, separating into Conscience Whigs in the North standing for antislavery measures and Cotton Whigs in the South speaking for slavery and its economic system. Lincoln, too, was forced to deal increasingly with slavery as the most pressing issue in the U. S. in the 1850s. From the mid-1850s forward, it became the main focus of his political attentions.[6]

In early 1854 Douglas introduced the Kansas-Nebraska Bill to organize new areas west of the Mississippi. Later in the spring Congress passed the act, the controversial content of which quickly drove Lincoln out of the shadows and back into the political arena. The new legislation dramatically undercut Lincoln's previous political stances and threatened to further destroy the faltering political party to which he had been tied for a full generation. First, Douglas's legislation repealed the Missouri Compromise (put together in 1820-21), which disallowed slavery on the frontier north of 36° 30' (except for Missouri) and allowed it below that line. Now, through popular sovereignty, residents of the new territory could vote slavery up or down, north or south, through their own ballots. Second, popular sovereignty, if followed, derailed Lincoln's Wilmot Proviso position: no expansion of slavery into the newly organized western territories. The Kansas-Nebraska legislation also further jarred Lincoln's Whig Party, which had not done well in the election of 1852. If popular sovereignty became the new *modus operandi*, southern Whigs were likely to join southern Democrats in supporting slavery's expansion; both groups had much to gain in the change, and Lincoln's no-extension principle had much to lose.

After Lincoln kept silent for several months while studying the Kansas-Nebraska Act and its implications, in late summer and then particularly in fall 1854, he began to make known his strong and energetic opposition to the new legislation. On 7 September he wrote to Illinois State Senator John M. Palmer that he wanted the "Nebraska measure ... rebuked and condemned every where." A few days later in an editorial in the *Illinois Journal*, Lincoln asserted that the "Kansas and Nebraska territories are now as open to slavery as Mississippi and Arkansas were when they were territories."[7] Over the next three weeks Lincoln delivered speeches opposing the Kansas-Nebraska Act, all leading up to his well-known

Peoria presentation on 16 October 1854, which many consider his first great speech.

The Peoria speech not only provided Lincoln's most complete and telling opposition to the Kansas-Nebraska legislation, it also revealed that his reactions to slavery were in clear transition. Indeed, if one wishes to understand the major contents of the political agenda that Lincoln organized in the mid-1850s and carried forward into the White House, one would do well to examine the Peoria speech carefully. Lincoln began by rehearsing his well-known position: he would follow the constitution in protecting slavery where it already existed, but he opposed its extension into the West. Drawing on his recent research (and Lincoln was a remarkable researcher considering he had less than one year of formal schooling), he asserted that the Founding Fathers, opposed to the expansion of slavery and wanting Congress to keep it out of new territories, would have voted against the Kansas-Nebraska legislation. Lincoln put the distinction between then and now succinctly: "Let no one be deceived. The spirit of seventy-six and the spirit of Nebraska, are utter antagonisms; the former is being rapidly displaced by the latter."[8]

Lincoln also moved to newer and clearer positions on slavery. He had always stood against slavery, but now he became more outspoken, denouncing slavery as a great moral wrong, robbing Negroes of their economic rights, besmirching the "republican robes" of the United States, and denying his country's worldwide influence as a democratic and republican country. It was a "lullaby" argument, he went on, to assert that slavery would not exist in Kansas and Nebraska because of the climate, growing conditions, or economic pressures. Plus, Lincoln did not want slavery in the territories because it would undermine the free labor system for white workers and their families that he hoped would be the bulwark of western settlement and development. Of note, Lincoln did not call for social equality for blacks, which he thought impossible, and he was silent on the internal improvements and other economic issues that were mainstays of Whig ideology in earlier years. Seeing that slavery and its possible expansion into the West had re-emerged with a vengeance in 1854, Abraham Lincoln was ready to do battle to limit the peculiar institution to its current spread.[9]

In the political arena Lincoln walked cautiously in the next few years, gradually moving to the forefront of American political leaders. His exact destinations were not always clear. Still, every year or two Lincoln participated in an event that enlarged his political understanding and kept his name in front of voters.

One year after Lincoln's determined opposition to Senator Douglas's Kansas-Nebraska Act brought him to the forefront of anti-Nebraska men, he ran for the other Senate seat in Illinois. (Until the early twentieth century, state legislatures, not individual male voters, elected U.S. senators.) The disappointing outcome of the Illinois legislature's vote in 1855 on that position illustrated the growing fluidity of political parties nationally and locally, as well as Lincoln's desire to give way in helpful compromise. Although he gained the largest number of votes in the first Illinois House and Senate ballots, he was unable to secure enough votes to fulfill his dream of winning a U. S. Senate seat. Lincoln's Whig Party had broken up, slavery was replacing economic issues as Illinois's chief political argument, and no party had yet arisen as a home base for antislavery voters. As Lincoln's vote numbers dwindled in the 1855 competition, he decided that rather than hold out stubbornly to the end and possibly bring about the election of a proslavery man, he would urge his supporters to vote for Lyman Trumbull, an antislavery Democrat. (Ironically, in the earlier votes when Lincoln was within five votes of a win, Trumbull refused to encourage his handful of supporters to throw their votes behind Lincoln—and perhaps give him victory.) Lincoln's compromising strategy worked; Trumbull won. Even though he was disappointed at losing the contest for the Senate seat, Lincoln stressed, instead, that Illinois had gained an antislavery man to offset Douglas's popular sovereignty views. He could not have realized how much his support for Trumbull and his followers would pay dividends in his run for the presidency in 1860.

The next year Lincoln gained the political home he needed when, somewhat reluctantly, he joined the new Republican Party. Lincoln worried that the Republicans would be too radical, too abolitionist in their platforms, and thus unable to gain sufficient voters to become a national party of substance. Putting aside those hesitations, he became a Republican and even garnered 110 votes as runner-up for his party's vice-president nomination in the election of 1856. In concluding that Lincoln had little or no national reputation until the Lincoln-Douglas debates in 1858, historians overlook his growing publicity as a leading anti-Nebraska man in 1854-55 and his enlarging recognition in the Republican Party in 1856.

In 1857-58, Lincoln had to wrestle with a controversial court decision and a difficult opponent. In 1857 in the Dred Scott decision, the Supreme Court declared slaves not citizens but instead transportable property. Chief Justice Roger Taney, speaking for the majority of the court, also opined that slaves could thus be taken into new western territories. This landmark decision, of course, undermined the Republican Party's— and Lincoln's—no-expansion platform. Lincoln, while expressing his disagreement with the decision, also counseled a wait-and-see attitude rather than overtly negative reactions.

One year later the debates with Douglas launched Lincoln to new, unexpected heights. Lincoln's role in the controversy over the Kansas-Nebraska Act, his rhetorical tussles with Douglas, and his Cooper Union speech in New York in 1860 were the three events that made Lincoln a national figure—and also brought him to the attention of Oregonians.

In their memorable debates and campaigning in 1858 Douglas and Lincoln did not so much introduce new subjects as reiterate and elaborate on their familiar views as well as try to catch one another with difficult questions.[10] The Little Giant trumpeted the virtues of popular sovereignty as the best answer to the pressing dilemmas concerning slavery, and Lincoln urged on audiences the need to keep slavery out of the western territories. Throughout the seven debates Douglas also painted Lincoln as a Black Republican (or, in more racially charged words, as a "Nigger lover") who wanted social equality and the vote for Negroes. In contrast, Lincoln depicted Douglas as an insensitive pragmatist who cared not a whit whether constituents voted slavery up or down.

Douglas likewise charged Lincoln with changing his stances depending on where the debate in Illinois was occurring—in the antislavery northern counties or the more proslavery south. He also accused Lincoln of, unpatriotically, opposing the Mexican-American War, misrepresenting the views of the Founding Fathers on slavery and territories, and siding with the radical abolitionists. But the most negative of Douglas's attacks were in the form of race baiting. Negroes were subhuman, with no more capabilities than an animal, Douglas asserted. How could Lincoln call for equality between the races when blacks were not the equals of whites in intelligence, moral capability, or natural rights?

Lincoln's answers probably satisfied most contemporary Republicans and perhaps more than a few Democrats, but they obviously jar modern sensibilities. Those who subscribe to a Lincoln myth, making him superhuman and saint-like in all his actions, have difficulty accepting what Lincoln said about race in 1858. As historian Allen Guelzo has discerningly noted, in the fourth debate at Charleston on 18 September, Lincoln "began with the words every Lincoln admirer since then wishes he had never uttered." Hoping to answer Douglas's continual accusations that he was an advocate of racial mixing, Lincoln told his listeners, "I will say then that I am not, nor ever have been in favor of bringing about in any way the social and political equality of the white and black races." Lincoln did not advocate for black suffrage, their serving on juries, or black-white marriages. "I will say," he added, "in this that there is a physical difference between the white and black races." That meant the two races were unlikely to live "together on terms of social and political equality." This being the case, Lincoln was "in favor of having the superior position assigned to the white race."[11] Although distasteful to twenty-first-century observers, this position on race set well with most residents of Illinois in 1858, as it did with contemporary Oregonians when they included a plank in their constitution of 1857 keeping blacks out of the state.

Lincoln lost his battle to replace Douglas in the U. S. Senate in 1858, but he gained much from his debates with his long-time rival. Lincoln's strong performance against Douglas and his able articulation of the antislavery position helped encourage his supporters and added notably to his mushrooming reputation. That notice led eventually to an unexpected invitation: would Lincoln come to New York to give a speech on a subject of his own choosing? After details were ironed out, Lincoln agreed to travel east to speak before an elite gathering of Republicans in New York City.

The presentation at Cooper Union on 27 February 1860, Lincoln scholar Harold Holzer opines, is "the speech that made Abraham

In February 1860 Abraham Lincoln delivered a key speech at Cooper Union in New York City. One historian claims it was "the speech that made Abraham Lincoln president." (Library of Congress, Prints & Photographic Division, LC-BH8277-242.)

Lincoln president."[12] Before a crowd of several hundred, including many leading Republicans (some of whom wanted to find an alternative to New York Senator William Seward as the party standard-bearer), Lincoln performed superbly. He impressed the audience with his scholarly presentation on the opposition of the Founding Fathers to the spread of slavery into new federal territories. Even more important for Republicans, as well as for Lincoln's own possible candidacy, he proved to their entire satisfaction that the Founding Fathers stood for the no-extension-of-slavery principle that Republicans in early 1860 were advocating. Near the end of his presentation, Lincoln admitted that he and others could, like letting sleeping dogs lie, accept slavery where it was in the states; but they must keep it out of the West, not "allow it to spread into the National Territories." If their "sense of duty" helped them to keep the pernicious institution out of the West, then, he had one final admonition for them. "LET US HAVE FAITH THAT RIGHT MAKES MIGHT, AND IN THAT FAITH, LET US, TO THE END, DARE TO DO OUR DUTY AS WE UNDERSTAND IT."[13]

• • •

As Lincoln climbed the American political ladder in the 1850s, Oregonians were transitioning from a new territory in 1848-49 to official statehood in 1859. That shift in the Far West included several revealing parallels with Abraham Lincoln's political journey in the same decade.[14]

Oregon's territorial organization followed that of other recently established federal territories. The president named a territorial governor, secretary, three judges (a chief justice and two associates), and sometimes other officials, including a surveyor-general, a U.S. attorney, and a U. S. marshal. If the governor did not serve simultaneously as an Indian agent, another person was appointed to that position. The federal government kept its hand tightly around much of the territorial organization by paying salaries and per diem for territorial officers and judges. But locals retained parallel power by popularly electing a territorial delegate, who had a seat without a vote in the U. S. House of Representatives. Adult white male residents of a territory also elected a territorial House and Senate, whose enactments the governor could not veto (at first) but that must follow all constitutional and federal guidelines.

The territorial system fostered discontent and disagreements. A president's appointed officials were usually friends of the chief magistrate or his supporters, and probably no more than a third claimed residency in areas where they served.[15] Most appointees knew little about the people and places where they were sent. Indeed, the territorial officials, like earlier colonial governors, were men torn by two conflicting loyalties: they needed to please the London or Washington leaders who had selected them, but they also must deal with residents of colonies or territories. Conflict more than consensus usually characterized the western territorial systems.

Nearly always territorial appointees reflected the political positions of the presidents who named them. Thus, the first territorial governor of Oregon, Joseph Lane, originally from South Carolina, was a loyal Democrat appointed by Democratic President James K. Polk. Lane arrived on 3 March 1849, took his oath of office, and declared the Oregon Territory open for business only one day before the end of Polk's presidential term. After several months of delay, Polk's Whig successor, Zachary Taylor, removed Lane from office and, as we have seen, offered the Oregon governor's chair to Abraham Lincoln. After

Lincoln's rejection of the position, Taylor turned to another Whig, John P. Gaines, who accepted the appointment. He seemed in trouble from the day he arrived. When Whigs came as territorial officers they were rarely successful in working out peaceful agreements with the more numerous Democrats of Oregon. Later, when Democratic presidents served in the 1850s, their appointees in Democratic territories stirred up fewer problems. During these years, Joseph Lane dominated Oregon territorial politics. First elected territorial delegate in 1851, Lane was reelected until 1859, when he became a U.S. senator and served until 1861. He became the vice-president candidate on the proslavery John Breckinridge ticket in 1860, reflecting well the Democratic and sometimes prosouthern perspectives of many Oregonians.[16]

Opponents of the Oregon Democrats were neither numerous nor well organized. Governor Gaines, an arrogant and self-impressed man, had upset many Oregonians with his unwise confrontations on the possible capital relocation from Oregon City to Salem and his mean-spirited attacks on his opponents. Very popular in the early 1850s, Lane, with

Joseph Lane was the Oregon political leader in the 1850s. He was the first appointed territorial governor and later was elected territorial delegate. His prosouthern stances led to his defeat in Oregon and his retirement from politics in the 1860s. (Library of Congress, Prints & Photographic Division, LC-DIG-ppmsca-26845.)

his military bearing and experiences, his Jacksonian ties, and his decision to relocate to Oregon, easily won the territorial delegate vote in 1851, with his only competitor another Democrat. No Whig had run. Even leading Whig newspapers in Oregon, the *Oregon Spectator* and the Portland *Oregonian*, supported Lane for delegate.[17]

The celebrated Lane was the leading political figure in Oregon, but he soon enjoyed a strong supporting cast. None were more important than Matthew Deady and Asahel Bush. A sophisticated and learned man from Ohio, Deady passed the bar in that state and came to Oregon in 1849. At first appointed as a territorial justice, he served in that position until he was named a U. S. district judge in Oregon in 1859. A voracious reader, a man interested in the full gamut of ideas and activities, Deady quickly became a well-known Democratic leader, although he rarely ran for elective office. Joining Lane and Deady was Asahel Bush, a journalist and printer reared in Massachusetts, who immigrated to Oregon in 1850. Before the year was out, Bush had control of the *Oregon Statesman*, which became the chief mouthpiece of Oregon Democrats and the strongest newspaper in the territory. Early in the 1850s, Lane, Deady, and Bush, cabal-like, formed the core of what one opponent termed the "Oregon Clique" or "Salem Clique," bent on dominating the entire political terrain of the Oregon Country.[18]

The emergence of this important triumvirate of new political leaders signaled a transition in Oregon politics. In the first years of the 1840s the mission and the Hudson's Bay Company's spheres of influence still dominated Oregon, but Oregon Trail immigration brought a new generation of leaders who moved to the forefront of Oregon politics by the beginning of its territorial period. The new leaders like Lane, Deady, and Bush, bringing American national issues into the Oregon arena, moved away from the Lee-and-McLoughlin tussles of the earlier years. Quite simply, the Salem Clique had invaded and captured the Oregon political scene early in the 1850s. In their movement to the front of Oregon politics, the three newcomers provided a revealing example of cross-continental political influences at work in the Far Northwest.

Opponents of the Clique had trouble gaining traction against the Democrats. Loosely joined together as anti-Democrats, disparate groups of old Whigs, temperance advocates, and antislavery supporters, they could not find able leaders or a few agreed-on, hard-core issues around which to rally. They were on the slippery slopes of defense, with little or no signs of the powerful offense that drove the Oregon Democrats. Indeed, Oregon Republicans came to experience what their national co-party members did: not until the Douglas-Buchanan rupture in the late 1850s split the Democratic Party were the Republicans offered an opportunity to capture the White House, as they did with the election of Lincoln in 1860. In the same election, with the same divided Democrats, Oregon Republicans also won with Lincoln.

As these shifting political crosscurrents were buffeting Oregonians and their political leaders, they had to address, simultaneously, several perplexing questions. Chief among these were dilemmas over land holdings and how these decisions would determine attitudes and actions toward Indians of the Oregon Country. The land question seemed to settle quickly, but white residents of the Pacific Northwest exhibited little awareness of how much struggles over lands led to conflict with Indians. When the U.S. Congress passed the Donation Land Act of 1850, it followed—and extended—most of what the Provisional Government had done earlier in its land policies. In fact, news of 320-acre parcels for each white adult male (or 640 for a married couple) enticed hundreds of new settlers. Not surprisingly, those newly arrived settlers, as well as others who came to the Oregon Country to participate in mining strikes popping up in several parts of the territory, exacted enormous mounting pressures on Indians and their lands.

The most horrendous of the white-Indian conflicts broke out in southern Oregon, but others exploded in nearby areas, including "North Oregon" (Washington Territory). Foreseeing the impact of the popular Donation Land Act, Oregon's first territorial delegate, Samuel Thurston, urged Congress to move quickly to do what they were attempting in other areas of the country: extinguish Indian titles on their lands, promise money and goods in exchange, and move Natives to reservations, which should be distant from the fertile farm and mineral-producing lands white newcomers coveted. Indians reluctantly gave in— under continuing pressures and promises—to the treaties nearly forced upon them and even more reluctantly removed to reservations, including the Siletz, Grande Ronde, Warm Springs, and Umatilla reservations in Oregon and the Yakama, Nez Perce, Colville, and others in what are now Washington and Idaho.

In southwestern Oregon, dissatisfied tribesmen rose up against the slowness of the treaty process and the increasing numbers of settlers and miners invading their lands. In turn, settlers, goldseekers, and regular and volunteer soldiers armed to combat Natives, especially those in the Umpqua and Rogue valleys. From the early 1850s until 1856, the two sides were in continual, if sporadic, conflict. The bloody Rogue River Indian War, in which one of Abraham Lincoln's closest friends, Dr. Anson G. Henry, served as Commissary and Quartermaster General, achieved what the ambitious and greedy newcomers wanted. Indians were defeated, their lands taken and made ready for settlement, and they were removed to reservations. It was a part, the most tragic part, of the frontier story.[19]

To the north in the new territory of Washington, established in 1853, the youthful and enthusiastic first territorial governor, Isaac Ingalls Stevens, was an energetic negotiator who pursued Indians even more vociferously than did leaders in Oregon. As one historian has written, Stevens's "methods featured fast talk, bluster, intimidation, and when he finished he had stampeded virtually all groups of the territory into signing treaties."[20] When these treaties were delayed in Washington and encroaching farmers and miners increasingly pressured eastern Washington tribes, they too rose up in the Yakama War and in other later battles. Gradually pushed back by soldiers with superior weaponry, the Indians surrendered, and most moved to the new reservations. By the end of the 1850s, much of the fertile former Indian land in the present-day states of Oregon and Washington was in the hands of the federal government or incoming settlers, with most of the Indians on reservations.

•••

On 17 August 1857, sixty delegates met in Salem to piece together a new constitution they hoped would lead to statehood for Oregon. In the thirty-one meeting days that followed, through intense verbal exchanges, partisan dealings, and a few compromises, the convention produced the constitution. These intense efforts provide an illuminating, insightful glimpse of the political attitudes of many Oregon territorial leaders—and perhaps of most Oregonians at that time. From the early

1850s onward several efforts had been mounted to move Oregon into statehood, but political factionalism and shifting party allegiances in Oregon, and the seeming disinterest of a Congress three thousand miles distant were insurmountable barriers to statehood advocates. Then, in June 1857, even though Congress had not issued an enabling act calling for a new constitution, Oregonians voted 5,938 to 1,679 to take on the large step of constitutional writing.[21]

The delegates reflected well the occupational and political landscapes of Oregon. Of the sixty attendees, about half (thirty-one) were farmers, seventeen were lawyers, and the other twelve editors, mechanics and miners, surveyors, physicians, and one civil engineer. Revealingly, three-fourths (forty-five) of the delegates were Democrats of that party's varied stripes and one-fourth (fifteen) were anti-Democrats. Only John McBride of Yamhill County was a Republican and vigorously antislavery (perhaps the only abolitionist at the convention), with persons such as Jesse Applegate (notable Oregon Trail pioneer), Thomas Dryer (editor of the *Oregonian*), and David Logan (lawyer and acquaintance of Abraham Lincoln) vaguely Whig (soon to be Republican) and clearly anti-Democrat.[22]

The Oregon Democrats favored statehood, especially since as the majority party they could hope to control the convention proceedings and the outcome. Caucusing on the first day of the convention, the Democrats, speaking words of unity and solidarity, elected Matthew Deady as president of the meeting. But the Democratic unanimity was more chimerical and the anti-Democratic criticisms more successful than most anticipated. Verbal tussles concerning judicial organization, a bill of rights, religion and politics, and corporations proved more heated and complex than expected. These debates revealed the rents among the Democrats as well as the wide chasms between them and their opponents.

Even more significant for revealing existing attitudes and future political alignments in the Oregon Country were the more-than-warm debates over slavery and free blacks in Oregon. For the most part, the convention followed the agreed-on decision to avoid the subject of slavery (this avoidance so upset Applegate that he left the meeting), to keep it out of the constitution they were writing, and to refer the controversial issue to the people of the territory for their vote (a form of popular sovereignty). Discussions on civil rights and race, however, were more contentious, but in an unusual way: it became quickly clear that both Democrats and anti-Democrats wanted a white society and only white voting rights in Oregon as a state. The debates came over whether Chinese and mulattoes—and other nonwhites—should also be lumped in with the near-unanimous stance to keep out free blacks. After hot crossfires on words and groups, the convention agreed that voting rights should be limited to adult white males, but the question of whether free blacks would be allowed in Oregon would, like the issue of slavery, be put before Oregon voters in a separate referendum.

The votes on the proposed new state constitution and the two other issues provide a revealing glimpse of Oregonians' attitudes on the eve of the Civil War. As expected, voters strongly supported the proposed constitution, 7,195 to 3,125, and rejected slavery by an even larger margin, 7,727 to 2,645. Surprisingly, the largest margin in the 1857 vote came with Oregonians excluding free blacks, 8,640 to 1,081. Oregonians made clear, much like Abraham Lincoln in Illinois, they wanted statehood but no slavery and, even more, they wanted to keep free blacks out of their new state.[23] But Lincoln had not gone as far as Oregonians; he did not stump for excluding blacks from Illinois.

•••

While Oregon wobbled through its territorial period, several of Abraham Lincoln's acquaintances and close friends moved there and provided him with new links to the Far West. The first of Lincoln's friends to arrive in Oregon was David Logan in late 1849. Just twenty-four years of age, Logan had already displayed flashes of brilliance, but also disappointing behavior. The oldest son of Lincoln's second law partner, Stephen F. Logan, David read law in the Logan-Lincoln office and passed the bar in 1844, when barely twenty years old. After serving in the Mexican-American War under Edward D. Baker, another Lincoln friend, Logan returned to Springfield to enter into a law partnership with his father.[24]

The partnership never came to pass. Why not? Had an errant son alienated his stern, demanding father? Had his later difficulties with alcohol already begun? Had the father decided his son needed disciplining, seasoning, out in distant Oregon? Historian David Alan

Johnson suggests affirmative answers for all these questions, although he admits evidence is insufficient to prove all these shortcomings.[25]

Strong evidence does exist to conclude that David Logan was a young man endowed with huge strengths—and abundant flaws. Like a team of unmatched horses, he alternatively pranced and stumbled throughout his career in Oregon. Unfortunately his drawbacks and the attacks of his enemies kept him from realizing his life-long dreams of gaining a seat in Congress. The promise that his acquaintance Abraham Lincoln saw in Logan's early years in Illinois never came to full florescence in Oregon.

Whatever the reasons, Logan came to Oregon in late 1849, looking for a job to sustain himself. After a few weeks spent operating a ferry on the Willamette River, he moved to Lafayette in Yamhill County, where several other immigrants known to Lincoln would also settle. Logan quickly gained the reputation of a top-flight lawyer and, as a Whig, jumped into Oregon politics. Indeed, Logan's career in the next fifteen

David Logan was one of Abraham Lincoln's close acquaintances who moved to Oregon. Logan became a Whig and then Republican leader. But his personal shortcomings and erratic actions kept him from winning a much-desired seat in the U. S. Congress. (Oregon Historical Society Research Library, image 86816.)

years—from 1850 to the end of the Civil War—illustrated the whirligig of change that dominated Oregon Country politics as it gradually shifted from a Democratic-dominated to newly secured Republican area. Abraham Lincoln, indirectly, and his acquaintances and friends such as David Logan, directly, were central players in this intriguing political shift.

In the nearly twenty letters that Logan wrote to his oldest sister, Mary, in Illinois during this decade and a half, he chronicled his quick emergence as a Whig and then Republican leader in the Oregon Country. The same correspondence reveals, unfortunately, the personal flaws that often undermined his clear, abundant strengths.

By the early 1850s Logan began to emerge politically in Oregon, which he described as the home of a "mongrel population" of "prompt, honest" men but also "bruisers" in need of education. The Democrats ruled Oregon; "this is no place for a *Whig*," he told his sister. Then he confessed, in a more somber tone: "I am Isolated and alone so I expect to live so to die." In bittersweet retrospect, he recalled the warm, sustaining memories of his sweetheart who had died in Illinois before he came to Oregon.[26]

In the next two or three years Logan's law practice greatly expanded. He was doing well financially and being named to territorial judicial positions. But his political aspirations were still blunted. "When I came to Oregon," he wrote, "I had reason to expect an appointment from government, but instead of that I have not even met with encouragement from the *Whigs*."[27]

In 1854 Logan began his Oregon political career by election to the territorial legislature. Three years earlier he had run for the same position but lost a bitter battle to Matthew Deady, who had also moved to Yamhill County and became an unusually underhanded opponent of Logan for years to come. Indeed, Deady bragged of getting Logan drunk in the contest of 1851 and then accused him of raping a young Indian woman in late 1854. Deady claimed he had solid, documented accounts from eyewitnesses to the horrendous incident on the "Main streets of the town" (Jacksonville), but he never clearly revealed those accounts. Nor was the damning accusation ever trotted out again in several of Logan's subsequent contentious campaigns for local and national offices in

Oregon. Unfortunately, the normally sedate, lawyer-like Deady seemed to relish juicy details of men's aberrant sexual behavior and betrayed an unwarranted tendency to blast Logan on several occasions. Might the lack of corroborative evidence and its absence in other attacks on Logan in the *ad hominem* style of Oregon journalism suggest that it was evidence from rumor-mongering rather than bald truth? Perhaps the acerbic and caustic tongue of Logan had sent Deady and fellow Democrats on their long, slanted, anti-Logan trail.[28]

Three years later Logan was elected from the Portland area to the Oregon Constitutional Convention. Serving on the judiciary committee, Logan was quickly recognized as a man of abundant wit and analytical brilliance. But there was the other side, too. As John McBride, another Lafayette resident and convention member, recalled, Logan, "with his sarcastic tongue, made many a member subside in silence to his seat."[29] Although Logan opposed slavery, he was explicitly critical of radical abolitionists. And his racial views seemed of a piece with his Oregon contemporaries in voting to keep out Negroes, mulattoes, Chinese, and Native Hawaiians. At the close of the convention, Logan voted against the proposed constitution, disliking the section on the judiciary and opposing other statements he condemned as Democratic partisanship. Still, he later signed the constitution and advocated its passage.

Meanwhile, Logan's political affiliations were in transition. Arriving in Oregon as an "Old Whig," as were his mentors—his father and Lincoln—Logan's political stances began to differ markedly from those of the national Whig Party and, later, those of the Republicans. When Lincoln's Whig friend Dr. Anson G. Henry, during the Kansas-Nebraska controversies of 1854-55 spoke for the Missouri Compromise and opposed its repeal, Logan, who had served on a Whig political committee with Henry in Illinois, denounced the doctor's resolutions: "they were too ultra, and tinctured with abolitionism, to pledge the whig party of Oregon to."[30] Logan also criticized the new Republican Party and stayed with the Whigs much longer than most other Whigs. In 1856, he harpooned the Republicans as "negro worshippers" and wrote his sister that he would "see the Republicans Dead before I'll vote with them."[31]

But it was in his strong support for popular sovereignty that Logan broke most decisively from the Whigs, Republicans, and Abraham

Lincoln. Like Lincoln's two close friends, Anson Henry and Edward D. Baker—and many other Whigs and later Republicans in the Oregon Country—Logan backed the Kansas-Nebraska Act and its call for popular sovereignty. Historians before the 1960s, quite possibly taking their cues from the frontier thesis of Frederick Jackson Turner, speculated that popular sovereignty appealed especially to frontiersmen like Oregonians of the 1850s because it allowed them control of their own affairs and kept an intrusive, unwelcome federal government more at bay.[32] They thought and spoke like previous generations of frontiersmen. Partly true, undoubtedly, but the complex political party realignments in Oregon were also important. The minority Whigs and then, increasingly, toward the end of the 1850s, the Republicans had to come up with an issue that would attract larger numbers of supporters. In addition, they needed to find a tough stance to employ against the powerful Joseph Lane and Salem Clique Democrats. At first many who later became Republicans only opposed popular sovereignty in its allowing slavery to extend into the new territories, but it was difficult for them to distinguish the slavery issue from others in which they were open to popular sovereignty.[33] Once the Oregon Democrats began to experience their intraparty clashes, the Republicans increasingly sounded the tocsin for popular sovereignty, leading them toward the Douglas Democrats but away from the Lane and President James Buchanan Democrats.

David Logan became the leading voice for popular sovereignty among the Whigs and then the Republicans. In July 1858, when Oregonians thought they would soon become a state (the delay went on for several more months), Logan was nominated as the Republican candidate for the U.S. Senate, but Democrats Joseph Lane and Delazon ("Delusion" to his opponents) Smith were elected. Nearly a year later, in April 1859, Logan the Republican and Lansing Stout the proslavery Democrat locked up in a dramatic election for the U.S. House, with Stout winning by a scant sixteen votes, 5,646 to 5,630. It was, one historian has written, a "campaign … more bitter than any other in Oregon's history." Then, in 1860, Logan ran once more for Congress, losing again to another Democrat, George K. Shiel, with the latter winning another close election by just one hundred and three votes.[34]

Abraham Lincoln listened with obvious interest to reports about Logan's political campaigns in Oregon. On 4 July 1860, he wrote to Dr.

Henry, telling him, "We should be too happy if both Logan and Baker should triumph." One month later Lincoln's letter to Simeon Francis reported, "We were very anxious here for David Logan's election." Then, hearing of Logan's most recent loss in late summer 1860, Lincoln wrote to an Oregon acquaintance, telling him "it is [a] matter of much regret here that Logan failed of his election. He grew up and studied law in this place."[35] And a few weeks later he answered a letter from his distant cousin, John T. Hanks, then residing in Oregon, saying he wished Hanks had not opposed Logan in the summer 1860 election because he had known Logan for a long time and supported him.[36]

So, on the eve of the momentous election of 1860, David Logan had risen to the top of the Republican ranks in Oregon. He had made clear in the late 1850s that he disagreed with the national Republican Party—and Lincoln's stance—on slavery. As Logan wrote in 1859, "I intend so far as the 'negro' question is concerned to be identified hereafter, with that political party, that favors the submission of the question of slavery to the people of the organized Territories—and is opposed to any kind of Federal intervention therewith." In faraway Oregon, David Logan and most of Lincoln's other Republican friends sounded more like Douglas Democrats than Lincoln Republicans. That positive position on popular sovereignty was the stance they would take into the election in 1860 and, ironically, help Lincoln to win in Oregon.

• • •

The most lively personally—and rabid politically—of Lincoln's close friends in Oregon was Dr. Anson G. Henry. Born with an evident cocklebur in his diaper, Henry never succeeded in finding a way to rid himself of the irritant. It was a spur to his incessant activity in Illinois and Oregon. Although he was trained as a medical doctor and first came to Springfield, Illinois, in 1832 to set up practice, Henry quickly converted to politics, Whig politics, and became Abraham Lincoln's confidant and firm political friend in the next two decades. Even after Henry moved to Oregon in 1852, the good doctor remained close to Lincoln, encouraging him, backing his decisions and policies, and importuning his White House colleague for political appointments.[37]

When Anson Henry arrived in Illinois, patterns of behavior that defined his career were already in place. Born in 1804 into an undistinguished upstate New York family of little financial standing, Henry had bounced from teaching, mining, business, and politics to medicine. All lacked sufficient remuneration. Now married and with an expanding family, Henry came to Springfield with but $5.30 in his pockets and no position in sight.[38]

Henry repeated in Springfield what he had tried elsewhere. First medicine, administration, and then politics—mainly politics. As usual, he became so enmeshed in Whig Party dealings that his medical practice suffered. Bonding with Lincoln, Henry became part of the Whig Junto, which also included Edward D. Baker and John T. Stuart (Lincoln's first law partner). Lincoln, Baker, and Stuart were the speakers, the candidates, the "faces" of the Whig organization. Henry was something of an office manager and wrote hundreds of letters to national and state officials to build up the Whig Party. Later, in pushing for Henry's selection as an Indian agent in the West, Lincoln wrote of him: "Dr. Henry was at first, has always been, and still is, No. [Number] One with me. ... I believe, nay, I *know* he has done more disinterested labor in the Whig cause, than any other one, two, or three men in the state."[39]

Lincoln also admitted earlier that he was deeply indebted to Henry personally. When Lincoln's troubled courtship with Mary Todd in 1840-41 crashed and he fell into a deep depression, Dr. Henry stepped into the agonizing situation. He helped Lincoln through those troubled times when "the hypo" crouched at his door, threatening to upset all that was dear to him. Again, in touting Henry for an appointive position, Lincoln admitted that the empathetic doctor might be "necessary to my existence."[40]

But not all men and women of Illinois reacted to Henry as Lincoln did. The doctor was outspoken, partisan, and sometimes too direct, especially in his reactions to opponents or what he considered the unfaithful among his own party. As one historian has discerningly noted, Henry was a "fiery fighter with a capacity for making two bitter enemies for each warm friend."[41] Henry never seemed to understand that his headlong, be-damned approach to partisan politics might undermine his occupational successes in the Springfield area. Anson Henry was devotedly political, rarely politic.

Henry's penchant for politics and pugnacity on public issues shortened his work as a doctor in Illinois. When his relocations elsewhere proved equally unsuccessful, he returned to Springfield and tried to land government appointments. His efforts to gain a postmastership or to become secretary of the Minnesota Territory or to be elected a probate justice of the peace all came to naught.[42]

Henry and his supporter Lincoln did not give up. On 22 March 1850 Lincoln wrote to cabinet member Thomas Ewing, asking that the secretary give "consideration to the question of appointing Dr. A. G. Henry to some Indian agency."[43] This time the importuning paid off; Henry was named an Indian agent in Oregon. The doctor never took up the position, however. The details are vague, and Henry's detractors then and historians much later have used the missing facts to pillory him. Evidently, in Panama on his way to the West Coast, Henry encountered his close friend Edward Baker, who was then recruiting men to build a railroad across the Isthmus of Panama. Henry, always on the scout for much-needed funding, agreed to remain in Panama as doctor to the men there and to also help with the recruitment of more men to the project. Still, he accepted $750 as part of his Indian agent's salary.

A dozen years later when his political enemies in Washington Territory accused Henry of absconding with the $750, he wrote an explanation in his own newspaper, *The Washington Standard*. If what Henry wrote was entirely true, he fell victim to bureaucratic snafus, never was paid his personal expenses to go to Oregon, and thus kept the $750. Henry was not prosecuted then or later, suggesting the government realized the $750 was fair compensation for what he attempted to do. But Henry did prosecute his journalistic accuser, vigorously beating him with a cane.[44]

When other ventures proved fruitless, in 1852 Henry organized and led a train of ten wagons up the Oregon Trail to the Pacific Northwest. They left Illinois on 6 April and arrived in Oregon the next October. Although overlanders in the early 1850s were often beset with disastrous attacks of Asiatic cholera, the Henry train came safely through to the Columbia, down it to Portland, and up the Willamette to Lafayette in Yamhill County, where other residents of Illinois's Sangamon County and Springfield had immigrated and beckoned Dr. Henry to relocate. He was granted a Donation Land claim of 320 acres and confided to his overland trail diary, "Very much pleased with the country."[45]

True to form, Henry soon forgot his farming; his medical practice was moderately launched and his political career enthusiastically rekindled in a new setting. With his unrelenting desire to set his neighbors straight he was soon telling them what they should believe and how they should vote. Lafayette, then second or third among Oregon towns in size, became a hotspot for Whiggery and thus a comfortable home for Henry. He announced his willingness to serve his community as a doctor, made presentations at temperance meetings, involved himself in agricultural organizations, and was named deputy surveyor of Yamhill County. Henry maintained contact with Edward Baker, now a thriving lawyer in San Francisco, and shared his worries about the future of David Logan, worries that Baker shared and enlarged.[46]

In early summer 1854 Henry was elected to the lower house of the Oregon Territorial Legislature. Among his several attempts to gain elective office, this was his only victory. While in the legislature, Henry was viewed as the leader of the Whigs, which included David Logan, and spoke explicitly on temperance and schooling issues, the latter deriving from his service on the educational committee.[47]

But another controversial issue captured most of Henry's attention. The entire country was convulsed following Stephen A. Douglas's introduction and Congress' passage of the Kansas-Nebraska Act. Not surprisingly, Henry plunged into the fray and vociferously broadcast his views. His speeches on this vexing issue in 1854-55 prefigured most of the political debates that whetted the doctor's political interests from then through the election of 1860. The terrible institution of slavery, its possible detrimental expansion into the territories, popular sovereignty, the repeal of the Missouri Compromise in the Kansas-Nebraska Act, and the Dred Scott decision were at the center of the doctor's charged comments before the legislature and would be for the next half dozen years. For the most part, Henry's views coincided with those of Abraham Lincoln, but unique features of the territorial political landscape of Oregon also introduced new wrinkles not a part of Lincoln's political credo.

In his views, Henry broke company with Oregon's Democrats and even with some Whigs on the Kansas-Nebraska imbroglio. Like Lincoln, Henry had come to believe that energetic opposition to the expansion of slavery should be the first and most important cause of the Whigs. He summed up that stance and attendant issues in a series of resolutions and presentations he made in the legislature. "I shall oppose," Henry asserted:

> *with all the power the God of nature has given me any and everything that shall have a tendency, directly or indirectly, to fix the bonds of slavery on any human being now free; or that shall extend the boundaries of slavery. I will stand by the right; stand by the abolitionist in restoring the compromise line of 1820; and I will stand by the slaveholder in maintaining and enforcing the fugitive slave law, and the compromise measures of 1850 in letter and spirit.*[48]

But in one large area, his position on popular sovereignty, Henry separated himself from Lincoln and joined an increasing chorus of opinion in Oregon. As mentioned, the growing desires of territorial Oregonians to control their own destinies and to find a way to compete more equally with the powerful Democrats in their region were motivating factors among Oregon Whigs—and, later, Republicans—to support popular sovereignty when their national parties did not.

In a rather complex and sometimes tortured way, Henry tried to clarify when he supported popular sovereignty, and when not. Although the majority opinion of the people should rule in most issues, Henry reasoned, it should give way on the Missouri Compromise, retain that agreement of 1820-21, and turn aside efforts for slavery expansion. To fellow Whig David Logan, Henry's ideas were too abolitionist and not to be followed, although Logan too eventually supported popular sovereignty. So did Lincoln's—and Henry's and Logan's—friend Edward Baker, when he came to Oregon in 1859-60 and won an Oregon senatorial seat in 1860. In their support of popular sovereignty in the 1850s, a position motivated largely by territorial concerns and Oregon's political scene, three of Lincoln's political friends and allies in Oregon—Logan, Henry, and Baker—diverged markedly from the views of Abraham Lincoln and the national Whig and Republican parties.

After Henry's active stint in the Oregon legislature ended in 1855, he moved on to other pressing regional issues. When the Rogue Indian War erupted into new ferocity in fall 1855, Henry jumped into the conflict, volunteering as Commissary and Quartermaster General. And, as always,

Henry had strong opinions about the origins, purposes, and meanings of the war, which he presented in a stormy message in Corvallis, which was printed as a pamphlet. Primarily a stirring indictment of the coverage of the war in Asahel Bush's *Oregon Statesman*, and Governor George L. Curry's actions, Henry's talk attacked these opinions and actions and, conversely, supported the deeds of the Oregon volunteer citizen soldiers. Henry dismissed the "false impressions" and incorrect information in the *Statesman*, driven, he believed, by Democratic political bias. That misleading journalism had to be countered.[49] Henry seemed to enjoy continuing his role as gadfly and critic, although his pro-citizen and army volunteer position, as well as his anti-Indian perspectives, enjoyed little or no support in subsequent scholarly studies of the Rogue War.[50]

After the white-Indian conflict died down when Natives were relocated to newly opened reservations, the ever-active Henry was off in new directions. Building on his recent experiences in Oregon as a land surveyor, he took on several contracts as a surveyor in Oregon and especially in Washington Territory, in the Puget Sound area. In time, these experiences helped Henry gain the presidential appointment from Lincoln as surveyor-general of Washington Territory in 1861.[51]

These actions did not sideline Henry's major, unrelenting hobby: politics, and lots of it. In the Whig Convention of April 1856, Henry received eight votes for Oregon's congressional delegate, a nomination that ex-Governor John P. Gaines obtained but lost in the run-off against incumbent Joseph Lane, the Democrat. In addition, although Henry was not a delegate to the Constitutional Convention in late summer 1857, he kept close watch on the discussions and decisions that transpired at the gathering.

In 1857 Henry set out to change the political face of Oregon. Realizing that the residency requirements adopted at the Constitutional Convention were very lenient, Henry fired off a letter to Edward Baker in California, inviting his long-time Illinois friend to come to Oregon to compete for one of the senatorial seats in the soon-to-be-organized state. Baker expressed his willingness to come and may even have boarded a steamer in San Francisco headed north—and then changed his mind and disembarked. For whatever reasons, Baker did not come, but Henry did not forget his earlier invitation. Probably, it was Henry who suggested in the spring of 1859 that Baker be again asked to enter the fray for a U. S. Senate seat in Oregon. As we shall see, Henry was instrumental in Baker's finally coming to Oregon in late 1859 (Baker himself) and early 1860 (Baker with his family) and successfully competing for one of the Senate slots.[52]

Even when out of Oregon and working off and on as a surveyor in Washington Territory, Henry kept an eye on Oregon politics. Although Henry told Lincoln in 1859, "I have taken but little interest in local Politics of Oregon," his activities told a variant story. So did his thoughts. In the same letter to Lincoln, the doctor asserted that Joseph Lane controlled the "Pro Slavery wing of the Democracy, & their old Democratic Champion (the editor of the 'Oregon Statesman') [was] leading the free state wing." Seeing and understanding this rent in the Democratic fabric, Henry continued, "The Republicans, who compose one third of the voters, ... ought to unite with the true old fashioned democracy." If the Republicans married themselves to the "old-fashioned Democrats," they could control Oregon politics. It was a union Henry pursued and encouraged. Indeed, he added to Lincoln, "when you hear of my having turned Democrat dont be surprised, for you may know that my course will be prompted by an honest desire to secure for Oregon a free Constitution."[53]

So, as the election year of 1860 dawned, Henry would not lend support to any divisive Republican efforts. Instead, as he told Lincoln, he would look for ways to fuse with like-minded Democrats. This was the pragmatic agenda that Henry and several other leading Republicans followed into the path-breaking election of 1860.

• • •

Simeon Francis and Edward D. Baker, Lincoln's two other close friends who immigrated to Oregon, were there for much briefer periods of time than David Logan and Anson Henry. Logan had resided in Oregon for nearly a dozen years before Lincoln gained the White House, Henry more than eight years. Francis had been an Oregon resident only fifteen months, Baker less than a year. But Francis and Baker were long-time friends and political companions of Lincoln in Illinois, and even if their stays in Oregon were very brief before Lincoln became president, they too did much to further Lincoln's cause and to shape Oregon politics in the Civil War era.

Simeon Francis, a journalist, also became a skilled political activist. He rode those two lively horses, often compatibly and vigorously, in his first years in Illinois. Born in Connecticut in 1796, Francis served his apprenticeship as a newspaperman in Connecticut and New York before moving to Illinois in 1831. There, with his three brothers, Francis launched the *Sangamo Journal*, later renamed the *Illinois State Journal*. The newspaper became the state's leading Whig periodical, and, over time, Abraham Lincoln and Francis became close friends. Francis sustained Lincoln's politics and opened the pages of his periodical to Lincoln's writings. James Matheny, best man at Lincoln's wedding, recalled much later that he had taken "hundreds of editorials from him [Lincoln] to Simeon Francis." Or, as another early biographer put it, Lincoln operated more out of Francis's office than out of his own law office.[54]

Politics—Whig politics—first drew Lincoln and Francis together. When Simeon Francis and his brothers swung their support behind Lincoln, that encouragement did much to spawn his political career. Francis, along with Dr. Henry and other members of the Whig Junto, were also strongly in favor of borrowing the necessary funds to launch the new state government-sponsored program of internal improvements that Lincoln advocated in the Illinois legislature.[55]

Sometimes Francis's involvement with Lincoln got him, unwittingly, into perplexing situations. In 1837, Lincoln spoke effusively in support of his friend Dr. Henry for the position of probate justice of the peace, with Francis then leaping into the bitter battle by publishing in the *Sangamo Journal* an anonymous letter signed "Sampson's Ghost." It was a vicious attack on Henry's Democratic opponent, James Adams. The emotional and unwise war against Adams failed: Henry lost badly to Adams, and Francis ended up with editorial mud splattered across his face.[56] Three years later, Stephen A. Douglas, incensed by something published in the *Journal*, attempted to publicly cane Francis. But the sturdy editor, said to be "second to none in Whig bravado," grabbed the diminutive Douglas by the hair until he was "pulled away from him [Douglas]."[57]

Then in 1842 a more sensational series of events involved Francis and Lincoln. A journalistic war similar to the Henry-Adams battle broke out in the *Journal*, which this time was attacking and denigrating

Simeon Francis, another of Abraham Lincoln's close friends who moved to Oregon, supported Lincoln's presidential efforts in 1860. Later, Lincoln named Francis paymaster at Fort Vancouver. Courtesy of Tom Lapsley Collection.

State Auditor James Shields. Several of the letters jabbing Shields, an emotional, lively, and record-breaking Democratic politician who went on to senatorships in three states, came anonymously from the pen of "Rebecca" of a mythical Lost Townships settlement. Lincoln, Mary Todd (Lincoln's wife to be), and one of Mary's friends were involved as authors of these pointed, satirical letters. Once Shields found out that Lincoln was the writer of some of the letters (Francis provided that information), he challenged the long-armed Lincoln to a duel. Choosing broadswords as weapons, which gave him a decided advantage, Lincoln tried to defuse the conflict, which he did. But the fallout from the drama did not redound well for Lincoln or Francis's *Sangamo Journal*.[58]

One outcome of the near-duel with Shields was redemptive, however. The collaboration in writing the Rebecca letters in the late summer and early fall of 1842 brought Lincoln and Mary Todd back together after a canceled engagement in January 1841. Simeon Francis and his wife went several steps farther: when Lincoln and Mary Todd's courtship had foundered, the Francises opened their home as a haven for Abraham and Mary's friendship to rekindle as they renewed their stuttering steps toward matrimony. It was Sim and Eliza Francis, along with Dr. Henry and his wife, Eliza, who did most to reunite Abraham and Mary and to help bring about their marriage on 4 November 1842.[59]

Sim (or "White Bear") Francis often had itchy feet, which surfaced in his desire to leave Illinois. Once Lincoln made it into Congress, he was expected—and repeatedly asked—to recommend his friends and political allies for patronage positions. Among those he tried to help were Simeon Francis and Anson Henry. As alluded to in the previous chapter, when Lincoln was offered the office of secretary of the new Oregon Territory in August 1849, he turned down the position and told Secretary John Clayton that he [Lincoln] would "be greatly obliged if the place be offered to Simeon Francis. ... He will accept it, is capable, and would be faithful in the discharge of its duties." And then Lincoln went on to say that Francis had "for a long time desired to go to Oregon." In the next few weeks Lincoln reminded his Washington correspondents of his support for Francis and reiterated that if named to the Oregon position Francis would do credit to himself and the Taylor administration. When Lincoln rejected the governorship of Oregon, he told another Taylor cabinet member: "I am still anxious that, Simeon Francis shall be secretary of that Territory." That appointment did not come to Francis, so Lincoln wrote again to Washington recommending Francis, this time for surveyor-general of Oregon.[60]

Francis did not give up on an appointment, and neither did Lincoln. In September 1850 Lincoln wrote asking for a Francis interview with the new secretary of the interior, whom Lincoln did not know. Although Lincoln's letter did not so state, Francis evidently hoped for an appointment as an Indian agent in the West. This time he was successful, as the *Illinois State Journal* announced on 16 October 1850. It is thought that when Anson Henry resigned from his assignment to go to Oregon as an Indian agent, Francis was named as his replacement. But Francis never went. The next spring the *Oregon Spectator* told the rather negative story that neither of Lincoln's Illinois friends had come to Oregon to serve as an Indian agent in 1850.[61]

In the mid-1850s a major shift in Francis's career occurred. Feeling the pressure of recent journalistic competition coming to town, Francis and his family sold the *Illinois State Journal* to two young, ambitious newspapermen wanting to capture all the non-Democrats in Illinois, including old Whigs, new Republicans, and nativist Know-Nothings. The upstarts were linked to the "Edwards clique," an elite group of

Springfield residents related to Lincoln through his wife Mary. (But, Francis clarified, "*Lincoln* does not belong to the Edwards clique.") Hearing that Dr. Henry had withdrawn from politics, Francis wrote to him in Oregon that this was a "wonderful coincidence, the fact *that I am also*" out of politics. Once released from his heavy and daily journalistic demands, Francis invested in a business, which, sadly, fell into ruin largely as a result of the dampening financial impact of a nation-wide depression, the Panic of 1857.[62]

Now the pull to Oregon became more insistent. Francis sold out in Illinois and arrived in Portland late in 1859. On the eve of his long-delayed trip he wrote to Lincoln that the "elections in the free States render it quite certain, I think, that the Republicans will have the next President,—if they select the proper candidate. ... Pardon me—I believe you are the man for the times; and your friends should present your name to public attention in a manner that will make the people believe they are in earnest."[63]

But that positive, encouraging perspective jostled for dominance with a somber mood of self-pity and accusation once Francis and his reluctant wife landed in Portland. In a long, complex letter to Lincoln just a few days after arriving, Francis first told his long-time political ally about their Illinois friends now in Oregon. Edward Baker had, within days, come from California to visit Oregon; "he is coming here on a political mission," Francis opined. "His object is to go to the Senate. ... My opinion [is] that he will be successful in his enterprise." He had also heard good reports about David Logan. "As a legal man," Francis noted, Logan "leads the bar here. ... I think he has passed the crisis [overcoming alcoholism?] and hereafter will be all that his friends desire." And as for Dr. Henry, "I find he has been boxing the compass here as a politician, but that he is now right."

Then, in his letter written one day after Christmas 1859, Francis turned suddenly sour and accusatory. He would "be frank" with Lincoln, "if I never have been before." When he had to sell his paper because of threatening competition, he lamented, "no friends came to me to say they would stand by me. ... I never had [a] cheering word from you or Judge Logan, or any of those for whom I had worked with all the little ability I possessed." His newspaper was gone, his business had failed, his friends had abandoned him. "I am now surrounded with strange faces—strange scenes." These were the words of a disappointed, even depressed, sixty-two-year-old man, with an unhappy wife, and in a new, alien country. Abraham Lincoln did not immediately respond.[64]

This cheerless letter proved to be an uncharacteristic low point for Simeon Francis. His wife did not like Oregon, and he did not yet have a position to support himself. But work on the Portland *Oregonian* soon came, and Francis bounced back. Two months later, in February 1860, he would write a strong, influential letter of support for Lincoln as president, providing the first major call to Oregonians for them to consider the tall, rail-splitting lawyer from Illinois for their next president. And in the coming months Francis proved a powerful support to Lincoln in Oregon in his 1860 presidential bid.

• • •

Edward D. Baker may have been the most influential of Lincoln's Illinois friends who relocated to Oregon. But his stay there was the briefest of the four. A superb orator, an enthusiastic leader, and an energetic politician, Baker was thrice elected to the U. S. Congress. He was Lincoln's warm acquaintance, competitor, and fellow Whig. So close was Baker to Abraham and Mary Lincoln that they named their second son, Edward Baker (Eddie) Lincoln, after Baker. And in March 1861 when Lincoln could have chosen any of his friends or political allies to introduce him before his inauguration as president, it was Baker he selected. Lincoln's links with Baker help to illuminate the sixteenth president's expanding knowledge of and connections with the American West.[65]

Born in London, England, on 24 February 1811, Baker immigrated to the U. S. with his family at age five. When he was a teenager, his parents moved to Illinois, where he read law, became an attorney, and married a young widow with two children. In 1835 Baker relocated to Springfield and quickly connected with Lincoln in law and Whig politics. Very soon, Baker's power and eloquence as a soaring speaker gained wide attention; his oratory, as well as his stump speaking, captured his audiences. Three years after Lincoln was elected to the Illinois legislature, Baker was selected to join him in that legislative body.

The union between law and politics that so often produces American politicians also included a third ingredient in Baker's case. He emoted over things military, often leading military marching groups in the 1830s and 1840s in Illinois. Baker loved performance—whether as orator, a preacher (he was a lay minister in the Campbellite or Christian Church), or strutting soldier. Lincoln's third law partner, Billy Herndon, encapsulated Baker's character: "quick—active & full of energy—having great fancy—more of fancy than imagination. He was lively—spontaneous—generous—profuse. ... He was bold brave—chivalrous—restless—uneasy. ... Cut and carved his own way through life."[66]

The restlessness and military eagerness surfaced after Baker was elected to the U. S. House of Representatives as a Whig in 1844. Unlike Lincoln, Baker zealously supported the declaration of war against Mexico. Resigning his seat in Congress, Baker helped raise and lead a regiment (which included David Logan) to fight in Mexico. Injured, he returned to Illinois and was reelected to the House for a term beginning in 1849. He again left Congress, this time to help build a railroad in Panama.

During the twenty years Baker and Lincoln competed and worked together in Illinois, they showed both similar and different faces. Both were motivated to jump aboard the uncertain Whig express in Illinois that pulled hard, but usually unsuccessfully, to thwart the designs of the more numerous Democrats. Although they competed for the same position in the U. S. House in 1842 and 1844, they did so, for the most part, amicably. In fact, with Baker's support, Lincoln was Baker's successor in Washington, D.C., in 1846.

In other ways, the two close friends were very different politically and personally. Baker, for example, was a rabid expansionist, particularly pertaining to the Oregon Country. In Congress in the mid-1840s, Baker, in a quick and memorable rebuttal of a colleague from Massachusetts, argued that the U. S. should go "for the whole of Oregon; every grain of sand that sparked in her moonlight, and every pebble on its wave-worn strand." On the floor of Congress, and rereading American history, Baker asserted that Oregon "was ours—all ours! Ours by treaty—ours by discovery." A bit later Baker urged President Polk not "to surrender to any foreign power [England] any territory to which, in his opinion, we have a clear and unquestionable title."[67] It was a revealing and intriguing stance for a British-born American politician to take.

Baker's bombast and grandiloquent metaphors were most often absent from Lincoln's straightforward and usually strongly rational presentations. Even more notable, unlike Baker, Lincoln did not speak out on the Oregon Question in the 1840s. Moreover, he was sharply critical of Polk's leadership in the Mexican War, when Baker was not. On these two western controversies, the Oregon Question and the Mexican-American War, Edward Baker and Abraham Lincoln took very different positions.

Other differences between Baker and Lincoln also became apparent. Baker, though he spoke at temperance meetings, loved to imbibe, play cards, dance, and sing. One Lincoln biographer provides a captivating thumbnail sketch of Baker's personal qualities: "Impulsive, eager for glory, Baker won many friends—among them Lincoln—with his personal warmth, commanding presence, generosity, and *joie de vivre*."[68] But while gaining increasingly larger retainers for his legal work, which could have led to more than comfortable living, Baker was a notoriously profligate spender and not dependable with his funds. Indeed, his one-time law partner Stephen Logan (also a law partner of Lincoln) reportedly said of Baker, "I could not trust him in money matters. He got me into some scrapes by collecting and using money."[69]

Few of these descriptive words fit Lincoln. Most saw him as quiet, pensive, sometimes moody, reticent (even "shut-mouthed"), and somber. True, he too was a first-rate speaker and gathered the trust and allegiance of many, but they were rarely Lincoln disciples or fans; usually friends, acquaintances, and supporters.

Things did not go exceptionally well for Baker when he abandoned his seat in Congress and became involved in building the railroad across Panama. The swamps, the climate, the diseases, and distances—all seemed to conspire against success. Then Baker himself came down with a fever and dysentery and had to retreat to the U. S. to recover. Dissatisfactions piled up, and in 1852 Baker on the spur of the moment decided to move to California. It was to be his home for the next seven years.

Some argue that Baker went to California to promote Whig Party fortunes in that far-off Democratic land. Perhaps, but the evidence is not conclusive.[70] What is clear is Baker's energetic entry into California public life. His speeches, his legal work, and his political activism as a stalwart Whig overnight connected him with numerous political leaders, journalists, and other sociocultural figures.

Moreover, in the constantly realigning, litigious, and violent society that defined Gold Rush California, Baker was often called into court and also asked to make several funeral orations. His strong defense of gambler and duelist Charles Cora led to a hung jury but did not save Cora from a vigilante hangman's noose. His memorial addresses honoring two men killed in duels—William L. Ferguson and, more importantly, U. S. Senator David C. Broderick—added much to Baker's reputation as an oratorical demigod.

They did not win elections for him, however. Defeated as a Whig in 1855 in a run for the California Senate, he tried again as Republican in September 1859, unsuccessfully, for a seat in the U. S. House. California, largely Democratic, kept Whigs and then Republicans out of any state office and all U.S. congressional offices in its first ten years. Baker's energetic participation in the founding of the Republican Party, for his own benefit, and his support for the Republican candidate John C. Frèmont in 1856 won him friends and attention but not the offices he craved.

Baker's second unsuccessful plunge into California political waters in 1859 made him all the more approachable to entreaties from Oregon. Even in 1857 Baker had begun to think about Oregon as less flooded over with Democrats. Following his defeat in the U. S. congressional race in 1859, Baker was ready for the blandishments of his friends and other Republicans in Oregon.

Dr. Henry had been planting seeds of interest in Baker's political garden since 1857. In the Republican state convention of April 1859, Henry and Thomas Dryer, another leading Republican and editor of the *Oregonian*, began to tout Baker as the candidate who could rally Republicans, work with like-minded Democrats, and win over independents.[71] Now other Republicans arrived to nourish those earlier plantings. Soon after Baker's loss in early fall 1859, a small group of Republicans from the north visited Baker to urge him to come to Oregon, campaign for the Republican cause, and perhaps run for office himself. In the same months a similar invitation came from Dryer and Logan, who also traveled to California to speak with Baker. They too asked him to move forward the Oregon Republican cause with his captivating oratory and skills as a pragmatic politician, and they also suggested a possible run for the U.S. Senate.[72]

This time Baker did not hesitate. The insatiable appetite of a political carpetbagger had been whetted. Coming north by steamer, Baker arrived in mid-December 1859 and immediately wrote to Anson Henry, who was evidently out of town. Baker urged him to return quickly: "Please come and see me right away," he told his old friend.[73] Meeting with leading Republicans and looking over the country, Baker immediately decided Oregon provided fertile openings for his next political forays. After returning to California, he brought his family into Oregon in early 1860 and girded up his loins for the coming election. His presence and very active role in the intense campaign of the following months clearly made a difference in Oregon politics and sharply redirected the trajectory of his own political career.

•••

Lincoln's four friends from Illinois in Oregon were not his only personal connections to the region, even though they were his most important links with the Far Northwest. Other Illinois acquaintances had moved to Oregon and kept in contact with Lincoln. Among these was David Watson Craig, a journalist who had trained with Simeon Francis and studied in Lincoln's law office before coming to Oregon in 1853. He soon established a reputation as a diligent, trustworthy newspaperman and later became an editor of the Oregon *Argus*. He also helped found the Republican Party in Oregon. It is said that Lincoln subscribed to the *Argus*, enjoying its strong Republican bent and its biting criticism of Oregon's Democrats.[74]

Another former resident of Sangamon County was David Newsom, who immigrated to Oregon in 1851. He had made use of Lincoln's legal services while in the Springfield area before becoming an Oregonian and establishing an expanding, very successful farm near Salem. Over the years, he wrote dozens of letters to Illinois readers about Oregon and farming, especially to the leading Whig-Republican newspaper, the *Illinois State Journal*. Later, Lincoln gave him an agricultural appointment in the Willamette Valley. Still another long-time acquaintance of Lincoln's was A. R. Elder, who had grown up with Lincoln in Kentucky and later was his neighbor in Illinois. Elder kept in contact with Lincoln and was subsequently appointed an Indian agent in Washington Territory.[75]

Overall, dozens of former residents of Springfield and Sangamon County relocated to Oregon, and many settled in Yamhill County, several in Lafayette, where David Logan and Anson G. Henry resided for part of the 1850s.

Later, William Henson Wallace, William Pickering, Samuel C. Parks, and Sidney Edgerton became important contacts with Lincoln. All acquaintances with Lincoln in Illinois, they were appointed to political positions in the Washington, Idaho, and Montana territories during Lincoln's presidential administration. On the other hand, Amory Holbrook, whom Lincoln met on one of his political junkets in the East, took a different direction. Ambitious to receive political patronage, Holbrook was increasingly critical of Edward Baker, Dr. Henry, and other Lincoln's appointments when he thought them too much influenced by Baker—and when they left him with no political plums.[76] As we shall see, Holbrook's sourness continued—and turned bitter—in the years to come.

These friends and political acquaintances were immensely important personal links for Lincoln in the Oregon Country. They kept him abreast of political crosscurrents in the Pacific Northwest, and most of the men diligently promoted his political prospects in the territories and new state in the region. Of all the territories and states west of the Mississippi, Lincoln was more directly connected, personally, with Oregon than with any other area. These acquaintances also helped establish the Republican Party in the Far West, with Baker the first Republican elected from Oregon or California. The personal influences became even clearer in the path-breaking election of 1860.

Chapter 3: Lincoln, the Oregon Country, and the Election of 1860

In the closing months of 1859 and the early weeks of 1860, Abraham Lincoln exhibited his willingness to run for the presidency. He had been reluctant to think in that direction immediately following his loss to Stephen Douglas after the momentous debates in summer and fall of 1858. But now, he admitted to his friend Lyman Trumbull, "the taste *is* in my mouth a little"; he could begin to see himself as a viable candidate for the White House.[1] Still, as he surveyed the American political landscape in the opening days of 1860, Lincoln urged his admirers and friends to be cautious, not to alienate others with a too-precipitous announcement and campaign. It was better to be venturously conservative, thinking of possibilities but carefully scrutinizing the political terrain before making any large decisions. The Republicans particularly needed to understand the dynamic issues separating the Democrats into the Buchanan-administration Democrats and the dissenting Douglas Democrats, and perhaps see how they could take advantage of this widening split.

Two thousand miles to the west, Oregon Republicans were equally ambitious but cautious as they peered into the political future of their new state in early 1860. They needed a stronger party organization, a top-drawer speaker to rally the troops, and careful consideration of how they might capture disaffected Democrats in coming electoral contests. Republicans in the Far West realized they might have to break from their national brethren on several issues in order to win their first statewide offices. As on the national scene, Democrats in Oregon were searching for ways to keep their party sufficiently united to hold on against the rising Republicans.

By the end of 1860, a political revolution had taken place, with huge implications for the nation as well as for residents of Oregon. Republicans had ousted the Democrats from the White House and gained the presidency for the first time. On the heels of the Republican victory, disillusioned southerners began to take their states out of the Union. This rupture meant that Lincoln would have a clear majority in Congress. His win also meant that Republicans would now control the powerful levers of patronage, able to name hundreds—even thousands—of their supporters and friends to public office. In the Oregon Country, Lincoln's win indicated he would be appointing territorial officials and thus launching the Republican Party in a new and more powerful way in the Pacific Northwest. Truly, the election of 1860 brought about a political revolution in the nation and in the Oregon Country. It also helped to forge several more Lincoln links with the Far Northwest.[2]

• • •

National and regional politics were experiencing similarly divisive times on the eve of the election of 1860. A fratricidal civil war had broken out among the Democrats over the issue of "Bleeding Kansas." Journalist Horace Greeley had coined the term to describe the political disagreement within Kansas as to whether it should be a slave or free state. President James Buchanan and administrative Democrats accepted the Lecompton Constitution, one of four proposed for Kansas, that allowed slavery in the state. Pointing to what he considered an illegal use of popular sovereignty that did not allow the will of the people in the Kansas Territory, Stephen Douglas broke with the president, declaring the Lecompton Constitution fraudulent and unacceptable. The division between the two wings of the Democratic Party had exploded into a broad chasm as the 1850s came to a close.

The Republicans, on the other hand, were on an upward swing, looking to bring additional voters into their new party and capture the White House in 1860. Buoyed by their surprisingly good showing in their initial run for the presidency in 1856 with John C. Frèmont, the Republicans were considering how best to expand their reach, win over unhappy Democrats, and name a presidential candidate who would draw rather than alienate voters.[3]

Similar divisions and challenges faced voters in the Oregon Country. By 1860 Salem Clique Democrats, captained by Asahel Bush, editor of the *Oregon Statesman*, had broken with Joseph Lane, the region's leading Democrat for nearly a decade. Competitions, clashing personalities, and differences on national issues had rent the party. Bush was siding with the Douglas Democrats, and Lane remained loyal to the Buchanan administrative Democrats. It became increasingly evident in the early days of 1860 that, though the Democrats were clearly in the majority in Oregon, they were in serious trouble, with the possibility of losing that year's elections if they continued their political feuds.

The new state's Republicans were not blind to what the Democratic divisions could mean for them. But if the Democrats had too many leaders jockeying for leadership, the Republicans lacked one around whom they could rally. Most of all they needed an oratorical commander to general their new party. David Logan could compete with the state's best from the podium, with Delazon "Delusion" Smith, Joseph Lane, and other Democrats, for example; but his unpredictable political and personal actions made him suspect. So the Oregon Republicans looked elsewhere and spotted the imposing figure of Edward D. Baker, who was making himself increasingly well known in California even though he had been unsuccessful in his runs for office. David Logan and Dr. Henry knew Baker well from Illinois days and urged fellow Republicans in Oregon to bring Baker north to stump for their nascent organization. Meanwhile, although *Oregonian* editor Thomas J. Dryer had championed the "100% Americanism" of the short-lived Know-Nothing Party in Oregon, the movement and its nativistic platform had not gained many adherents in the mid-1850s and was essentially moribund as the election of 1860 loomed.

The details of Baker's coming to Oregon and his stated purposes remain vague. Some clearly wanted Baker to rally Oregon's Republicans with his dazzling voice; others desired his relocation to Oregon; and still others seemed to hope that he would relocate and head up the party in its battles in 1860. Finally, others, especially Logan, began by favoring Baker's relocation but became increasingly hesitant and then oppositional when Baker's presence seemed to blunt their own political aspirations. Whatever the explicit reasons and Baker's understanding of the offer, by early 1860, after a brief exploratory visit in late 1859, Baker was in Oregon with his family and hit the political trail. His presence made an immediate difference in Oregon's political landscape and launched him to the forefront of the Republicans, much to the joy of Dr. Henry and to the growing consternation of David Logan.[4]

Meanwhile Simeon Francis had arrived in Oregon, and within a few weeks his extensive journalistic talents and experiences were put to work in behalf of the Republicans. After preparing an essay in Illinois touting Lincoln for the presidency, which remained unpublished, Francis used the same material to author a key and widely circulated newspaper story bringing Lincoln to the attention of Oregon voters as a viable presidency candidate. On 11 February 1860 he told readers of the Oregon *Argus* that "circumstances have placed Mr. Lincoln before his country and will place him before the [Republican] convention as one of the men worthy of their high behest as a candidate for the first position in the world."[5] Some Republicans already had a strategy in mind: they would launch a more explicit campaign under the oratorical generalship of Edward Baker and tout possible candidates for the national election, including Abraham Lincoln.

•••

At the same time that residents of the Oregon Country were hearing more about the Republicans from Edward Baker and for the first time about Lincoln from Simeon Francis, Lincoln and his supporters were trying to avoid being caught in the quicksand of national Republican politics. Lincoln carefully managed these tentative strategies, urging his lieutenants in Illinois to be more civil with one another and to clear beforehand, with him, any statements they made about Lincoln, his political stances, or his intentions. Meanwhile, he traveled and spoke more often, in Ohio, Indiana, Iowa, and Kansas in 1859. Then, in February 1860, he gave his important pre-nomination speech at Cooper Union in New York City. Indeed, studying the large impact of Lincoln's speech from the vantage point of a century and a half, a leading Lincoln scholar asserts that the Cooper Union presentation paved the way to Lincoln's Republican nomination and election in 1860.[6] Newspapers in New York and New England (where he traveled and spoke after Cooper

Union) immediately and strongly invited readers to think of the tall and talented westerner as a good presidential possibility. Even the ever-modest Lincoln thought he had done well, telling his wife Mary that "the speech at New York ... went off passably well and gave me no trouble whatever," but he had to admit that the nine other presentations, following in quick succession, caused him some "difficulty" since "reading audiences ... had already seen all my ideas in print."[7]

In the weeks following his trip to New York and New England, Lincoln counseled his followers to maintain balanced political positions and avoid any controversial actions. During these days freighted with such significance for Lincoln, as well as later in the year in his run for the presidency, he displayed several political faces that proved attractive to a wide variety of voters in the march to his nomination. This mix appealed to some conservatives and radicals and especially to moderates like Lincoln himself. Known for his support for Henry Clay's system of internal improvements, his strong Unionism, and his willingness to let slavery alone in the South, Lincoln struck observers as much less

Abraham Lincoln, by careful planning and astute maneuvering, won the Republican nomination for the presidency in 1860. A fractious and wide split in the Democratic Party allowed Lincoln to gain the White House as the first Republican president. (Library of Congress, Prints & Photographic Division, LC-DIG-pga-00380.)

radical than William H. Seward, his main opponent for the Republican nomination, and that leader's alienating statements about a "higher law" doctrine and an "irrepressible conflict." While clearly detesting slavery, Lincoln avoided the vociferous attacks of abolitionists on slavery and slaveholders. An advocate of no extension of slavery into the territories—the central tenet of the Republican Party—Lincoln also opposed Stephen Douglas's popular sovereignty doctrine and the Dred Scott decision, but he did so without denouncing those who differed from him in their views about these matters. As much as anything, Lincoln's moderate positions positioned him as a possible second choice for those already committed to other Republican candidates as their first choice.[8]

These middle-of-the-road stances, which Lincoln and his lieutenants adroitly coordinated, worked to perfection. In early May 1860, Lincoln gained the Illinois Republican nomination, and a week later his party's nomination at the national Republican Convention in Chicago. While capturing the Illinois nomination he was branded the "railsplitting candidate" of the Republicans. Lincoln's relative John Hanks and a colleague, at the behest of a prescient Illinois politician, appeared on the convention floor with two fence rails, said to have been split by Lincoln and Hanks. Accompanying the rails was a wide banner with the splashed wording "ABE LINCOLN: The Rail Candidate of the People in 1860." Most importantly, Lincoln gained the full support of the Illinois Republicans at Decatur, which became so important a few days later in Chicago.[9] The Railsplitter candidate, Honest Abe, the Man of the West images were born, and all played central, unifying roles in the election to come.[10]

Lincoln's careful campaign strategies prevailed the next week at the Republican Convention housed in the jerry-built Wigwam at Chicago. Lincoln remained at home in Springfield but worked closely with his loyal Republican captains at the convention. David Davis, Norman Judd, and Leonard Swett of Illinois, with the candidate's consent, billed Lincoln as Illinois's favorite son and the acceptable second choice of other state delegations. After supporters of the front-runner, Senator Seward of New York, were stymied in their efforts to gain a first-ballot victory, Lincoln dramatically cut into Seward's lead on the second ballot and won on the third. As Doris Kearns Goodwin puts it succinctly, "it is clear that when opportunity beckoned, Lincoln was the best prepared to answer the call"—"better prepared," that is, than his major competitors Seward, Salmon Chase of Ohio, and Edward Bates of Missouri.[11]

Oregon played a role in Lincoln's nomination, but not in the way some writers asserted early in the twentieth century. Selecting their first delegates as a new state, Oregon Republicans were forced to make quick and not entirely satisfactory decisions when the date for the Chicago convention was pushed forward. That meant some of the chosen delegates could not travel to Chicago before the convention opening, clearing the way for proxies. When Leander Holmes, a leading Oregon Republican could not make it to Chicago, Horace Greeley, the country's best-known journalist and editor of the widely read *New York Tribune*, was named Holmes's proxy and took his place. Greeley's clear and pivotal role in the stop-Seward movement not only helped Lincoln; it also spotlighted the Oregon delegation with its famous proxy member. Some have argued that when Oregon switched four of its votes from Bates to Lincoln on the third ballot, it ensured Lincoln's nomination. That was not the case. Lincoln was still one and a half votes short of victory until Ohio changed four of its votes to the Lincoln column, thereby pushing him over the top.[12]

Another of Lincoln's insightful strategies helped win his election in 1860 and impacted the course of Oregon politics in 1860. Seeing that the Democrats were not only falling into disarray but also approaching the precipice of splitting into warring sides, Lincoln urged Republicans to delay holding their national convention until after the Democrats met. In other words, to adopt a wait-and-see policy and to take advantage of any difficulties the Democrats encountered in their countrywide politicking.

The month before Lincoln's nomination Democrats gathered in Charleston, South Carolina. Despite their fractious differences, the Democrats hoped to put together a party platform and nominate a candidate that would unite rather divide the party. But the conflicts that separated the Democrats—slavery in the territories, "Bleeding Kansas," and popular sovereignty—quickly surfaced and immediately undermined any possible unity. When southerners could not obtain guarantees protecting their right to bring slaves into new territories and a new, more demanding slave code, they exited the convention. Reconvening in Baltimore in June, the Democrats tried again, but they were too fractured, unable to agree on a compromise platform or candidate. They fell into two groups, with northern Democrats swinging behind Stephen Douglas and Herschel V. Johnson of Georgia and southern Democrats nominating John C. Breckinridge, the sitting vice-president from Kentucky, and Joseph Lane of Oregon as his running mate.

Lincoln had been right—again. The wait-and-see tactics benefitted the Republicans. The Democrats, torn asunder by their views on slavery, its protection, and expansion, were now two separate parties. By July 1860 Lincoln and other leading Republicans were predicting the party's victory in the fall elections.

• • •

Oregon Republicans and Democrats, even while reacting to these dramatic happenings on the national political scene, were also trying to plot and plan the agendas for their own participation in their first national election. Republicans expressed their jubilance over Lincoln's nomination, even though they had spoken more openly for Bates and Seward before May 1860. Largely unknown in the Oregon Country before his nomination— save through the support and presentations of his Illinois acquaintances now in the West—Lincoln quickly gained, as we shall see, his party's mounting support in Oregon in the summer of 1860.

Much more problematic and contentious were the stumbling steps of Oregon's Democrats from spring to fall. Not only were the Democrats at odds with one another on several policies at national and state levels, they were also rent with personality conflicts. And the gradual development of Washington Territory and its political leanings also played a not-inconspicuous role, especially in the person of its controversial territorial delegate, former territorial governor Isaac Ingalls Stevens. All these issues plagued Oregon's Democrats, dividing them, making them more susceptible to intraparty squabbles, and some of them more open to the "fusion" offers coming from the pragmatic Edward Baker and other malleable Republicans in early 1860.

In more than one way the personal conflicts, national issues, and Washington territorial politics were conjoined. As we have seen, the key Democratic figure of the past and present, in early 1860, was Joseph

Lane. He had dominated Oregon politics since he arrived in 1849, as the appointed territorial governor, then became the territory's elected delegate, and next one of its first two U. S. senators. But in the late 1850s Lane's star began to decline in Oregon even as it seemed to brighten in Congress and on the national scene. Championed earlier in the decade by the indefatigable *Oregon Statesman* editor Asahel Bush and the Salem Clique, Lane lost that support. Indeed as 1860 approached, Bush and his followers had become harsh critics of Lane.

Probably Lane's support for the Buchanan administration and its position on the proslavery Lecompton Constitution in Kansas did most to upset Bush, who agreed with Douglas's vociferous denunciation of the faulty constitution. Lane's other problems in 1858-59, including his inability to get Congress to pay the war bill for fighting Indians in the 1850s and his failure to push Congress to support Oregon statehood, as well as his unwillingness to follow all of Bush's suggestions on territorial printing, further angered the Salem journalist. In 1859, Bush and his political crony and later senator James Nesmith, sent increasingly critical missives to Lane in Washington. Nesmith described one of Lane's attempts to defuse conflicts as "a senseless unmeaning mess of trash." And in the last letter that passed between Bush and Lane for the next twenty years, the editor told the politician his correspondence was alienating, untrue, and thus unacceptable. Thereafter, Bush was more than an ex-friend of Lane's; he had become his bitter enemy.[13]

The opposition in Oregon to Lane mounted steadily in 1859 and crested in 1860-61, although Lane and his followers won some of the conflicts that embroiled them. When Lane stood with the southern delegates and their proslavery stance in the aborted Democratic Convention in Charleston, he did quite well in the contested votes that followed. Those who opposed Douglas particularly took a second look at Lane's availability for the presidency, but it was not to be. Later in May in Baltimore, Lane again won some support for the presidency at the southern Democratic Convention. Instead, after Breckinridge was named for the top slot, the delegates by acclamation selected Lane as his running mate.[14]

But Lane's stock was rapidly falling in Oregon. His identification with slavery, his running on the Breckinridge ticket, and his support for secession alienated Oregonians, particularly Douglas Democrats.

Lane was not considered for reelection to the Senate after Oregonians turned sour on him. After his loss in the presidential election of 1860, Lane spent his final years quietly on his farm near Roseburg. The gradual disappearance of Joseph Lane from the forefront of the state's Democratic politics markedly influenced the election of 1860 and the Civil War years in Oregon.

• • •

Meanwhile, happenings in Washington Territory to the north revealed other developments in the political landscape of the Oregon Country. The political events of the 1850s in Washington both paralleled but also broke with the course of events that shaped Oregon's history. Soon after the territory was officially organized, President Franklin Pierce named I. I. Stevens the first territorial governor of Washington. He dominated the region for most of its first decade. As his biographer writes, Stevens "strode through the Northwest's formative years (1853-1861) as a colossus among Lilliputians."[15] In his years as territorial governor (1853-57) and later as territorial delegate (1857-61), Stevens earned the reputation of a "young man in a hurry." During these frenetic years of leadership, Stevens directed a railroad survey from the Midwest to the Pacific Coast and served as superintendent of Indian affairs, even while he tried to keep his gubernatorial duties in hand. His years as a territorial delegate were equally action-packed.

Stevens led. Small in size but large in ambition and assertiveness, he organized politics, the railroad survey, and Indian affairs, and he expected others to follow. He built up something of an Olympia clique of Democratic power and kept Whigs—-and, later, Republicans—at bay. Most observers, his contemporaries as well as those later, saluted Stevens's go-ahead directiveness. For instance, Oregon political leader Joseph Lane lionized Stevens as the "most indefatigable of all the senators and representatives in Congress," the "best-working man that I ever knew … all the time on duty, [and] seems never to tire or let up."[16] Stevens would return the favor in action, nominating Lane for president in the southern Democratic Convention at Baltimore in 1860.

Stevens and others in the new territory seemed ill prepared, however, for the changes that mining booms and newly arriving immigrants

THE LATE GENERAL ISAAC I. STEVENS.—[PHOTOGRAPHED BY BRADY.]

Isaac Ingalls Stevens, a small, extraordinarily energetic man, was appointed the first governor of the Washington Territory and later was elected its territorial delegate. His prosouthern sympathies led to his political demise. He supported the Union, but lost his life as a northern general in the Civil War. Harper's Weekly, 20 September 1862. *(Courtesy of the OSU Libraries Special Collections and Archives Research Center.)*

forced on them. Mining rushes, the great people-movers of the American West, brought hundreds of newcomers to the Colville area and later across Washington to the Fraser River boom in nearby Canada. These miners and others who came to settle in the Puget Sound region and other scattered parts of Washington called on the governor, territorial legislature, and military forces to provide protection.

In responding to these sometimes emotional calls for action, Stevens's energetic, self-assured, and decisive activities often raised large welts of discontent. Particularly was this the case in his handling of Indian affairs and in his relations with Gen. John E. Wool. Like most residents of the territory, Stevens wanted the regular army to protect newcomers—those coming up the trail, those in the mining camps, and those on farms and nascent towns. Whether Stevens's actions in support of the settlers were politically motivated or sincere is not entirely clear (it may have been both), but he did urge—sometimes nearly commanded—the military to act decisively. Conversely, Wool, reflecting a strong opinion among many officers, wanted to keep newcomers out of the traditional hunting and gathering areas of Native tribes. When Wool and other army leaders refused to carry out the wishes of Stevens and ambitious and worried settlers, the Washington residents castigated the military as cowardly, unsympathetic, and unwilling to address settler needs. These conflicts between Native groups, territorial leaders, and regular army and volunteer officers, as will become clear, lasted for more than a decade, into the mid-1860s and beyond.

When the military refused to do all that Stevens urged them to do, he took control himself. And when not all settlers followed his commands, he declared martial law and imprisoned a handful or two of settlers who had refused to follow his orders. A comedy of errors followed, with Justice Edward Lander challenging the governor and the governor detaining and jailing the judge. Lander threatened Stevens with contempt, and the governor promised to pardon himself. But, sensing rising negativity toward his martial edict, Stevens revoked it and backed off from his controversial actions.[17]

President Franklin Pierce was displeased with Stevens's martial law actions and even spoke of replacing him with Oregonian Joseph Lane. Reading the presidential discontent as a sign that Stevens might not be reappointed territorial governor, the territory's Democrats urged him to run for their congressional delegate in 1857. Stevens won easily over his colorless and ineffectual Republican opponent, Alex Abernethy, the younger brother of George Abernethy, who had served as governor of Oregon Provisional Government. Many observers viewed Stevens's overwhelming victory in 1857 as a vote of support for his offensive actions toward Indians and his martial law declaration. As one territorial politician and historian later put it, "A vote against Isaac I. Stevens is a vote against the Indian war as carried on by people of the territory."[18]

Before 1860, although Washington territorial Democrats were divided in their reactions to Stevens's actions and to Kansas-Nebraska issues, that division did little to help the Whigs, Free Soilers (who were also against the expansion of slavery to the western states), or Republicans. These opponents, by and large, were unable to capitalize on the Democratic split. But the division continued—and even widened. Driving the wedge of separation even deeper into the Washington Democrats was the national conflict between President Buchanan and Douglas Democrats over the issues of slavery and a proposed state constitution in Kansas.

Anti-Stevens Democrats in Washington sided with Douglas, Stevens Democrats with the president. In 1859, Stevens easily defeated William H. Wallace for the delegate position, but not as handily as he had two years earlier against Abernethy. In 1859-60 politics changed little in Washington Territory and continued to mirror national trends, even though national controversies over slavery and its possible extension had less impact on the Far Corner than east of the Mississippi. Then came the election of 1860, which, as it did in Oregon, changed political alignments to the north in Washington, leading into the Civil War era.

•••

As the unpopularity of Stevens and Lane mounted in their home bases, that faltering support opened more possibilities for opponents. In Oregon, three different strands of influence, once conjoined, transformed the new state's politics; even as Lane's power base began to crumble, two other lines of action opened. Indeed, they had begun even before Lane seemed to be in trouble. The Douglas Democrats, under the able leadership of Asahel Bush and later of James Nesmith, increasingly pushed for popular sovereignty and parallel castigation of the Buchanan administration and the strong southern states-rights support of slavery. These "Hards," as distinct from the "Softs" of the Buchanan wing, were looking for ways to wrestle political leadership and power away from Joseph Lane. At the same time, the recent Republicans, just coming to the fore at the beginning of 1860, were also searching for a way to carve out a larger and more significant cut of the Oregon political pie. Might there be a way for the Hard-Douglas-Bush Democrats of Oregon to bundle with the Republicans in order to snatch away the political power base Lane had enjoyed for nearly a decade? Some among the Hard Democrats and Republicans thought so and began to search for ways to build temporary bridges of union to rally, together, against the Lane wing of the Democrats.

Ironically, even though Lincoln had fought against Douglas's popular sovereignty since 1854, some of his Republican friends in Oregon were leading proponents of a "fusion" agenda that would bring together Republicans and Douglas Democrats. As early as February 1859, Dr. Henry wrote to Lincoln to praise him for his valiant contest with Douglas the previous fall but also to explain that he thought Republicans in Oregon, making up about one-third of the new state's voters, ought to fuse with the Hard or Douglas Democrats to make Oregon a truly free state. He warned Lincoln not to be upset when he heard that Henry had backslidden into the Democrats. Henry would neither give support to Lane's proslavery forces, nor would he support divisive Republicans. Six months later Henry again sang a similar tune to Lincoln. David Logan had lost his very close election to Shiel, Henry argued, because Republicans of a radical bent had overemphasized abolitionism and alienated moderates, especially Douglas Democrats who might have supported Logan against his proslavery opponent. Instead, his fellow Republicans should have emphasized "the Non-intervention plank [i.e, popular sovereignty]." But better times might be coming. The next year two new senators from Oregon would be elected, and Henry was convinced that "we will elect an out & out Republican & a Popular Sovereignty Democrat, that will make a good Republican in a few months." Henry seemed persuaded such coalition tactics were the agenda Oregon Country Republicans ought to follow.[19]

So was Edward D. Baker, who had already flirted with popular sovereignty before he came to Oregon. In California, Baker faced the same huge barrier that blocked Republicans in Oregon: there were too many Democrats to overcome. But if one reached out to Douglas Democrats, through an agreement on popular sovereignty, there might be slim possibilities for victory. In his run for Congress in California in 1859, Baker told Oregon politicians later, he had advocated the "'doctrine of non-intervention by Congress, or anybody else, with the people of the territories as to their domestic institutions; ... I thought it wise and moderate and just to permit them to govern themselves as to slavery as well as other domestic affairs, as they thought fit.'" California Republicans did not follow Baker's lead in support of popular sovereignty and his calls for fusion with Douglas Democrats, but he imported those positions to Oregon and soon put them to work in his new political home.[20]

Even Simeon Francis, a latecomer who did not arrive until December 1859, was immediately talking about fusion politics. Although Francis did not express himself on the efficacy of coalition efforts, he did not

Edward D. Baker, a close and long-time friend of Abraham Lincoln, came to Oregon in 1859-60 and won election as a U.S. senator in fall 1860. An outstanding orator, skillful politician, and enthusiastic military leader, he was killed in the Battle of Ball's Bluff in fall 1861. (Library of Congress, Prints & Photographic Division, LC-DIG-ppmsca-08348.)

oppose them either, instead reporting neutrally about Baker's coming to Oregon and his first actions. Baker was politically ambitious, Francis told Lincoln. Francis predicted that the Republicans and the "Anti-Lecompton democrats will get about the same number [of votes]" and "together they will elect the two Senators—of which he is likely to be one." Baker's goal was a seat in the U. S. Senate, Francis added.[21]

Concurrently, as the Republicans pondered a possible marriage of convenience with anti-Lane Democrats, Douglas Democrats such as Asahel Bush were considering the growing need to work with Republicans. In early 1860 Republicans and Hard Democrats were drawn together out of political necessity and their common distrust and increasing dislike of Joseph Lane and his Soft Democrats. This new willingness for coalition surfaced in spring and summer of 1860.

As Republicans and Democrats met in counties across the state to elect members of the state legislature, which in turn would name Oregon's two new U.S. senators, coalition politics began to emerge. For example, at Republican county gatherings, Baker and others urged their party members to avoid naming candidates for the Senate seats, sometimes to support Douglas Democrats at the county level, and in other counties be willing to take a wait-and-see position but always to avoid partisanship and conflict. Democrats seemed willing to make similar compromises. The legislative competitions elected nineteen Buchanan-Lane Democrats, eighteen Douglas-Bush Democrats, and thirteen Republicans. Clearly, the Republicans held the deciding votes between the two Democratic wings, but they could not elect a Republican senator in the fall without strong Democratic crossover support. As summer came on, it was increasingly clear that fusion politics might decide the election of the two senators in the fall.[22]

In midsummer Lincoln's connections with Oregon resurfaced. Busy with his run for the Republican nomination in May 1860, Lincoln was barely able to keep up with only the most necessary correspondence. His letters to faraway Oregon were on hold for the first half of 1860, as were most missives to him, but they began to flow back and forth from July onward. On Independence Day, replying to an earlier letter, Lincoln told Dr. Henry that "to-day, it looks as if the Chicago ticket will be elected. I think the chances were more than equal that we could have beaten the Democracy *united*. Divided, as it is, its chance appears indeed very slim." Lincoln also indicated he was "just now receiving the first sprinkling of your Oregon election returns—not enough, I think, to indicate the result. We should be too happy if both Logan and Baker should triumph."[23] Although initial reports gave Logan victory in his head-to-head battle with Shiel for a seat in Congress, he eventually, as we have seen, lost by just one hundred and three votes.

Exactly one month later Lincoln answered three letters from Simeon Francis with his own addressed to "Friend Francis." Now Lincoln was even more convinced of the future: "I hesitate to say it, but it really appears now, as if the success of the Republican ticket is inevitable." The "democracy was so divided between Douglas and Breckinridge" that he expected victory even in states that Frèmont could not capture in 1856. "I should expect the same division would give us a fair chance in Oregon." Then he expanded his comments on Oregon politics: "We were very anxious here for David Logan's election. I think I will write him before long. If you see Col. Baker, give him my respects. I do hope he may not be tricked out of what he has fairly earned."[24] (No letters from Lincoln to Logan after Logan left Illinois are extant.)

As the crucial senatorial (and presidential) election loomed in early fall, Lincoln and his Oregon friends turned their attention to that notable event. Baker wrote on 1 August, belatedly congratulating Lincoln for his nomination victory and expressing his "great hope of a Republican Senator in Oregon—and ... [in] possibly both States [Oregon and California] in November. I think you will not need them—of course I should be delighted if you were to win them."[25]

Six weeks later Dr. Henry wrote Lincoln a long and illuminating letter, spelling out the complex politics of Oregon and the first machinations of the state legislature in trying to elect two new senators. Six Lane Democrats, finding they were falling behind the rising numbers of fusionist Douglas Democrats and Republicans, "left for Home, for the purpose of breaking a quorum." They would not return until promised one of the senatorial positions, but Henry did not think that would happen. Most troubling to Henry, however, was that David Logan had permitted "his name to be used against Baker, and [he has] done all in his power to defeat him [Baker] & failing in this, used his influence to prevent the Election of Senators. This course surprised Evry body acquainted with the circumstances. Logan had joined with me & others in urging Baker to come here, with the express understanding that if we beat [Joseph] Lane & [Delazon] Smith, he [Baker] was to be the Republican Senator--But for the delay, caused by this most extraordinary course of Logan, I think the Senate would have organized on Monday, & Senators, (Baker & Nesmith) would have been Elected that Evening."[26] The erratic Logan, having supported Baker's coming to Oregon to stump for the Republicans, probably turned sour about Baker's appearance because the newcomer from California was stealing the limelight and, perhaps, the political position that Logan thought he deserved.

The deadlock continued for nearly two weeks. In addition to the missing Democratic state senators, those voting could not make up their minds. Some turned in blank ballots to void a possible election, some threw away their votes to forestall an election, and still others refused to vote. When the absent Lane Democrats returned, the gridlock continued. In all, nearly thirty ballots were taken until finally James Nesmith and Edward Baker were named senators. The fusion had worked, with Republicans supporting Nesmith and Douglas Democrats voting for

Baker. For the first time since the beginning weeks of its statehood, Oregon had two U.S. senators.

More importantly, the election of Nesmith (formerly a political ally of Joseph Lane) and Baker illustrated that coalition politics could work in Oregon. The Republicans and the Hard Democrats, thinking in partisan but also realistic terms, realized they could not elect one of their own unless they worked, for the moment, to achieve this immediate, short-range goal. They could break bread with erstwhile opponents if these temporary agreements led to important wins at the ballot box. In addition, the two groups could agree on popular sovereignty even if their interpretations of the concept differed. Douglas Democrats in the state legislature voting for the Republican Baker informed party members around the state they had supported Baker because of his backing of popular sovereignty.

Once the results were known in the senatorial contest, three correspondents rushed off letters to Lincoln to inform him of the extraordinary outcome. On 2 October, a jubilant Edward Baker told his lifetime competitor and friend about his election to the Senate. Revealingly, although Baker promised Lincoln "you have a true and warm friend at your side," he did not admit to his support for popular sovereignty, which Lincoln had opposed for several years, and most recently in the debates with Douglas in 1858.[27]

On the same day, Amory Holbrook, an unsuccessful candidate in the senatorial contest and known to Lincoln, wrote to express his reservations about the process. Speaking against the fusion efforts that brought the Nesmith-Baker election, Holbrook declared his fears that the compromising "has not helped us [the regular Republicans]" and could endanger Lincoln's possible success in Oregon during the coming November elections. Obviously, Holbrook was upset that the carpetbagger Baker had come to Oregon, gained immediate attention, and won the Senate seat but in doing so, Holbrook suggested, robbed "the soundest & most earnest Republican[s]" in Oregon" from their rightful positions. When Baker omitted Holbrook from the patronage lists for Oregon he sent to the president-elect, Holbrook's letters to Lincoln turned toxic, especially in his castigation of Baker but also in his disgust with Lincoln.[28]

The most positive, uplifting letter about the senatorial elections came from Dr. Henry one day later. "Our most sanguine hopes have been realized," Henry wrote; "Baker is now a Senator from Oregon. No other man but him would have successes under the circumstances." And he added euphorically, "Altogether it is the most remarkable political romance that has ever been enacted in the history of our Government." Henry was certain that the fusions had led to success. The tireless political doctor went on to note a less positive side of the dramatic events. "At the very moment when we were confident of success, we were stunned with the proof of base treachery in our Republican camp."[29] Although Henry named no names this time, he was obviously referring to the contrary actions of David Logan he had spelled out two weeks earlier to Lincoln. Hearing of Logan's untoward actions and his later criticisms, Lincoln, it is said, asserted uncharacteristically that he would not name Logan to any office in the future.[30]

Baker's unanticipated win in early fall 1860 garnered national attention. The West Coast correspondent of *The New York Times* celebrated Baker's senatorial election in Oregon as a win for that state as well as for California, where Baker had gone to campaign for the Republicans even as he was making his run in Oregon. Baker's election meant that Lane would soon "have to 'stand out' in the cold," and Oregon had, according to an interviewee, "one of the soundest Republicans in the Union" headed to Washington." Now, according to another respondent, "the Pacific Coast has got a man in the Senate who" would not "persist in representing [the] Mississippi ... [but support] the Pacific Railroad." The fusion action, the correspondent emphasized, "carries Oregon against the administration ... and for LINCOLN probably."[31]

From the beginning of 1860, few observers, if they even knew about Lincoln, thought he had much chance of capturing the Oregon vote. As one reporter for the Republican *Oregonian* put it, since Lincoln dealt only with "abstract issues" and failed to hit slavery "head on, in all its bearings" in his debates with Douglas, he did not deserve the support of Oregon voters.[32] In the early months of the election year most Oregon Republicans favored Edward Bates for the presidency. The resident of a slave state, a political conservative, and not a proslavery man, Bates appealed to many Oregonians of midwestern backgrounds from Missouri and adjacent areas.

Events clearly moved in Lincoln's direction as 1860 progressed. The widening split among the Democrats, the willingness of Republicans and Douglas Democrats to fuse, and the Baker-Nesmith win in the senatorial race—all these happenings helped Lincoln's chances in Oregon. And though some Republicans such as Avery Holbrook and David Logan wanted to avoid any coalition moves and castigated Baker's compromises, some devout Republicans, though also opposing fusion, strongly backed Lincoln.

The most notable of these was Jesse Applegate, Oregon's archetypal pioneer. Applegate—who had arrived in the Northwest via the Oregon Trail in 1843 as a key participant in the "Great Emigration"—spoke out against the possible Republican-Hard Democrat alliance and opposed Baker as a senator. As some Republicans pushed forward the compromise, Applegate viciously attacked them: "A more corrupt set of men never combined for an unrighteous purpose than the Republicans who made Baker the nominee of their party for the Senate," he told an acquaintance. And he had "expressed [himself] freely ... [to] these mercinary and treacherous writches." He would make sure "the actors, aiders, or abettors of this plot against the rights of the people, and the interests of the State, shall ever enjoy an emolument, or abuse a trust."[33] Conversely, in the run-up to the presidency, Applegate gave numerous presentations, "full of eloquence, logic and humor" in support of Lincoln.[34] Opposition to fusion and Edward Baker did not sour Applegate on Lincoln.

Unquestionably the fusion compromise on popular sovereignty between the Republicans and Douglas Democrats and the senatorial election success of Nesmith and Baker greatly impacted the presidential election in Oregon in November 1860. These occurrences illustrated a newly understood truth to those willing to consider compromises: wise political observers in Oregon, pragmatically accepting some views of opponents, could lead to partial success rather than defeats and losses. These negotiations helped Lincoln win a surprising victory in Oregon. On 6 November, in an exceptionally close and very divided election, Lincoln garnered 5,345 votes, Breckinridge 5,075, Douglas 4,131, and John Bell of the Constitutional Union Party 213. Even Lincoln admitted his victory in Oregon came from "the closest political bookkeeping that I know of."[35]

A week after the election, Alfred R. Elder, a long-time Lincoln acquaintance dating back to their Kentucky boyhoods, wrote from Oregon to congratulate Lincoln. "We have made a noble fight," Elder told the president-elect; "we have conquered the enemy." Although not all the votes were in, "all parties conceed the State has gone Republican. Oh! what a jubilee we will have. Glory to God! ... Long before this scroll reaches you, you will have heard of the election of 'Ned' [Baker] to the Senate. 'Old Sim' [Simeon Francis], God bless his old soul, Dr. Henry and Your humble servant were there as of yore, fighting shoulder to shoulder, for our gallant Baker. It was a great victory for Oregon, and, not only for Oregon but, for the United States."[36]

Others agreed with Elder's euphoric missive, although in less effusive terms. Simeon Francis also sent his congratulations, telling Lincoln he was convinced "that our success in Oregon in the election of Senator [Baker], carried the State and California,—not, however, without much and hard labor."[37] Francis had done his part in the push for Lincoln, as a newcomer in early 1860 and then even more influentially from the editorial chair of the *Oregonian*, which he had assumed in early 1860.

The Wide Awakes, the young, semimilitary marchers who led rallies and parades for Lincoln throughout the country, came alive in Oregon during and after the election. At torchlight rallies they sounded their "hurrahs" for Lincoln; in some towns they joined with speakers and bands, waving handkerchiefs, together adding "fuel to the flame of enthusiasm."[38]

The enthusiastic responses of Republicans and other supporters of Lincoln and the new Senator Baker were revealing symbols of the path-breaking impact of the election of 1860 on the Oregon Country and the nation. Not only was the first Republican elected to the White House; his party would now, not without considerable conflict and turmoil, gain the majority in Congress and face an unexpected and traumatic war. Lincoln and the Republicans would also, for the first time, have control of potential patronage. That appointive power, as we shall see, did much to shape the political landscape in the Pacific Northwest, especially in Washington Territory and the two new territories to be organized in Idaho and Montana. Moreover, Lincoln's victory in Oregon turned the tide politically in the new state. Four years later Lincoln won again—with a larger margin—in what had previously been a decidedly Democratic area since its first white settlements. In nearly all the presidential elections in Oregon stretching through 1900, the Republicans were more often victorious than the Democrats. One can argue, with good evidence, that Lincoln's wins in 1860 and 1864 made him something of a political founding father for the Republicans in much of the American far northwest.[39]

Chapter 4: Lincoln and Pacific Northwest Politics, 1861-64

Abraham Lincoln's connections with the Oregon Country turned decidedly more political when he moved into the White House in 1861. In the first ten to fifteen years of his political career in Illinois, Lincoln espoused the Whig program of internal improvements. But when controversies over slavery escalated to a fevered pitch in the late 1840s and early 1850s, Lincoln, even while embracing the Wilmot Proviso principle of no extension of slavery into the territories, moved clearly into the antislavery (but not abolitionist) camp. Then a third stage of Lincoln's links to the Oregon Country emerged when he assumed the presidency. He resurrected his earlier backing for internal improvements, combined that support with his recent antislavery stances, and advanced both as a chief executive. This new stage revealed itself in his political involvements in the Pacific Northwest, his patronage decisions in the region, and his support for congressional legislation eventually influencing the economy of the Pacific Northwest. These political and economic decisions, in turn, obviously impacted partisan and civil rights matters, as well as military decisions and Indian policies.

•••

The most time consuming and controversial of Lincoln's ties to the Pacific Northwest in the early 1860s were his political participations and patronage appointments. An astute and strong party man, Lincoln looked for ways to advance his Republican Party throughout the country and paid a good deal of attention to launching it in the new states and territories of the American West. Since Oregon had become a state in 1859, Lincoln's appointments were now much less numerous than in other parts of the Far Corner. Conversely, Lincoln was much involved in naming officials in Washington (organized as a territory in 1853), and in the new territories launched during his presidency, Idaho (1863) and Montana (1864). Although some presidents considered such political activities onerous, Lincoln enjoyed political discussions and giving positions to relatives, friends, and political contacts. He thought of patronage as an acceptable part of the American political system and worthy of as much attention as he could give political appointees during an all-consuming, horrendous war. In the days leading up to his inauguration—and in the weeks and months afterward—Lincoln's private papers were full of memoranda concerning possible appointments in western states and territories.[1]

At the other end of the political pipeline reaching from the White House to the Oregon Country, Lincoln's Republican political friends out west were on the horns of a dilemma. Since their leader had been elected to the presidency, these party members would get a much larger share of appointee political plums, but who would decide on the men for these

From 1862 to 1864, Abraham Lincoln made key political appointments in the territories of Washington, Idaho, and Montana. He also supported congressional legislation establishing transcontinental railroads, homesteads, and educational facilities impacting the Oregon Country. (Library of Congress, Prints & Photographic Division, LC-DIG-ppmsca-19211.)

positions? Would the newly elected president make the decisions, would Lincoln's friends and supporters select the candidates (largely from their own numbers), or could a compromise agreement be worked out for them to be selected? Surprisingly—and yet maybe not—the Republicans often could not amicably settle differences of opinion about patronage. In the Oregon Country, Republicans were much less willing to work out disagreements than was Lincoln. Indeed the fractious differences among the Republicans, as much as competitions with Democratic opponents, kept the Republicans from enjoying fully many of the political fruits coming their way during the Civil War years.

The Republicans entertained little disagreement on another matter. In their view the Democrats, particularly those who sided with the seceding southern states or opposed war on the South, were Rebels, even "Traitors." Republicans of the Oregon Country gleefully adopted the negative nicknames for their Democratic opponents: "Secesh" or, even worse, "Copperheads," especially for those who did not support the Union cause.

The Democrats, though often in the majority in all subregions of the Pacific Northwest, were also so divided on the war, the Union, and other controversies that they could not sustain a united front against the new, ambitious Republicans. During Lincoln's presidency, the Democracy had to heal past wounds that had decisively divided them in the late 1850s and agree on new compromise measures if they were to regain the full sway of their numerical superiority. Not surprisingly, dissenting Democrats of the Oregon Country often labeled their opponents abolitionists and "nigger lovers," and their president as a would-be tyrant coercively warring against the South. These ongoing—and mounting—conflicts between the two major parties played out in several venues and forms.

Lincoln's political connections with subregions of the Oregon Country also shifted because the careers of several of his important political friends of the 1850s had dramatically changed. By 1862, David Logan was largely absent from Lincoln's political notebook after his continual divisive actions during the election of 1860. Edward (Ned) Baker took his senatorial seat in December 1860, introduced Lincoln at his inauguration in March 1861, and raised a regiment of soldiers for the Civil War. He lost his life, however, in the ill-planned Battle of

Ball's Bluff in October 1861 and thus could no longer shape Lincoln's patronage decisions on the West Coast. Simeon Francis also disappeared from most of Lincoln's correspondence after the president named him army paymaster at Ft. Vancouver in 1861.

Only the indefatigable—and often irascible—Dr. Anson Henry remained on central stage in the Oregon Country. He leaped into the political gaps left after the other Lincoln friends vanished or went in other directions. Working with Baker and Francis before their careers and lives changed, Henry compiled lists of "acceptable" candidates for territorial posts, denouncing opponents (usually Democrats but also dissenting Republicans), and encouraged Lincoln to follow the good doctor's suggestions in Pacific Northwest politics. These guidelines, especially those Lincoln adopted, obviously influenced Republican politics in the Oregon Country during his presidency.[2]

• • •

The political tracks in Oregon following the election of 1860 and the outbreak of the Civil War are more complex than merely two competing parties, side by side, sniping at one another. Rather, crossovers, shifting allegiances, and new combinations were more typical than extraordinary. Many Democrats found a modicum of agreement with Republicans in Union clubs and support for the war. Some Republicans, especially those who fused with Douglas Democrats to elect Republican Baker and Democrat Nesmith in 1860, could support Democrats for state office and on a few measures. But Democrats who had followed Buchanan and then Breckinridge and Joseph Lane in 1860 could not find much fellowship with the Republicans. Truth to tell, during the disruptive times of the nation's worst war, political irregularities seemed as usual as party loyalties.[3]

Republican enthusiasm was quickly dampened. By 1862 the party lacked a clearcut leader around whom they could rally. Baker was dead, Logan had disappeared, and Dr. Henry and Simeon Francis had gone off to Washington Territory to take up Lincoln appointments. Journalist Thomas J. Dryer, opinionated and outspoken editor of the *Oregonian*, was also gone, having won a Lincoln appointment after traveling to Washington, D.C., to present his case. His position as U. S. minister to the

Sandwich Islands (Hawaii) was brief, and decidedly unsuccessful, largely because of his alcoholism and inattention to duty. Leander Holmes also briefly emerged as a state leader and then inexplicably disappeared. The Republicans of Oregon, only five years old in 1862, wobbled following the loss of these leaders and their lack of clarity on pressing issues. They were not abolitionists, and there were no Radicals among them such as Senator Charles Sumner of Massachusetts, whom Lincoln wrestled with in Congress. Oregon Republicans opposed slavery but did not want free blacks among them. However, they did favor a transcontinental railroad and a homestead act, which were part of the Lincoln and Republican platform of 1860.

Additional disappointments added to Republican woes in the early 1860s. Most significant were the losses of important political positions. Chief among these was the controversial decision of Oregon Governor John Whiteaker, a proslavery man, to name Benjamin Stark, a Democrat opposed to Lincoln's policies, to finish out Edward Baker's term in the Senate. Republicans and even some Democrats rallied unsuccessfully to keep Stark out of the Senate.[4] Adding insult to injury, as far as the Republicans were concerned, in fall 1862 the Oregon legislature elected Benjamin F. Harding to replace Baker in the Senate. Even John R. McBride of Lafayette, the only Republican to hold major office between in 1861 and 1864, failed in his renomination bid in 1864.George H. Williams, a Democrat who converted to the Republicans in 1863 and won a U.S. Senate seat the next year, was the only other Republican from Oregon to serve in the U. S. Senate through 1865. Although the Republicans won the presidential vote in Oregon in 1860 and 1864, with Lincoln heading their ballot, they had difficulty winning other national seats in the state.

On one issue, however—support for the Union—Republicans were in agreement. It became the glue that held the new party together during the war years, and worked so well and invitingly, in fact, that many (probably most) Democrats came aboard the good Union ship. Certainly squabbles carried over about what to do with slavery, what should be the correct reactions to the Dred Scott decision (1857), and what should be the Oregon Country's position on blacks in the region. But once Fort Sumter was fired upon, patriotic support for the Union began to spread like an expected sunny day. As long as the war was viewed as an effort to defeat a secessionist South and bring it back into the Union and the subjects of slavery, emancipation, and black rights were downplayed—as they were, by in large—most Oregonians discovered a uniting consensus under the expanding tent of Unionism.

A series of occurrences following the fall of Fort Sumter testified to the rising tide of Union sentiment in Oregon. Union rallies broke out in 1861 in Portland, Eugene, and Salem, and a huge meeting in Corvallis drew more than five thousand. The enthusiasm for the Union cause reached new heights the next year, with support for Lincoln and the North replacing the earlier advocacy of popular sovereignty. The fusion between the Republicans and the Douglas Democrats that led to the election of Senators Nesmith and Baker and Lincoln's win in Oregon in the election of 1860 continued into 1862. This ongoing reorientation of political parties led to another victory in June for the fusionists when John McBride was elected to Congress and Addison C. Gibbs (a Douglas Democrat who later became a Republican) to the governorship. These and other Union Party candidates swept Oregon, carrying all but one county. Later that fall another Douglas Democrat—and Unionist— Benjamin Harding was named a US senator.

After watching the initial actions of McBride and Harding, Dr. Anson Henry wrote to President Lincoln to give him the Oregon Republican perspective. "Mr. McBride is a Republican 'Dyed in the Wool', a young man of great promise," Henry told Lincoln; "he contributed more largely to the Election of Col. Baker than any Republican in the State." And sending along confirmation of Harding's support for the administration, Henry asserted that that evidence showed "how fully you are endorsed by Senator Harding." "Both Gentlemen," Henry added, are in "<u>every way</u> worthy of your Confidence." Henry also thanked Lincoln for his letter of March 1862 that "contributed very largely to harmonize and strengthen the Union element, and the results are just what I then predicted they would be [the election of Union candidates.]"[5] Even the new Governor Gibbs, still then a Democrat, wrote to Lincoln to promise that "any thing I can do to aid your administration in putting down the rebellion will be done with pleasure."[6] Union sentiment seemed to be sweeping up Republicans and Douglas Democrats alike by the end of 1862.

Still, not all Republicans marched in lock step with Lincoln. Some expressed strong reservations about his leadership and actions in the Oregon Country. Among these was Amory Holbrook. A New Englander who accepted appointment as U.S. Attorney in Oregon Territory and worked his way up to become a leading Republican, Holbrook tried, unsuccessfully, for a U. S. Senate position in 1860, only to lose to Edward Baker. Afterwards, he found Lincoln friends, Senator Baker and Dr. Henry, insurmountable barriers to his political aspirations. Frustrated and angry, he turned sour, as we have seen, and wrote increasingly negative letters to Lincoln, attacking Republicans in Oregon and criticizing Lincoln's patronage decisions in the state.[7]

For Oregon Democrats, particularly those who were pro-South and antiwar in their sentiments, these were equally difficult times politically. Most of all, these Democrats were leaderless. Joseph Lane, who had led the Democrats of Oregon for more than a decade, returned to the state after the disappointing outcome of 1860. Highly criticized for his prosouthern and secessionist stances and falsely accused of plumping for a separatist Pacific Republic, Lane retreated from the Oregon political scene.

No one arose to assume Lane's mantle. Governor John Whiteaker, holding views similar to those of Lane, increasingly lost favor with Oregonians after the outbreak of fighting. Matthew Deady, a fellow Democrat but an opponent of Whitetaker, once described the governor: "'Old Whit' is a ... cross between Illinois and Missouri, with a remote dash of something farther Down East. Although wrong in the head in politics, he is honest and right in the heart." Others could be much less charitable. The rabid Republican *Argus* editor bludgeoned the governor as "the biggest ass in the State" and added, "Whitaker is at heart as rotten a traitor as Jeff Davis."[8] Although both senators from Oregon—Nesmith (1860-66) and Harding (1862-65)—were Democrats, they were also Unionists. True, Nesmith was lukewarm in his support of Lincoln—he thought Lincoln was not up to the demands of Civil War leadership—but neither man diligently tried to resurrect the Democracy that ruled Oregon until 1860.

Other surprises undermined Democratic strength in Oregon. They lost two of their most influential leaders. After more than a decade as a stalwart Democrat, Matthew P. Deady left the party and became a Union supporter. He did not go so far as to become a Republican but could not support the Democrats, particularly those who opposed the Union, railed against the Constitution, and existed on "mere negation." "Like many other great parties and even nations," he told a friend, "the Dem party has run its course. It belongs to the past. It has gone to the tomb, and no power that I know can resurrect it."[9] Asahel Bush also swung his support to Lincoln and became a Unionist, without totally abandoning the Democrats. But the mercurial Bush soon found that he could not agree with Lincoln's Emancipation Proclamation nor his cashiering Gen. George McClellan. Deciding he had had more than enough journalism after being at the helm of the influential *Statesman* for nearly a dozen years, Bush sold the newspaper, abandoned politics, and entered a very successful career as a businessman and banker. The loss of the Deady and Bush voices seriously weakened the Democratic cause.

•••

Washington Territorial politics in the early 1860s illustrates the expanding role of Abraham Lincoln during the Civil War years in the Pacific Northwest, even while it also reveals the continuing upsets that roiled territorial politics in these years. More immediately apparent are the national-regional parallels that marked the course of politics in the early 1860s. The same break between Douglas and Buchanan that characterized national and Oregon Democrats also rent the party north of the Columbia. And among their opponents, Lincoln's appointees in Washington influenced the Republicans there as much as his friends David Logan, Dr. Henry, and Ned Baker had in Oregon.

Another remarkable parallel comes into focus in the loss of leadership of two similar political chiefs, Joseph Lane in Oregon and Isaac Ingalls Stevens in Washington. Both had been appointed territorial governors, both had later been elected territorial delegates, both were strongly prosouthern in the late 1850s, and both lost considerable prestige—and power—in their controversial roles in the election of 1860. Negative reactions to Lane's candidacy as vice-president on the Breckinridge ticket, for which Stevens served as national chairman, considerably reduced their popularity in the Pacific Northwest. Lane was not renominated for the U. S. Senate in Oregon, and Democrats in Washington chose not to renominate Stevens for territorial delegate. The Democratic division, the appearance of Lincoln's new territorial nominees, and the disappearance of Stevens from political leadership brought a dramatic shift in territorial politics in Washington.[10]

The contest for territorial delegate in Washington Territory in early 1861 illustrates the political complexities that invaded the Oregon Country on the eve of the Civil War. The ongoing split between Stevens and anti-Stevens Democrats hampered that party's attempt to find a consensus candidate. When Stevens returned from Congress for a reelection bid, he ran headlong into the conflicts among Democrats resulting from events of the 1850s and the 1860 election, as well as those his own actions had engendered. Early on Douglas (and anti-Stevens) Democrats made clear their strong opposition to Stevens's reelection. Controlling the nomination process, the anti-Stevens faction pressed him to drop out, which he did in late spring 1861. In place of Stevens as the Douglas Democrat candidate, they named Selucious Garfielde, a man with a checkered career of political affiliations. Unwilling to support Garfielde, the Buchanan-Breckinridge-Stevens Democrats backed Justice Edward Lander as their candidate. In opposition, William Henson Wallace,

HON. W. H. WALLACE.
STEILACOOM, W. T.

Lincoln appointed William Henson Wallace governor of Washington Territory, but Wallace was almost immediately elected its territorial delegate. The same scenario followed in Idaho: Lincoln named Wallace the territory's first governor and shortly thereafter he was elected its territorial delegate. (Oregon Historical Society Research Library, folder 1091.)

whom Lincoln had just named territorial governor of Washington, ran on a no-party platform in an attempt to capitalize on the Democratic split. The strategy worked well since the majority Democrats could not agree on a candidate and split their support between Garfielde (1,276) and Lander (747). Wallace captured the election with 1,585 votes. As in the national and Oregon elections of 1860, the divided Democrats had allowed the Republicans to gain offices without achieving a majority vote.[11] Wallace's victory was a great step forward for the Republicans, but it also opened the door of fractious disagreements that divided the new party in the Civil War years.

Those squabbles seemed to follow one after another as if linked. And they were, often tied to ambitious and selfish politicians whom Lincoln appointed to Washington. Soon after Lincoln's election in November 1860, he and his friends on the West Coast began to think about appointments for California, Oregon, and Washington Territory. To fill these appointments for the latter area, Senator-elect Baker, Dr. Henry, and several others had loyal Republicans in mind. From these far-western advisors, from members of Congress and Lincoln's cabinet, and from Republicans in Washington Territory came dozens of possible patronage nominations. Regrettably, some of the suggestions were more self-serving than valid. The first of Lincoln's appointees began to appear in Washington Territory in 1861-62. Unfortunately, they often did not get along. These disagreements made for unsettling politics among the Republicans and often kept them from leading the territory as well as they might have.[12]

By the end of 1861, arguments among the Republicans were as clear and numerous as the unwise and selfish acts and attitudes of several appointees. Two of Lincoln's appointments served for most of his presidency, William Pickering as governor (1862-66) and Anson G. Henry as surveyor-general (1861-65). Others, especially two territorial secretaries and Indian superintendents and agents, were in and out of their positions. Three episodes illuminate the unsuccessful side of Lincoln's patronage decisions in Washington Territory.

The first came about when William Henson Wallace, Lincoln's initial selection as territorial governor, abandoned the position even before he actually began to serve and was elected territorial delegate in 1861. With

Wallace gone to Washington, D.C., Lincoln's territorial secretary, L. Jay S. Turney, became the acting governor. He failed. At first Dr. Henry celebrated Turney's work as a fellow Illinoisan and loyal Republican. Henry wrote to a close friend, probably Oregon Senator Baker, that Turney's "whole conversation & comportment show him to be a warm & enthusiastic admirer of Mr. Lincoln and yourself."[13] Three months later Henry denounced Turney as "the most mortifying and ruinous thing for Republicans in this Territory." Although Turney claimed that he had Lincoln's ear, that they were close friends, and that the president confided in him, his foolhardy and mistaken actions and attitudes—and his imbibing, "he gets drunk"—were turning Washingtonians against the president.[14] Henry pushed the president to cashier Turney, which Lincoln did in October 1862.

Henry's quick, negative-turning reactions to Turney illustrated the doctor's frequent actions in Washington Territory. Those partisan deeds were both typical and unusual for territorial appointees, with negative and positive sides. No other surveyor-general in a western state or territory was as active politically as Henry. No other person from the Oregon Country wrote as frequently to Lincoln as Henry. When Wallace left for Washington, D. C., as the new territorial delegate, Henry assumed Wallace's unappointed position as Republican leader and the Lincoln representative in the territory. Even after William Pickering arrived in June 1862 as Wallace's replacement, Dr. Henry stayed in the vanguard of Republican politics. Self-assured, strongly opinionated, and opportunistic, Henry was also loyal to Lincoln, energetic in his support of his party, and tireless in his work for his political friends and colleagues. Those complex personal characteristics colored Henry's reactions to two other Lincoln appointees, Bion F. Kendall and Victor Smith.

The heated controversies that swelled around B. F. Kendall provide another illustration of the partisan politics of Washington Territory in the early years of the Civil War. A member of Isaac I. Stevens's railroad survey crew, Kendall came to Washington Territory, passed the bar, and began a "vigorous career" in public office. He was, one observer wrote many years later, "fearless, honest and outspoken. As a lawyer, officer and newspaperman he made friends, but also made enemies, public and private."[15] Early in the war, Kendall came to the attention of General

Winfield Scott, who told Secretary of the Interior Caleb Smith and President Lincoln that Kendall "executed a confidential mission for me of great danger & importance; taking him [Kendall] thro' nearly all the seceded States."[16] Scott's support and Smith's recommendation led to Kendall's appointment in late summer 1861.

The naming of Kendall, a Democrat, as Washington's Superintendent of Indians initiated a firestorm. For Dr. Henry, increasingly speaking (he thought) for the territory's Republicans, the appointment was unacceptable. It did not fit Henry's political designs for the territory. Henry, William H. Wallace, and William Pickering, like Senator Baker before them, expected to control patronage appointments that rewarded friends, families, and political allies. Although Lincoln generally agreed on these patronage expectations, he was never as partisan as his western Republican friends.

A few weeks after Kendall assumed his new position, Henry wrote him about possible appointments of Indian agents on reservations. Henry especially encouraged Kendall to support the Rev. James A. Wilbur, a Methodist minister, in his work with the Yakama tribe (at that time spelled Yakima). Sending on to Kendall a letter from Reverend Wilbur that expressed the minister's concerns about possible changes on the reservation, Henry pointed to the "confidence of the Christian community" in Wilbur and to his obvious "results under most disadvantageous circumstances, that has astonished every body." "Mr. Wilbur is an ardent Republican," Henry added, "but never muddles with politics by mixing himself up with our partisan squabbles."[17]

When Kendall did not follow Henry's suggestions, the doctor soon began sending negative letters denigrating the Indian superintendent's leadership. To one correspondent Henry wrote that Kendall was part of "a wide organized scheme" to overthrow "agents and employees ... [in] his agencies that were known to be friendly to you & myself." Kendall's actions in dismissing the Reverend Wilbur, Henry was convinced, had "most grossly offended the entire Christian community of both Oregon & Washington. ... There will be almost a universal demand for his removal and I dont see how Mr Lincoln can refuse to comply with it."[18]

Henry did his part to make sure the president should follow this path. If Kendall were continued as superintendent, he told Lincoln, Kendall and other like-minded "Secessionist" advocates would not only "grossly insult ... the whole Methodist Church" but damage a "main prop of the Republican & Union cause." Kendall was a "Sober temperate man," Henry admitted, but was "entirely unfit for his position, from principles, habits and associations." So the political doctor urged his friend Lincoln to sack Kendall and allow Washington's territorial delegate, William Wallace, to name his successor.[19] Henry's pointed criticisms, as well as others from Wallace, were more than enough. Kendall was removed in spring 1862.

A third episode furnishes still another illustration of Lincoln's links to the Oregon Country. These incidents, playing on partisanship and personal animosity, also include bizarre, even seriocomic, actions as well. In July 1861, at the suggestion of Secretary of the Treasury Salmon P. Chase, Lincoln appointed Chase's journalist friend Victor Smith from Ohio as collector of customs for the Puget Sound district, at Port Townsend.[20] A month later, again on Chase's suggestion, Lincoln also named Smith a special treasury agent (to check on government spending in Washington Territory). At the end of July, Smith arrived in Port Townsend, finding persons there upset that he—not they—had been named collector of customs. In record time, Smith alienated most residents of the new town with his supercilious attitudes and his abolitionism, which did not play well in any part of the Oregon Country. Soon thereafter, Smith began to call for the relocation of the customs house west to Port Angeles, which he cited as having a better harbor. His critics alleged he was also buying land at the new site, and removal of the customs office there would greatly enhance his investment. Criticism mounted so quickly that Smith headed off to Washington, D. C., to explain his actions to Secretary Chase and save his position.[21]

When Smith returned, with his job shaky but still intact, he found his opponents had taken over his customs house holdings. Threatening to unlimber the devastating guns of a revenue cutter, the *S. S. Shubrick*, at the buildings, Smith took the customs records to Port Angeles, where he attempted to re-establish the customs office. But Dr. Henry's pointed criticisms, as well as others from the two governors, Wallace and Pickering, were more than enough to sink Smith, especially after Henry went to Washington, D.C., to deliver the negative report.[22]

Even Lincoln, the man of unruffled temper, had had enough. On 8 May 1863 the president wrote to Secretary Chase, telling him that Victor Smith had been removed from the customs position. "Yet, in doing this," Lincoln explained, "I do not decide that the charges against him are true. I only decide that the degree of dissatisfaction with him there is too great for him to be retained." The president also promised Chase that he would find another position for Smith if the secretary wished. Chase remonstrated with Lincoln and even threatened to resign, but the president held firm in his decision. Smith was sent packing.[23]

The dismissals of Kendall and Smith clearly reveal how much internecine partisanship colored politics in the Oregon Country, involved President Lincoln, and influenced the political history of Washington Territory. The Kendall and Smith incidents, as well as several other similar happenings, likewise provide examples of the inaccuracy of describing northwesterners as no more than "spectators" to the events and ideas convulsing the nation in a civil war. The links between region and federal government, often through the person and office of Abraham Lincoln, continued clear and strong.[24]

These three incidents were but tips of a much larger iceberg. Republicans were at one another, denigrating each other's character, urging their perspective as the only one to be heeded, and, ironically, undermining the importance of their links with Lincoln and opening the way for Democrats to reassume political control in Washington. And it happened. In 1863, after Wallace accepted the governorship of the new territory of Idaho, the territorial legislature named Democrat George Cole the new territorial delegate. An opponent of the Emancipation Proclamation and the "coercion" emanating out of the White House and aimed toward the South (an oft-sounded charge from opponents of the war), Cole went to Congress obviously representing the Copperheads of the Oregon Country. As a resident from the Walla Walla area, he also reflected the expansion of that region of the territory and its growing political strength. Not surprisingly, Republicans from Puget Sound looked with alarm at such developments.[25]

● ● ●

The formation of two new territories—Idaho in 1863 and Montana in 1864—resulted largely from fevered mining rushes, overnight population expansion, and ambitious politicians. Earlier, the Oregon Trail, the Mormon exodus west, and other water and road transportation routes brought newcomers to what became Idaho, but the mineral rushes in the early 1860s onward did most to entice immigrants. Gold and silver strikes were the powerful magnets drawing thousands, first to north Idaho near Lewiston on the Clearwater River and then by 1862 south to the Boise Basin. In summer 1862, just three years after its founding, Idaho City (about forty miles northeast of Boise) had overtaken Portland as the largest city in the Pacific Northwest. The next year its population stood at 6,275, only 584 of which were women. Also in 1862 "Fabulous Florence," located in the north, boomed to nearly eight thousand residents, but two weeks later most of the tsunami of residents had washed away. These and other mining boomtowns greatly increased traffic up the Columbia and overland and brought renewed calls for better government and more law and order in the hinterland of Washington Territory, which then covered a vast expanse of land from the Pacific Coast to modern-day Montana and Wyoming. Leaders and investors profiting from these strikes and residing in Walla Walla, Lewiston, and later the Boise Basin, wanted more local power and fewer ties to distant Olympia.[26]

Ambitious politicians were already thinking of establishing a new territory to the east of present Oregon and Washington, but they and members of Congress could not agree on the thorny issue of boundaries. Washington delegate Wallace, his right-hand man Dr. Henry, and their friend Oregon Congressman John R. McBride were pondering such expansion in 1862. In fact, Henry, funded by his Olympia-area colleagues, traveled to Washington, D.C., as a lobbyist. He suggested a line extending north from Oregon's northeastern boundary for the boundary between Washington and Idaho; that proposal was eventually accepted, but not without a good deal of political debate and recrimination. After intricate maneuverings and last-minute pressures, Congress passed the Idaho bill, and Lincoln signed it on 4 March 1863.[27]

The president had not said much during the awkward, uncertain steps toward Idaho's territorial organization. Generally, however, he favored such incorporation because it offered the possibilities of founding the Republican Party in a new area and including, in this case, another mineral-rich area. Lincoln also followed the appointment suggestions of Wallace and Henry, et al., save for replacing one of their justices with his own Sidney Edgerton, a substitution important to the organizing of Montana Territory a year later. The president also found a judicial position for his Illinois lawyer friend Samuel Parks.[28]

One week after Wallace completed his position as Washington's territorial delegate in March 1863, he began as Lincoln's appointed governor of Idaho Territory. In these moves, Wallace's motivations and decisions are not easy to understand; he did not leave much comment on his transition from Washington to Idaho. He could have run again for Washington's territorial delegate but chose to become Lincoln's appointed Idaho governor. Why did he select the latter position now when earlier he had chosen Washington's delegateship over being its governor? And why select Idaho over Washington when the latter's ten-year existence as a territory promised more prestige than a new one shakily cobbled together in recent months? The dean of Idaho historians suggests that Wallace probably worried that he would not be reelected in the Democratic-leaning territory of Washington whereas, as Lincoln's appointee, he was assured of a position in Idaho.[29] Perhaps he decided wisely since Washington Territory selected Cole, an avowed anti-Lincoln, pro-South man, to replace Wallace in 1863.

The earlier pattern of Wallace's career in Washington quickly repeated itself in Idaho. After accepting Lincoln's appointment as governor and pushing the president's programs in the new territory, Wallace decided to compete for Idaho's first territorial delegate. It was a tough, exciting battle that Wallace won because he carried the more populated Boise area, where 70 percent of the territory's voters resided. Elected in November, Wallace left the next month for Washington, D. C. Besides being a strong Lincoln and Union man, Governor Wallace had spoken for the organizing of an even newer territory encompassing the mining boomtowns of what became Montana. Even though in his gubernatorial chair less than a year and absent from Idaho half that time, Wallace was a balanced leader among newly arrived residents badly conflicted over politics and Civil War issues. He also pleased Republicans like Dr.

Henry in Washington Territory by serving as their spokesman after the Democrat Cole became their delegate.[30]

Why Lincoln chose Caleb Lyon to follow Wallace as Idaho's second governor baffled contemporaries. It still does. About Lincoln's wrongheaded decision, Wallace wrote directly and revealingly to his wife from the capital: Lyon is "a bad appointment I fear the President was pledged to this appointment before I reached this city otherwise this appointment would not have been made."[31] Lincoln confirmed Wallace's conclusions in telling Lyon that "Gov. Wallace ... is very anxious for a different man to be appointed Gov. of that Territory. I told him my promise to you was absolute, but if he could persuade you out of it, all right, but that I would keep my word with you."[32]

In Idaho, Lyon was as out of place as a city sophisticate at a frontier barbecue. Some consider him Lincoln's worst western territorial appointee. Reared in New York, Lyon was an energetic man of poetic interests and linguistic talents but innocent of the demands of political leadership and out of touch with miners, Mormons, and hardscrabble farmers. He quickly proceeded to alienate nearly all residents with his foolish and questionable antics. Whether in his attempts to verse uneducated laborers on the joys of the classics, in his flamboyant dress, or in rumored crooked financial dealings, Lyon failed in every way and was soon gone.[33]

In his two years of dealings with Idaho, Lincoln may have appointed as many as twenty or more men to office. Some he knew well, such as Wallace, Edgerton, and Parks; others were acquaintances of friends, like Justice Alexander (Alleck) Smith, Dr. Henry's son-in-law, and Lyon, an acquaintance of Lincoln's New York political cronies; and still others who were Lincoln's own political colleagues, such as John B. McBride, the Oregon congressman whom, after he failed in his reelection bid in 1864, Lincoln named a justice in Idaho. There was a strong Oregon connection among the appointees. Some referred to these men as Lincoln's Yamhill contingent, since several came from that area of Oregon. These included McBride, Alleck Smith, and Territorial Secretary William B. Daniels, brother-in-law of McBride. In the press of an all-consuming war, Lincoln could not pay much attention to Idaho, but his connections are clearly evident in the territorial appointments made during his presidency.[34]

One year after Idaho's organization in 1863, continued demographic eruptions in the huge, open spaces of the northern West led to the establishment of Montana Territory. Politics again played a central role. After Lincoln named Sidney Edgerton chief justice of Idaho, Edgerton served in the isolated mining camps of present-day Montana and experienced the difficulties of trying to travel between those areas and the distant, hard-to-reach capital of Idaho in Lewiston. Edgerton and his nephew Wilbur Fisk Sanders, a courageous vigilante leader against the vicious Henry Plummer gang (who were robbing and abusing travelers), called for a new territory to bring much-needed order to the mining camp populations flooding into western Montana. They were aided in their efforts by Wallace, the Idaho governor and delegate, who wanted the new territory to the east. Dr. Henry was a valuable ally too, fresh and optimistic from his work with Wallace in bringing about Idaho territory a year earlier. Another supportive boost came from the Idaho legislature, which preferred a new territory rather than facing the chaos, violence, and vigilantism perplexing Idaho leaders in 1863 and early 1864.[35]

Advocates of the new territory hit upon an intriguing method to push their cause. They would send the dependable and enthusiastic Edgerton to Washington, D. C., with an eye-popping quantity of gold, some of it sewed into his clothing. Hungry for dramatic show-and-tell stories like this, Congress moved quickly. Indeed, even before Edgerton arrived, enticing rumors of Montana's mineral riches had reached Washington, and James M. Ashley, chair of the House's territorial committee, had already introduced legislation to establish Montana. Many years later Edgerton revealed that he had "a number of interviews" with Lincoln, who "was earnestly in favor of the [Montana territory] bill." Edgerton also remembered Lincoln's looking at the gold nuggets and half mumbling to himself, "Talk about bankrupting this country; it can't be done, it can't be done. There is gold enough in the Rocky Mountains to pay off our national debt in three years, if we could get it out."[36]

Lincoln selected Edgerton as governor of Montana. It seemed a wise choice, but proved not to be. Edgerton, an abolitionist and Radical Republican, could not deal with opposition or lead a divided constituency. Exhibits of Edgerton's shortcomings came soon. In October 1864 Montanans were to choose their territorial delegate. Governor

Edgerton championed his nephew Sanders for the position and harassed anyone who did not agree with the two of them. The two dyed-in-the-wool Republicans mounted a strong, one-sided campaign supporting the Union and harpooning all opponents as Copperheads and traitors. There were only two political parties, Edgerton declared, "one for the country and one against it."[37]

The assertive campaign backfired. The duo alienated independent-minded voters. Those not aligned with either extreme flocked into the camp of their opponents. Sanders lost; the Democratic candidate Samuel McLean won.

Edgerton seemed unable to grasp what was happening. He could not understand that he needed to work with some of his opponents—they probably were in the majority—if he were to govern Montana. He could not. His slashing, attacking methods continued when he demanded that all legislators must sign an "Iron Clad Oath" that they had never carried arms against the Union. Lincoln did not make such a demand. The governor's bitterly partisan approach kept him and his opponents at war and prevented them from addressing pressing issues in the new territory.[38]

Tied down with his multitudinous pressing duties, Lincoln was virtually uninvolved in Montana's territorial politics in the months from its inception to his assassination. There is no correspondence between the president and Montana's leaders, and they, by and large, did not contact him. Meanwhile Edgerton's problems expanded. A territorial secretary, the officer in charge of handling the territory's monies, had not arrived. The governor's political burdens also kept him from dealing with pressing Indian problems. And he not only alienated opponents but fellow Republicans when he made unilateral appointments without consulting them.

All these dilemmas were too much for Edgerton. When a territorial secretary finally arrived in September 1865, the governor was only too happy to flee east, without official permission to do so. He hoped to gather further support in Washington, but his Radical Republicanism put off the new president, Andrew Johnson, who sacked Edgerton. What Edgerton could not learn as a territorial governor, Lincoln had perceived as a national leader: one had to find ways to lead as many persons and as diverse a population as possible. Be willing to compromise, avoid attacking opponents, keep open to new ideas and change. None of these learned lessons is evident in Sidney Edgerton's quick and unsuccessful journey through Montana politics in 1864-65.[39]

•••

President Lincoln influenced the Oregon Country in still other ways, but these were through congressional legislation rather than through patronage appointments. In the first year and a half of his administration, Lincoln backed several legislative bills that markedly shaped the Oregon Country and the remainder of the trans-Mississippi West. Illustrating his Whiggish inclinations about leadership, Lincoln allowed Congress to push through, among others, the Pacific Railroad Act, the Homestead Act, and the Morrill Land-Grant College Act, all in 1862. Even though Lincoln was not the ramrod driving these legislative enactments, he supported all of them as a Republican Party leader and then as president.[40]

Lincoln had been a long-time promoter of railroads. As an ambitious Whig and Republican politician he had spoken repeatedly for railroads, which he viewed as a necessary avenue to move farmers and "mechanics" upward and outward in an increasingly market economy. Lincoln also had served as an attorney for railroads. When he entered the White House, his other motivations for encouraging transcontinental railroads included keeping Oregon and California from leaving the Union to form a separate, possibly slave-holding, Pacific Republic and tying the West, generally, to the country east of the Mississippi.

President Lincoln quickly and easily supported the Pacific Railroad Act, which gave the Union Pacific and Central Pacific railroads sixty-four thousand acres of land per mile of track laid. Two years later, in 1864, with financiers balking at investing in the railroads, Lincoln urged Congress to double the size of land grants, make more financing available, and charter another transcontinental railroad, the Northern Pacific, stretching across the northern West to the Pacific Coast. None of these railroads crossing the West was completed during Lincoln's lifetime, but his supporters hailed him as a "railroad man" in their support of his candidacy.

Lincoln's involvement in agricultural matters was even more forthright. Ironically, Lincoln had foresworn farming while still a young man, but as an aspiring politico he realized he could not alienate agriculturists. That lesson, learned early in Illinois's prairie politics, carried over onto the national scene. Some contend that the Homestead Act, which Lincoln warmly backed, may have been the most important piece of agriculture legislation to pass through Congress. Knowing of Lincoln's advocacy of a homestead act, some enthusiastic voters walked a gangplank of expectancy by stating that a vote for Lincoln was "a vote for your own farm."

The Homestead Act of 1862 embodied Lincoln's values as well as his dream for the future of the West. He wanted Americans to find a way to realize their ambitions as he had in political realms; for most of his countrymen that meant owning arable land. The Homestead Act endeavored to do that by giving bona fide settlers 160 acres of farmable land if they resided on it for five years, "proved [it] up" (made improvements), and paid a small registration fee. Residents of the Pacific Northwest, especially those arriving after the Donation Land Act expired in 1855, could now claim 160 acres of rich agricultural soil. The problems in the system, including the crooked land deals and excessive involvement of land speculators, were not yet evident in the 1860s and 1870s. Lincoln supporters could and did claim him as a "land man," and he envisioned providing virtually free land to worthy settlers and returning veterans.[41]

Earlier as a loyal Whig, and later as a Republican convert, Lincoln agreed with the high value those two political parties placed on education. He also personally valued formal education, even though he had spent so little time in organized schools. It was not surprising, then, that Lincoln backed what became the Morrill Land-Grant Act, giving 30,000-acre parcels of land to any state equal to the number of their U.S. senators and representatives. Thus, the act provided a minimum of 90,000 acres for all states. The land granted was intended to help establish colleges "to teach such branches of learning as are related to agriculture and the mechanical arts." Eventually in the Pacific Northwest, these land grants helped establish Oregon State University, Washington State University, the University of Idaho, and Montana State University.

• • •

Lincoln's patronage appointments and his support for legislation emanating out of Congress were major connections with the Oregon Country, but they were not the whole story. Although the involvements were less numerous and less direct, Lincoln also had his hand in determinations about Indian affairs and military decisions. Even though the war east of the Mississippi and political challenges in Washington, D. C., devoured most of his time and energies, Lincoln still managed to put shadowy handprints on other actions in the Pacific Northwest.

Lincoln did not know much about Indians. Although his grandfather Abraham Lincoln had been killed by Indians in 1786 in Kentucky and Lincoln himself had served briefly (with no armed conflict) in the Black Hawk War of 1832, he had little contact with Indians before and during his White House years. Generally, as president he left the troubling complexities of Indian policy making in the hands of energetic William P. Dole, a political appointee and friend who served as Indian commissioner throughout Lincoln's administration. Yet a few events involving Indian affairs forced themselves upon the president, and more than one involved the Oregon Country.[42]

Two incidents in the trans-Mississippi West dealing with Indians especially captured Lincoln's attention. Just as he was readying a preliminary version of the Emancipation Proclamation in August-September 1862, he had to deal unexpectedly and quickly with a Sioux uprising that inflamed southwestern Minnesota. Local politicians and frontier military leaders wanted to hang all three hundred and three Native American leaders they captured and claimed were fomenters of the uprising. Cautiously, Lincoln winnowed out from the list only those declared guilty of capital crimes (murder and rape), allowing thirty-eight captives to be hanged but saving the lives of two hundred sixty-five others in December 1862. It was a traumatic series of events that Lincoln avoided discussing thereafter. The other incident concerned the Cherokees and their chief, John Ross, in Indian Territory. When Union forces failed to protect the needy Five Civilized Tribes, Confederates marched in and gained their support. Belatedly, northern forces arrived, captured Ross, and sent him to Washington, D. C. Lincoln and Ross met and exchanged letters. Lincoln promised the Cherokee leader he would reform the sordid Indian Service, but was unable to do so while under the heavy pressures of his other burdensome duties.

Lincoln's links with Indians in the Pacific Northwest were neither as dramatic nor as personal as those involving the Sioux and the Cherokees' John Ross. Generally, Lincoln agreed with Commissioner Dole's "concentration" plan, removing Indians to reservations away from miners and settlers flooding westward. Although twenty-first-century Americans often want to make Lincoln into a committed advocate of racial equality, he was not. He abhorred slavery and wanted to free slaves, but he did not push for social and cultural rights for blacks. His attitudes toward Indians seemed to conceive of them primarily as barriers and threats to westward expansion. Still, Lincoln's handling of the Sioux uprising and his contact with John Ross reveal that he had more sympathy for the plight of Indians than did many mid-nineteenth-century Americans.[43]

Lincoln's dealings with Indian affairs in the Pacific Northwest indicate no well-thought-out plan. Rather, the happenings were a potpourri of rather unrelated events. The president sent treaties made with Oregon Country Natives to the U.S. Senate without commenting on them (his usual practice); he wrestled with naming or removing superintendents of Indians in the Northwest territories (especially in Washington); and he received negative reports about rascals stealing from Indians (without commenting on these negative reports). Here were several evidences of a leader who promised to reform an unsavory system but who seemed disinclined or unable to devote the necessary time to instigate those needed reforms.[44]

Two happenings provide fleeting glimpses of Lincoln's involvement in Indian policies in the Oregon Country, but also illustrate the difficulty of coming to specific conclusions because of the scarce information. For example, Lincoln's rather indistinct fingerprints appear on some of the squabbles surrounding the appointment of new Indian superintendents in Washington Territory. The president rejected Anson Dart (who had served in the 1850s in another administration) because of the negative reactions of Washington politicians and residents of the Northwest. Lincoln also became embroiled in the brouhaha after Democrat B. F. Kendall was named to the position and quickly demonstrated the leadership skills of an obdurate, tone-deaf stone by firing a Methodist missionary and alienating these churchmen and upsetting Dr. Henry, the latter of which was not difficult.[45]

These altercations delayed negotiations of other much-needed agreements with Indians and a new treaty with the Nez Perce. Miners and other settlers arriving pell-mell after the discovery of precious metals on the Nez Perce reservation overran Indian land holdings and arrogantly confronted Natives of the area. A new Indian superintendent, Calvin Hale, rammed through a treaty that reduced Nez Perce holdings by roughly 90 percent and sent the treaty off to Washington. Lincoln, without a blink of an eye or comment, submitted the treaty to the Senate in 1864. It was finally ratified in 1866, after Lincoln's death.[46]

Another Lincoln connection to Oregon Indian affairs, although promising much, came to little. John Beeson, an Englishman of Quaker heritage, returned east after standing up as a sympathetic advocate for the Rogue Indians of Oregon. He had stirred up controversy by supporting the Indians and criticizing the cupidity and aggressiveness of pioneers. Once in the East he pestered government officials to reform policies toward Indians. In his headlong enthusiasm and moral ferocity Beeson alienated Commissioner Dole, but he was "received sympathetically by Lincoln." In fact, the president told Beeson that he had known for some time the reformer's ideas and was mulling them over. In a conversation with Beeson, Lincoln promised that as soon as "the pressing matter of this war is settled the Indians shall have my first care and I will not rest until Justice is done to their and your Sattisfaction."[47] But nothing happened; Lincoln did not embrace Beeson's calls to reform the Indian Service and policies toward Indians. The needed time for reform had run out.

Lincoln made several similar statements to men such as Beeson and Bishop Henry B. Whipple, the famed friend of the Sioux Indians, in 1862 and thereafter. The president did not follow up on his promises, however. Some historians and biographers have loudly criticized Lincoln for his failures to act as an Indian reformer; others, correctly, see him as more sympathetic toward Native Americans than most Americans of his times but hamstrung by a war that ate up his and his contemporaries' attention. Perhaps Lincoln scholar Mark Neely, Jr., presents the most viable conclusion about Lincoln and Indians: "it remains difficult to describe Lincoln's Indian policy," Neely writes, "because he made so few statements on the problem and because he took little direct action in Indian affairs."[48]

• • •

In other areas dealing with the Oregon Country, Lincoln was more actively involved. One such area included challenges to the Union from secessionists and pro-South advocates. As rumors about dissenters spread, Lincoln set out to make sure that anti-Unionists did not remove California and Oregon from the U. S. to form a separate Pacific Republic. He also urged state and territorial leaders in the Oregon Country to combat the ex-Confederates who had moved to the region and who were fomenting disruption. Finally, he looked for ways to safeguard settlers of the Northwest after U.S. military forces stationed there were shipped east to battle against the South. These general and specific goals gradually evolved, sometimes in hesitant and chaotic form.[49]

In late June of 1861 Anson Henry wrote to the White House, telling the president, "There is a much stronger Secession feeling in Oregon than is generally believed." Lincoln's political doctor was convinced that the election of Edward Baker and James Nesmith in 1860 as the state's new U. S. senators and the simultaneous defeat of Joseph Lane and the Breckinridge Democrats in Oregon and California was "all that saved this Coast from going with the South." The timely arrival of General Edwin V. Sumner in San Francisco would also keep "the public property from falling into the hands of secessionists."[50]

Dr. Henry's worries were part of a long-time, widely held rumor about the Far West and Pacific Coast. For several years opinion makers had predicted that the West might separate from the East if its rights and interests were not respected and protected. In the late 1850s, and especially after Lincoln's election in November 1860 and the impending outbreak of war, proslavery and pro-Confederate and other separatist groups spoke of possibly seceding and forming a separate Pacific Republic. Earlier in 1860 newly elected California Senator Milton Latham gave his initial speech on the Senate floor, supporting slavery and arguing that if war came, Californians should join neither the North nor the South but "sustain ourselves [in] the relations of a free and independent state." Eight months later Californian Congressman Charles L. Scott called for "a separate republic."[51]

In Oregon, supporters of the Union mistakenly attacked pro-South advocate Joseph Lane as the leader of the separationists. In Washington

Territory, rumors circulated that bands of men were organizing a force to overthrow the government, take control, and separate the territory from the Union. No major leader or large contingent of voters in the Northwest came out forcefully for a Pacific Republic, but worries about such threats continued well into the Civil War years.[52] Some have contended that one of Lincoln's motives for strongly advocating a transcontinental railroad lay in his desire to lessen the possibilities of westerners leaving the Union, going out on their own. Clearly, the worrisome rumors added to the challenges Lincoln faced in the Oregon Country, and as we shall see, obviously influenced federal policies toward dissenters in the region.

Opponents of the Pacific Republic idea and staunch Republicans often pointed to Confederate supporters, "Dixie Democrats" as they called them, as ringleaders of the secessionist movement in the Northwest. Despite these accusations, those connections were never clearly proven, but ex-Confederates and Confederacy advocates were numerous in some sections of the Oregon Country and often were strong foes of Lincoln's policies. In southern Oregon and in Idaho and Montana territories, pockets of Confederate supporters were much in evidence.

Once Lincoln was elected and even before he entered the White House, pro-Southern advocates, nationally as well as in the Oregon Country, turned their big guns of criticism on him. They denounced him as an abolitionist and a Black Republican. In the Northwest some backers of the new Confederacy joined secret societies such as the Knights of the Golden Circle, others refused to support the Union, and still others happily condemned anyone who criticized the South. Jesse Applegate, a Republican and the epitome of Oregon Trail pioneers, opined that his state stank "with an element foul and corrupt, bordering … on actual treason." Another critic condemned the pro-South residents of southwestern Oregon as "enemies of freedom" who "would hang Lincoln." Republicans and other Unionists concluded, without strong supporting evidence, that Joseph Lane was clandestinely heading up a dangerous conspiracy and shipping in a cache of weapons to foment a secessionist Pacific Republic.[53]

The deeds of some anti-Unionists provided ammunition for their critics. Joaquin Miller, who would become the most widely recognized

Oregon author of the nineteenth century, epitomized the actions of a few radical pro-Confederate supporters. A contributor to the pro-South *Democratic Register* in Eugene, Miller spewed out his venom at the North and Lincoln in 1862. The president, he charged, would never leave office "unless hurled from it by the indignant people of the West." Although Miller's family was Republican and his brother fought for the Union, he asserted that, under Lincoln and the Republicans, the country was "now plunging into a vortex of oblivion ... day by day becoming an enslaved nation." Reading these inflammatory words, Asahel Bush, the leading Democrat (but a Unionist) and editor of the *Oregon Statesman*, lambasted Miller as a "miscreant and traitor. ... As soon as his one-horse paper is busted up," Bush added, "he will be found skedadling to the Southern Confederacy."[54] The end of Miller's journalistic assaults came quickly when General George Wright, as Lincoln allowed political officials and military leaders to do, shut down the *Register* as a newspaper conspiring with the enemy and undermining the Union cause. (In actuality, Wright denied Miller's newspaper and other anti-Union papers the use of the U. S. mails, effectively shutting them down.) In a similar vein, William T'Vault, a journalist in Jacksonville, castigated the Republicans as a "fanatical abolition party," a "negro-worshipping gang," headed by "their dictator Lincoln."[55]

But when Union critics locked on to the idea that all dissent was evidence of pro-South sympathies, they missed the complexities among their opponents. Some dissenters were upset with what they considered an increasingly powerful central government reaching into their lives with taxation, military duties, and the curtailment of their freedoms. Many of these residents were not first of all lovers of the South and the Confederacy. They were instead supporters of a popular sovereignty that would allow frontier men and women to remain free from an increasingly assertive central government under the leadership of Lincoln and to make their own decisions. As the leading authority on the politics of the Oregon Country during the Civil War years has written, "To those in the Pacific Northwest, the wisest and most practical solution to the slavery [and sectional] agitation was the application of Stephen A. Douglas's popular sovereignty. Many Oregonians pointed with pride to their own solution of the question by this means."[56] These were the independent-minded northwesterners who so often upset stalwart Union men and women in the region.

Support for the Confederacy bubbled up even more strongly in the Idaho and Montana territories. In Idaho, beginning with the gold and silver rushes in the early 1860s, thousands of young men of Democratic persuasion flooded into the area, which became a new territory in 1863. The first two territorial governors, William H. Wallace and Caleb Lyon, were Republicans, appointed by Lincoln. But Democrats in Idaho were in the majority in 1863 and beyond, electing Democrats to their territorial legislature. So strong was the Copperhead contingent that when a Republican-appointed judge tried to hold court in the outlying mining boomtown of Florence, a grand jury "promptly indicted Lincoln, the cabinet, several army officers, and the judge himself."[57]

By 1864, so many Democrats had moved to Idaho that they easily won that fall's elections. They gained the territorial delegate's seat and a majority of the lower house of the territory. But like many in Oregon, they were often as much advocates of local control and critics of what they considered a too-strong federal government as they were pro-southern sympathizers. They "wanted Union without coercion," one historian has written.[58] Whatever their true perspectives on political issues, these Democrats were continual headaches for Lincoln's appointed territorial governors.

Beset by ongoing political controversies, Caleb Lyon, who succeeded Wallace in February 1864 as Idaho's territorial governor, wobbled from the beginning. In addition, problems with Indian policies and his own alienating personality drove Lyon out of the territory for most of his gubernatorial administration. Although in 1864 Lincoln thought the rife dissention in Idaho was beginning to melt away, Lyon did not. He agreed with a West Coast military officer that a "strong Anti Union feeling exist[ed] throughout the Pacific slope." "An influx of desperate characters driven from the rule of law and order," Lyon continued, was also "strong in this [Idaho] Territory."[59] Lyon's inability to deal with these divisive political issues and those who dissented eventually led to the quick end of his stay in Idaho.

The civil war of politics and North-South conflicts spilled over into Montana, which became a territory in May 1864. It was especially difficult for new territories such as Idaho and Montana, for they were born into the territorial world, in the swaddling clothes of controversy— Montana even more so than Idaho. Large numbers of Missourians, for example, had moved into Montana, bringing with them a cast of mind favoring the South. Their views and influences helped buttress the antiwar Democrats already residing in Montana. Even though the impact of these southerners or Doughfaces (that is, northerners with southern sympathies) was exaggerated when they were derisively called Copperheads and traitors, they were, nonetheless, opponents of the Republicans, particularly those Lincoln sent in from the East. The dissenters also pointed to Lincoln's crackdown on dissent as excessive, as actions that must be opposed. But one Republican leader and a strong Unionist was surely misstating the truth when he warned that the "left wing" of Confederate General Sterling Price's army from Missouri was "skulking in the gulches of Montana, inciting treason."[60] Interestingly, Price and his "left wing" became the rumored bogeyman menace in several areas of the Far West, including other sections of the Oregon Country.

Heated rhetoric and misguided decisions threw new fuel on the intraparty and sectional fires already burning in the new territory. The major source of the unwise actions, as we have seen, was Governor Sidney Edgerton. A strongly committed Republican more in line with the Radicals in his party than moderates like Lincoln, Edgerton would brook no division in his political house. Instead, when he demanded that all members of the Montana assembly must take the "Iron Clad Oath" of their past and present allegiance to the Union, he also threatened that if they would not, they would not be paid. Some perjured themselves by claiming no Confederate attachment in the past, and only one member dropped out, refusing to sign the oath. Edgerton also chose to deliver what one scholar appropriately terms "a severe and tactless denunciation of the Confederacy" in his first address to the territorial assembly. Attacking his opponents and southerners generally, Edgerton asserted: "the issue is fully made up between loyalty and treason ... between them there is no middle ground."[61] The split between Republican stalwart Edgerton and Democrats sympathetic to the South or hesitant to support the Lincoln administration quickly widened.

Sidney Edgerton became the Lincoln-appointed governor of Montana Territory in 1864. A stubborn, partisan Republican he was unable to work well with the Democratic majority of that new territory. (Library of Congress, Prints & Photographic Division, LC-BH824-4889.)

Obviously the bitter sectional quarrels dividing the Union had lapped over into Montana. But the heated partisan politics of both Republicans and Democrats rose above the boiling point in the new territory. Shortly after Lincoln's death, less than a year after Montana had been organized and Edgerton had begun his administration, the territory wobbled on the edge of collapse because it could not find a way to resolve its political differences, especially under the governor's misguided leadership.

•••

Over time, Lincoln's essential noninvolvement in military affairs paralleled his separation from Indian policies in the Oregon Country. In a larger view, his general plans of how to deal with the West militarily in the Civil War, like his strategies for areas east of the Mississippi, gradually came into focus as the war progressed. Yet few of those plans touched directly on the Pacific Northwest.

Bit by bit Lincoln made clear his goals for military activity beyond the Mississippi River. First, he wanted to keep the Confederacy from advancing west through New Mexico and Arizona and on to California to capture its much-needed ports and its rich minerals. He also hoped to divide the South into separate parts by freeing the Mississippi River from Confederate control stretching from New Orleans north to Illinois. If need be, he would also invade Louisiana and Texas to make certain this important division occurred.

None of these plans had a major impact on the Pacific Northwest, but other military determinations, frequently tied to politics, did influence the area. Most often these decisions dealt with keeping dissenters under control, making certain the West Coast did not secede from the Union, dealing with settlers' complaints about and conflicts with Indians, and guarding the overland trails as immigrants entered the Oregon Country. Even in these areas, the evidence of Lincoln's presence was sometimes a bit indistinct.[62]

Although Lincoln's long arms did not reach out to direct military policy in the Pacific Northwest, the actions of military leaders and soldiers there were of a piece with his broader plans for the West. Even before he entered the White House, Lincoln made clear that he thought the West a fertile ground for agriculture and mining; those views solidified farther once he became president. That meant the West, including the Oregon Country, must be kept in the Union, safe from secessionist dreams of separation; and settlers and miners must be protected from Indians who might react to white entry into their hunting grounds and living areas.[63]

In April 1861, Brig. Gen. Edwin V. Sumner came west to become the new commander of the Department of the Pacific, which four months earlier had combined the departments of Oregon and California. Sumner undoubtedly knew that Lincoln had spoken of making the West safe for its residents and protecting and developing its mineral resources. These purposes would be at the center of military policies in the Pacific Northwest and California, and Sumner set out to achieve them.

For Lincoln, the West embodied his dream of a region ripe for economic development. But that development could not occur if secessionists and Indians continually undermined his purposes, turning the hoped-for dreams into a nightmare. The frontier military would have to make sure that these troublesome groups did not upset Lincoln's plan.

Sumner set in motion actions to protect the Union and its facilities, trying not to alienate those who questioned Lincoln's war policies. Among Sumner's quick actions was to bring Army Regulars from the Northwest to protect threatened Union sites in California and Nevada. Very soon public opinion swung toward the Union, and the secessionists lost a good deal of their support. The new departmental commander began to call for volunteers, and as soon as they arrived he sent some east to protect the overland trails leading into Oregon and California.[64] Unexpected consequences added new challenges to military direction in the Far West. Most Army Regulars stationed in the Oregon Country and California were called to fight in the troop-hungry eastern theaters. By the end of 1861, about two-thirds of the Regulars stationed on the West Coast had gone east. Trying to replace them with locally recruited volunteers to retain and protect the far-western areas became a new challenge. In Oregon the recruitment process turned into a more difficult contest because Democratic Governor John Whiteaker, favoring neutrality, did not support the war or the draft. An ardent pro-southerner with opinions similar to those of Joseph Lane, Whiteaker promised he would not call for troops for Lincoln to continue his "wicked and unnatural war upon the South."[65] Before he left the governor's chair in 1862, Whiteaker urged impartiality in Oregon to keep the state out of war. Since territories were not called upon to supply troops and if retention and protection were to be continued in the Oregon Country, Sumner had to import volunteers from other areas to the Pacific Northwest. He did so from California, with men from that state guarding communities, trails, and mining areas. The recruits from the south grumbled often and long about their boring duties in the Oregon Country rather than their being sent east to fight in the real war.[66]

Meanwhile, the Lincoln administration made decisions to help Sumner carry out its goals in the Pacific Northwest and California. When Whiteaker refused to help with the recruitment of needed troops, Lincoln's Secretary of War Simon Cameron allowed Senator Baker to do his own recruiting. In 1861, Baker's enthusiastic efforts led to a California regiment of more than six hundred members.[67] In addition, Lincoln chose not to enforce the draft on the West Coast, including Oregon, because in doing so he could more likely avoid anti-conscription controversies among westerners and achieve his retention and protection goals.

When Brig. Gen. George Wright replaced Sumner as commander of the Department of the Pacific in October 1861, he was even more diligent in pursuing the Lincoln administration's military agenda. He placed additional pressure on secessionist groups to discontinue their activities, kept out of the mails several newspapers he accused of pro-Confederate propaganda, and moved to keep Indians at bay, especially through brutal and vicious attacks on hungry and raiding Indians in the northern regions of California and southeastern Oregon.

Fortunately for Lincoln and his military men on the West Coast, conflicts with Indians in the Pacific Northwest were less numerous and less violent in the Civil War years than they had been in the 1850s and would become again after war's end. True, the flood of miners into Washington, Idaho, and Montana regions, overrunning Indian lands, fouling their water sources, and damaging their grazing areas, upset white-Indian relations; but those upsets did not break out into war until later. Still, something had to be done, so in 1863 Lincoln's appointee to the Indian superintendency in Washington Territory, Calvin Hale, moved to negotiate a new treaty with the Nez Perce. It was a ticklish, tense situation, so Hale had six companies of troops from nearby Fort Lapwai to stand by as the difficult negotiations were carried out and signed by the "treaty Indians" but not by other Nez Perce, including old Chief Joseph.[68]

Although several conflicts broke out between the military and Indians, including those in the Snake Indian War in eastern Oregon, only one huge battle with Indians, the Bear River battle (January 1863), occurred during the Civil War years in the Oregon Country. It resulted more from difficulties in the Rocky Mountain areas and Mormon expansion than from events in the coastal areas. But the conflict was also, in part, a result of the military's mission to protect settlers and immigrants on the overland trails into the Pacific Northwest. Rambunctious Brig. Gen. Patrick Edward Conner was sent from California to look into rumors that the Mormons were being disloyal to the Union. When he arrived in Salt Lake City in late 1862, he heard numerous stories of Shoshoni Indians attacking settlers and stealing their cattle, their harassments of traders traveling to the newly opened Montana mines, and their intercepting of immigrant trains on the overland trails. There were reasons enough and more for the hungry and pressured Indians to respond to Mormon and other settlers' incursions, but those reasons seemed of little matter to the red-haired Conner and his men, hungry for action and more than a little "Indian killing." On the freezing day of 29 January 1863, Connor's two hundred and sixty men surrounded and attacked Bear Hunter's Shoshonis near present-day Preston, Idaho. After four hours of intense fighting in which two hundred and twenty-four Indians were killed and one hundred and sixty women and children taken, the soldiers had won one of the most disastrous battles for Indians in the American

West. The horrendous engagement also suggested that Lincoln's policy of protecting settlers from Indians, if in the hands of a brutal leader like Conner, could lead to a virtual massacre of Native Americans.[69]

• • •

From 1861 to the end of 1864, Abraham Lincoln's ties to the Oregon County both tightened and expanded. The most significant of the new anchorings and expansions came in the field of politics. Through his dozens of appointments in the Pacific Northwest, Lincoln had essentially founded the Republican Party in the new territories and supported the new party in the state of Oregon. He had reached out, too, to War Democrats like newly elected Governor Gibbs of Oregon, to foster additional support for the Union. Lincoln's backing of congressional legislation in the form of railroad, homestead, and educational measures also added to his leverage in the Far Corner. Finally, he cemented further connections by urging residents of the Oregon Country to oppose secessionists and any others attempting to undermine the war efforts. These developments bonded Lincoln more closely politically with the Pacific Northwest, but other challenges remained, as the reelection year of 1864 would soon prove.

Chapter 5: Lincoln, the Oregon Country, and the Election of 1864

Abraham Lincoln was in a bind. For much of early 1864 the Civil War was not going well. Naysayers in his Republican Party talked of nominating another candidate who could win the war and the election of 1864. Leading journalists and other politicians were predicting a loss for Lincoln and the Republicans should he run again. In the midst of these disappointments and dilemmas Lincoln sat down to write an extraordinarily revealing document.

On 23 August, in a brief piece entitled "Memorandum Concerning His Probable Failure of Re-election," Lincoln revealed his somber and foreboding mood. "This morning, as for some days past," he began, "it seems exceedingly probable this Administration will not be re-elected." If that was the case, he continued, "Then it will be my duty to so co-operate with the president elect, as to save the Union between the election and the inauguration; as he will have secured his election on such ground that he can not possibly save it afterwards."[1]

That memorandum was the nadir of 1864 for Lincoln. Within three months, victories on the Civil War battlefields and triumphs in the fall state elections turned the tide in the opposite direction for the president. But in the opening months of the year, Lincoln's endeavors to lead the country to victory in the war and to be re-nominated and reelected were in question. Even if one does not accept the exaggerated statement that "the 1864 election was the most important electoral event in American history" (the election of 1860 was of equal importance, for example), one must agree that Lincoln's reelection was of central significance in moving toward the end of the Civil War.[2]

The election of 1864 and events surrounding it also provide other illuminating glimpses of links between Abraham Lincoln and the Oregon Country. During 1864, Lincoln's connections with his close friend Dr. Anson Henry and his contacts with other territorial leaders in Washington, Idaho, and Montana (most of whom he had appointed) reinforced political bonds between the president and the Far Northwest.

•••

In the opening months of 1864, Lincoln faced several perplexing challenges. Surprisingly, several of the vexing questions came from within the president's own party. Radical Republicans such as Charles Sumner, Benjamin Wade, and Zachariah Chandler in the Senate and Thaddeus Stevens, George Julian, and Henry Winter Davis in the House were greatly dissatisfied with Lincoln. They wanted him to press harder on antislavery measures, to lead a "hard war" against the South, and to lambast "traitors" in that region who had begun the war. These congressmen were also much upset with Lincoln's amnesty policies and his nascent Reconstruction plans, which they considered far too lenient and kind-hearted.[3]

Another growing discontent was even closer at hand—within Lincoln's cabinet. Presidential aspirations ate at Secretary of the Treasury Salmon P. Chase like a devouring disease. Those needs had driven Chase into the election of 1860, and even after his loss he thought he merited the office more than Lincoln. Perhaps one of his fellow Radicals from Ohio, irascible Ben Wade, had it right in explaining Chase's large self-appreciation. The trouble with Chase, Wade noted, was he thought there were four members of the Trinity, and that he was the fourth part. In fall of 1863, Chase's presidential lust was oozing out again. A few Radicals began to speak of him as a more assertive and thus more viable candidate than Lincoln for the Republican nomination in 1864. Although Chase tried to deny his ambitions and actions, the tracks seemed clear to others. As well as to Lincoln, who refused to become involved in the controversy beginning to swirl around Chase and his possible run for the presidency. Still, the Chase groundswell added to Lincoln's already huge load.

Even heavier than these political burdens was the war weariness that had descended on the North like a heavy, wet, and dark blanket.

UNION AND LIBERTY!   AND   UNION AND SLAVERY!

Abraham Lincoln's campaign for reelection in 1864 seemed to falter until Union victories in the field helped secure his victory as the "Union and Liberty" candidate. Lincoln's opponent, George McClellan, was a Unionist, but his Democratic platform called for peace and the acceptance of slavery, which his opponents castigated as "union and slavery." (Library of Congress, Prints & Photographic Division, LC-USZ62-945.)

For nearly three years Union supporters had prayed for and expected military breakthroughs that would push back the Confederates and defeat the South. That steady string of victories had not happened. Indeed, things seemed bogged down in early 1864. Lincoln still had not found the general who was clearly, diligently in charge and able to push the president's twin goals: simultaneously attack the South in several locations across the North-South battle lines, and defeat and destroy Lee's army. The president had been unable to divert many Northerners—and some of the generals—from emphasizing too often the "on to Richmond" campaigns, which Lincoln did not favor.

• • •

The leading authority on Civil War politics in the Oregon Country portrayed residents of the region as "spectators of disunion." Distance, frontier independence, adherence to popular sovereignty, and separation from major divisive issues—all these issues, according to Robert W. Johannsen, were reasons why Pacific Northwesterners were less involved than other Americans in the fractious Civil War. Overall, Johannsen believed, residents of the region were conservative, nationalistic people with an outlook akin to the Border States, neither uniformly northern nor southern in their outlook.[4]

That perspective is less tenable a half century after Johannsen offered it. First, like so much writing about the subject, this point of view casts the Civil War too narrowly, as primarily an experience of war, of armed conflict. Too little is said about national-regional politics, civil rights, Indian policies, and Union-Copperhead conflicts. And, in Johannsen's case, the story is too tied to the perspectives of Frederick Jackson Turner, our most important American historian but whose inordinate stress on the frontier underemphasized eastern influences on the West. A more nuanced view, demonstrating national influences on regional experiences, should portray the peoples of the Oregon Country as intensely interested in Civil War issues, especially as they played out in local contexts. They were clearly on the western end of a cross-continental political connection.

As we have seen, the earliest links among the Oregon Country, Abraham Lincoln, and national issues emerged in the 1850s. Lincoln's Illinois friends who came to the Pacific Northwest kept him abreast with the politics of the Far Corner. He, in turn, wrote to them about his attitudes toward and involvements in national issues. Even more clear evidence of Oregon Country connections with the rest of the nation came in the prominent roles Joseph Lane and Isaac Ingalls Stevens played as Democratic vice-presidential candidate and national committee chair, respectively, in the Breckinridge campaign of 1860. Edward Baker's recognized part in Oregon and national politics in 1860-61 illustrates still another Oregon Country-national connection.[5]

These bonds of interest continued in the first years of the Civil War. Most often they came in the leading newspapers of the region, especially in the Portland *Oregonian* and Salem *Oregon Statesman* but also in several other newspapers in the Pacific Northwest territories. Further evidences of the links appear in the private correspondence of such regional leaders as Matthew Deady; Senator James Nesmith; Lincoln's political crony in Washington Territory, Anson G. Henry; and in Lincoln's politically appointed governors, William H. Wallace, William Pickering, Caleb Lyon, and Sidney Edgerton. As the newspapers and personal letters reveal, residents of the Oregon Country were interested in and participated in national issues, but they usually saw them within the purview of regional needs and perspectives.

Such was the case in Oregon in the early months of 1864. The political patterns in Oregon followed a wobbly rather than a direct, straight-ahead predictable route. Although from 1861 onward most Oregonians were and remained Unionists, that configuration was by no means unanimous. In fact, by 1864, because of disappearances and losses, Democrats and Republicans alike were following different leaders. These changes also reshaped Oregon's connections to Lincoln.

The shifts involved some of Oregon's best-known politicians. For example, Joseph Lane, the state's leading Democrat, was gone from the scene, having retired from public life. Delazon Smith had died in 1860, exhausted from his efforts in behalf of the Democrats. The energetic and irrepressible Edward Baker had been killed at Ball's Bluff in 1861, robbing the Republicans of their newest and most dynamic speaker. At the same time Anson Henry left Oregon for Washington Territory as Lincoln's newly appointed surveyor-general.

The most revealing of recent changes was that of Asahel Bush. In the wide divide that defined the Democrats after spring 1861, Bush kept to the Douglas Democrats, embraced some fusion with the Republicans, and supported a modicum of Lincoln's Union efforts. In the loyal-disloyal dichotomy that separated Americans generally and Oregonians too, Bush clearly stood among the loyalists. But he also increasingly criticized the leadership of Lincoln, pointing to the president's draft and emancipation policies and the removal of Gen. McClellan as infringements on personal freedoms and obvious mistakes. Then, Bush suddenly dropped from the Oregon political stage, selling the *Oregon Statesman* and transitioning to a very successful career in business and banking.[6] These transitions left James Nesmith in the U.S. Senate and, less directly, Matthew Deady in the U. S. district court as the leading Democrats.

Generally, political happenings in Oregon in 1863 and early 1864 seemed less contested than those in the previous half-dozen years. Perhaps the acceptance of fusion, the rise of Unionism on the state level, and Lincoln's willingness to support some bipartisanship efforts nationally aided in turning Oregon politics onto a more placid route.

During the 1850s Asahel Bush, editor of the influential Oregon Statesman, *was a leader of the Democratic Salem Clique in Oregon. But in the 1860s he withdrew from politics, robbing the Democrats of a major anti-Lincoln voice. (Oregon Historical Society Research Library, Album 109.)*

Yet there were also unclouded evidences of differences among Oregonians. Six Oregon newspapers were "suppressed" (kept out of the U. S. mails), said to be "treasonable" in their coverage of Civil War and administration issues. These actions stirred up conservative or Dixie Democrats, who, like their Copperhead counterparts across the country, pointed to what they considered the tyrannical actions of Lincoln. Most Oregonians, however, seemed to think the periodicals had gone too far in their criticism of Lincoln's domestic and war policies, or at least they acquiesced in the suppressions. The censorship of newspapers, the suppression of the writ of habeas corpus, and the curbing of freedom of speech were parts of Lincoln's reluctant campaign to deal with critics and opponents who were scuttling war measures, attempting to forestall the draft, and otherwise undermining efforts to defeat the South.[7]

Other darker sides, earlier in evidence, came into clearer focus during 1863-64. Political participants later confirmed that supporters of a separatist Pacific Republic, although neither numerous nor much in the public square, nonetheless represented a rumored threat in Oregon and California. As the war wore on, diehard members of the movement spoke of the need to remove their regions from the military conflagration to the east. More organized were the circles of the Knights of the Golden Circle, a secret organization with the goal of uniting all slave regions and their supporters. As many as ten circles of the Knights were said to be scattered across western Oregon, up and down the Willamette Valley. To counter the Knights, Union Leagues sprouted around the state. Their purpose was to battle against the Knights, support Lincoln, and back Republican or Union Party candidates. Supported by Governor Gibbs, the League councils, keeping their activities secret, spoke only for candidates who remained explicitly loyal to Lincoln. Together, the Knights and Leagues were, obviously, more a symbolic than a shaping force in Oregon politics in 1864.[8]

• • •

Although the residents of the territories of Washington, Idaho, and Montana could not participate in Lincoln's bid for reelection in 1864, the men did take part in local elections and in that way exhibited their support for or opposition to the Lincoln administration. In June 1864, William Pickering in Washington, Caleb Lyon in Idaho, and Sidney Edgerton in Montana, all Lincoln appointees, occupied the governors' chairs in these three territories. But none was able to marshal unified support for Lincoln. Strong—if not expanding—Democratic numbers, plus the personality and partisan limitations of the governors kept them from rallying the territories uniformly behind Lincoln. Ironically, A. C. Gibbs, elected to be the Oregon governor in 1862 as a Douglas Democrat, proved to be the most effective of the Northwest governors as he swung increasingly toward the Republicans and explicitly announced his support for the Lincoln administration.

But perhaps the demographic shifts and resulting political makeup of the Northwest territories did more to determine the political outlook of these areas than the successful or inadequate leadership of Lincoln's gubernatorial selections. In 1864, Washington Territory illustrated, as would Idaho and Montana to the east, the population shifts that reshaped Northwest territorial politics in the Civil War era. Although Lincoln's patronage appointments of governors Wallace and Pickering and other mainstays like Dr. Henry seemed to promise a Republican trajectory to Washington's politics, the impact of mineral rushes and the gradual development of agriculture in the eastern sections of the territory beckoned thousands of newcomers with opposing political persuasions. A majority were Democrats, and most of them supported George E. Cole from Walla Walla in his successful election as the new territorial delegate in 1863. These newly arrived Democrats added to the party's strength, already evidenced by the territorial legislature's rejection of a resolution to support the Union one year earlier. (Under pressure of not receiving needed administration largèsse, the legislature reversed itself the next year.) Until creation of the new Idaho Territory lopped off more than half of Washington in March 1863, the eastern Washington mines were spreading into present-day Idaho, Montana, and Wyoming, drawing cards for hordes of miners, many of whom were Democrats, some of them decidedly pro-South and anti-Lincoln.[9]

In late 1863 and early 1864, a few months into Idaho's territorial existence, its close ties to Abraham Lincoln were, in some respects, exceptionally clear. As noted in the previous chapters, several of Lincoln's first appointments in Idaho were his friends or acquaintances of his friends. William H. Wallace, the territorial governor, was an acquaintance of Lincoln. The secretary was William B. Daniels from Yamhill County, Oregon, where he had been a neighbor of Lincoln's close confidant in the Pacific Northwest, Anson Henry; and he was the brother-in-law of Oregon Congressman John R. McBride, another Lincoln partisan. For chief justice of the territory Lincoln selected Sidney Edgerton, a political and lawyer acquaintance from Ohio. The two justices Lincoln appointed were Samuel C. Parks, still another lawyer and friend from Illinois, and Alexander (Alleck) C. Smith, Dr. Henry's son-in-law. Although one writer has exaggerated a bit in asserting that Lincoln had more connections with Idaho than any another western state or territory (in reality, he had more with Oregon), the Lincoln-Idaho ties were numerous and strong.[10]

The disparity between Lincoln's Republican and out-of-territory appointees and the growing Democratic populace of Idaho helps explain some of the difficulties that pervaded the new territory in 1864. When Wallace was elected territorial delegate and headed off to Washington, D.C., Secretary Daniels, hoping to be named as Wallace's replacement, served as acting governor, but he was not up to the task. Under pressures beyond his abilities, Daniels resigned, explaining to Wallace, "the sooner I get away from here the better."[11] That meant for much of 1864 Idaho had no elected governor in residence, only a reluctant territorial secretary trying to fend off the continuing political stresses.

The conflicts were many—and intense. Idahoans fought over whether Lewiston, Boise, or another location would be the territorial capital. Democrats called for a more equitable distribution of voting districts, allowing them to gain more seats in the territorial legislature. Legal authorities seemed unable to quell the violence that erupted in the form of robberies, murders, and other mayhem; these violent acts were particularly numerous in the outlying northern and eastern areas, some of which soon became part of Montana. Vigilante groups more than organized law and order were determining quick guilt and exacting swift and harsh penalties. And there was the ongoing problem of Congress not providing the needed funds to operate the territory.[12]

Only strong, on-site, and diligent leaders could handle this litany of problems. After the detrimental impact of the previous absences of territorial officials was compounded by the early failures of Wallace's replacement, Caleb Lyon, Idaho descended into chaos. Lincoln, his cabinet, and Congress paid too little attention to the struggling territory, allowing crooked officials to take advantage of the lack of oversight and abscond with funds. And other needed appointees just did not come. From late 1864 into early 1865 Idaho was on the verge of total collapse. Unionists and Copperheads, Yankees and Rebels, were in an intense competition, with no one from within or without providing necessary leadership.

The sloughing off of some of Idaho's eastern and northern regions, because of distance and failures of law and order, and their incorporation into Montana was an inadequate foundation on which to erect still another new territory. As we have seen, many of the same political challenges that divided Washington and Idaho territories were evident in Montana. Once Lincoln named Sidney Edgerton as governor and added territorial judges, the new territory gradually lurched forward in summer 1864, but a secretary for Montana did not arrive until after Lincoln's death. The president had appointed two, but neither accepted the office.

Finally, Thomas F. Meagher agreed to serve, but he did not arrive until September 1865, more than a year after Montana was organized.[13]

The conflicts and divisions that the Civil War, territorial organization, and partisan politics engendered in 1864 were all evident by the end of summer 1864. Edgerton would accept only Union sentiments—and, if possible, loyal territorial legislators; Lincoln and Congress were too harried to pay much attention to a faraway territory. And Democrats—probably in the majority—were dead set against marching lockstep behind Edgerton. Undoubtedly a young observer in a western Montana mining camp overstated the situation when she wrote a friend: "I verily believe that two-thirds of the people here are infidel and 'secesh.'" Another probably came closer to the truth in pointing out that Unionists were nearly nonexistent in all of Deer Lodge County. But Democrats were pushing past the Republicans in voting numbers, with political partisanship—Rebels versus Yankees—ruling the scene. Tempers were ready to explode, as they would in the coming fall elections.[14]

• • •

Lincoln seemed tied in knots with the manifold duties expected of him in the demanding earlier months of 1864, but he did find time to support at least two measures especially important to western expansionists in California and Oregon, and the three territories in the Pacific Northwest. The president remained interested in western railroads after signing the charter for the first transcontinental railroad in 1862. He followed up by determining the eastern terminus of the Union Pacific and the western end of the Central Pacific. When private and government funding seemed inadequate to build the line, he backed congressional legislation to reorganize financial support for the transcontinental road but, even more importantly, to double the size of its land grant. These changes were made in 1864.[15]

In the same year the Northern Pacific Railroad was chartered and granted twenty sections of land in states and forty sections in territories for each mile of track it laid in building a rail line from Lake Superior to an undetermined end point on the Pacific Northwest coast. The line contained great promise for those hoping to develop all parts of the Oregon Country. These railroad expansions were part and parcel of

Lincoln's desire to expand the West, to make it ready for new settlers and to make lands there available to veterans and westward-moving families.[16]

At the same time, Lincoln endorsed plans to send Indian people to reservations. Following the plans of his commissioner of Indian affairs, William Dole, and of many others of the time, Lincoln viewed the establishment of reservations as the best of still inadequate ways to handle white-Indian conflicts over lands in the American West. Lincoln said little about Indian affairs; in fact, he knew little about Indians. So, he was inclined the follow the advice of Dole and Indian agents in the Oregon Country when they called his attention to matters there or brought treaties to the Senate for its confirmation.

In early 1864, Lincoln sent several treaties to the Senate, often attaching supportive comments from Commissioner Dole and from the secretary of the interior. Some dealt with "Shoshonee Nation" tribes on the borders with Utah and Nevada; others with "Bannacks" in Idaho Territory. All were based on the prevalent idea of "concentration" and "relocation." Indians would be removed from contested regions— often in mining and rich agriculture areas—and confined away from settlements in less-desired areas.[17]

The most significant for the Oregon Country was the treaty negotiated with the Nez Perce in June 1863. In 1855, an earlier treaty with the Nez Perce considerably diminished their living areas and, by force of treaty demands, divided the Indians into treaty and nontreaty groups. After miners and other settlers forced their way onto Nez Perce lands set aside by the treaty of 1855, Indian agents Calvin Hale and two others traveled to Lapwai to renegotiate a new, greatly reduced reservation. Working hard to gain support from the treaty bands of the Nez Perce (but unsuccessfully with young Chief Joseph and the nontreaty bands), Hale formulated a new treaty that reduced the Nez Perce reservation by 90 percent. None of the nontreaty leaders signed the treaty, which took away their lands but promised financial support to help replace the lost lands. It was the discontent and disagreement of these nontreaty bands that became a major cause of the tragic Nez Perce War of 1877.

On 4 April 1864 President Lincoln submitted the Nez Perce treaty to the Senate. He mentioned Hale's work with "the chiefs, headmen, and delegates of the Nez Percé tribe of Indians in Washington Territory [actually, Idaho Territory, as of March 1864]." He sent along supporting materials from Superintendent Hale and Commissioner Dole, but detailed none of the controversies arising from the treaty making.[18] Lincoln's handling of this and other treaties reflected his essential agreement with those who favored reservations—the "concentration policy"—in handling the nettlesome problem of Indian policy. Although he increasingly wrestled with the rights and possible citizenship of former slaves, Lincoln had not moved along a similar route in dealing with the rights of Native Americans in the West.[19]

• • •

Additional heavy burdens of dissatisfaction and discontent fell on Lincoln as spring turned to summer. After the momentous victories at Vicksburg and Gettysburg in July 1863, Unionists hoped the tide of war had turned. Their anticipation for the end of conflict grew after U. S. Grant was given command of the Union armies the following March. Now, it was on to Richmond and the defeat of Lee and the Confederates.

That enthusiasm evaporated in the long weeks from May into June 1864. Gen. Grant locked onto Gen. Lee for a series of brutal and deadly encounters. Battles in the Wilderness (5-6 May), Spotsylvania (8-12 May), and Cold Harbor (1-3 June) led to the loss of nearly sixty thousand Union troops, with Lee's Confederates suffering only half that many. Unable to best Lee and move on to Richmond, Grant dug in near Petersburg (twenty miles south of Richmond) and began a siege that would last nearly nine months until near the end of the war.[20]

Not only was Grant stymied and even in a stalemate in his attacks on the Army of Northern Virginia, but Jubal A. Early, the able southern general, threatened Washington, D. C., in a daring sortie in early July. Crossing the Potomac into Maryland, Early swung northeast and advanced to within five miles of the White House. Hastily shifted Union forces rushed up from Petersburg to block Early and to push him back into Virginia but not until he had put a deep scare in the capital. Critics of Lincoln, already upset with the gridlock between Grant and Lee forces in Virginia, used the danger of Early's advance to further pummel the president.

The politics of war and the politics of Washington, D. C., overlapped during these months and made Lincoln's days even longer and more burdensome. Leading congressional critics pointed to the ferocious but standoff battles at the Wilderness, Spotsylvania, and Cold Harbor and asked why Grant's superior numbers had not allowed him to drive Lee from his fortifications. Some had erroneously predicted the war would be over by fall. More than a few of these overly optimistic politicians turned against Grant, labeling him "the butcher." Lincoln was not among them. Victory would come in time, the president sighed, but it might even take a year of tenacious fighting in Virginia and elsewhere to turn the tide.[21]

Party politics continued to add to Lincoln's load as he attempted to lead in summer 1864. Most of the Republican Radicals (sometimes described as the "Unconditionals" because of their assertive demands) opposed Lincoln's re-nomination, looking for other candidates to replace the president. When Chase's bid seemed to nosedive (but not entirely disappear), some Radicals pushed for Gen. Ben Butler or John C. Frèmont for the Republican nominee. Even though these political generals were inadequate—sometimes dangerously incompetent—as military leaders, they retained such political allegiance among Lincoln's Republican opponents that neither the president nor his lieutenants could overlook the competition from them. Other dissidents tried to mount a Grant candidacy, but the general refused to cooperate. When Grant was informed of a plan to advance his name for the presidency, he told a visitor that he wanted no part of the move. "I consider it as important for the cause that he [Lincoln] should be elected as that the army should be successful in the field."[22] The Radicals, hoping to stall decisions until they could rally more votes against Lincoln, called for delaying the Republican nomination from June until 1 September. Those delaying tactics failed, and in June in Baltimore Lincoln was renominated, with minimal opposition, as the candidate of the Republican or Union Party.[23]

Lincoln's re-nomination did little to solve the most pressing problems facing him in the late summer. The war weariness increased as Grant remained dug in near Petersburg, unable to dislodge Lee. Also, Radical Republican opposition mounted when Lincoln pocket-vetoed the Radical-directed Wade-Davis bill a few days after he was renominated.

More much demanding than Lincoln's agenda for Reconstruction, the Wade-Davis bill called for a majority of voters in each Confederate state to take an oath of past and future loyalty before it could be brought back into the Union. Some Radicals went so far as to call for a new convention to name another candidate for the Republicans. Others chimed in, with New York *Tribune*'s editor, Horace Greeley, probably the country's best-known journalist, flatly asserting, "Mr. Lincoln is already beaten. He cannot be elected."[24] Even Henry Raymond, *New York Times* editor, national party chairman of the Republican/Union Party, and a supporter of Lincoln, spoke gloomily to the president. "I hear but one report," Raymond wrote on 22 August; "the tide is strongly against us." If the vote were taken now, "we should be beaten." The next day Lincoln wrote his pessimistic memorandum.[25]

• • •

Spring, summer, and early fall 1864 elections in the Oregon Country revealed political alignments in the region. Indeed, well before these prepresidential votes, leaders and residents were lining up behind their candidates, and attempting to align others correctly. For example, Governor Gibbs of Oregon, a Douglas Democrat on his way to becoming a Republican, urged Lincoln to refrain from using "Republican" for his party designation and to switch to the "Union Party." He reminded the president that Oregon would elect a U. S. senator in 1864, and the adoption of "Union" for the party name would likely keep Douglas Democrats in line for fusion efforts. "But," he added, "if that name is changed [to Republican], the Pacific States may go copper head, and Oregon will probably elect a secessionist to the Senate." He concluded by calling himself a "Douglas democrat" who, nonetheless, was "a supporter of your Administration." He apologized for bothering Lincoln, but reiterated that this was "a matter of great interest to the people of this coast."[26]

To the north, Dr. Anson Henry was as busy as a frenzied beaver chewing away at any opponents of Lincoln and promoting the interests of those who supported the administration. Not until early 1864—after a trip to Washington, D.C.—had Henry succeeded in getting the president to oust the doctor's persistent enemy, Victor Smith, from his customs position in Washington Territory. Smith was a Republican but more of the Radical stripe and more a friend and backer of Secretary Chase than Lincoln. Those were traitorous actions to Henry, a view he tried to impress on the president and territorial officials. Conversely, Henry could warmly recommend Democrat William Winlock Miller to Lincoln because he was the son of their mutual friend in Illinois and because he was "the best specimen of a Union Democrat ... we have in this Territory ... I know you will like to make his acquaintance."[27]

These kinds of political jockeying and partisan sentiments much influenced elections in the Oregon Country, but they also revealed a clear trend in Oregon state politics. In spring 1864 John R. McBride, the sitting Oregon U. S. congressman, was up for reelection. But the Republican/ Unionists, after indicating they would not support McBride, flirted with several other candidates before nominating J. D. H. Henderson, a Presbyterian minister and political newcomer. One historian suggests that McBride might have lost not because he failed as a sound Republican and Lincoln supporter but because he had alienated western Oregonians by suggesting a branch of the U. S. Mint should be placed in The Dalles and not in the Willamette Valley. Oregon Democrats were also badly divided but more on how to react to the war, secession, and Lincoln's administration, and lost by a large margin to Henderson in the run for U. S. Congress. And they were not able to elect many Democrats to the state legislature, which boded ill for other coming elections.[28]

The following September the legislature met to elect a U. S. senator. The incumbent, Benjamin Harding, a Douglas Democrat known for his foot-dragging support for Lincoln, was not seriously considered for reelection. Instead, the Union-dominated body, on the third ballot, selected George H. Williams. The election of Williams illustrated the expanding strength of the Republican/Union coalition in the state and its support for Lincoln. Williams was a former chief justice of Oregon Territory and a regular Democrat in the 1850s and an unsuccessful Douglas Democrat in the senatorial run-off in 1860. By 1863 he had converted to the Republican Party and became a well-known leader, perhaps even toward the Radical end of the party's spectrum. His selection by the legislature in early fall 1864 symbolized the shift of Oregon politics in the Civil War era. A fusion of Douglas Democrats and Republicans and other Republicans won most of the elections in the 1860-63 period. In 1864, two years after the Oregon Union Party began, that Republican-Union combination gained victories—within the state and later in the reelection of Lincoln.[29]

In mid-1864, the three organized territories in the Pacific Northwest illustrated similar and yet divergent paths from those in the state of Oregon. A persistent tension undermined good government in those areas, and in most other regions under the territorial system. Lincoln had had a hand in creating the tension. By appointing, by and large, nonresident territorial leaders who usually were unacquainted with the new areas and peoples they were expected to govern, Lincoln sent appointees on something of a fool's errand. Meanwhile, shifting populations in Washington, Idaho, and Montana in 1864, particularly in the second half of the year, brought in increasing numbers of Democrats. Even though many were Unionists, they frequently disagreed with Lincoln's methods—and the Republicans—thus setting up a civil war of opinions that often derailed sound leadership and governments. In the classic words of noted American historian Carl Becker, the system asked (as in the American Revolution years) "who would rule" and "who would rule at home." The American territorial system in 1864-65 embodied an irreconcilable conflict between those coming from the outside, appointed "carpetbaggers," and those inside, ambitious and sometimes recalcitrant residents. Perhaps Lincoln did not so much name incompetent territorial leaders (as some historians have claimed) but placed appointees in a system destined for conflict and upset.[30]

The clash between appointed Republicans and majority Democrats played itself out in Washington, increasingly so. With Victor Smith and most of the intra-Republican controversies out of the way, Governor Pickering and Surveyor-General Henry could focus on lining up more support for Lincoln, not allowing Territorial Delegate Cole to blunt administrative policies, and keeping any other pro-southern men from gaining leadership in the territory. They tried. Since there were no major territorial elections at the time, Pickering, Henry, and their cronies turned their political energies toward rousting out any territorial politicians who did not wholeheartedly support Lincoln and the North. So did Simeon Francis. Writing to Pickering about the possibility of raising a new regiment of volunteers in Washington, Francis pressed the governor to "secure the appointment of officers for them from your territory. ... We want no secesh officers."[31]

Congress and Republicans in Washington Territory worried that the territorial legislature would not support the Lincoln administration. With this uncertainty in mind, Congress altered the territory's charter to allow the governor to veto the legislature's decisions. This revision meant that Republican Governor Pickering could hold a Democratic legislature in check and also counterbalance any efforts that Territorial Delegate Cole tried to get the legislators in Olympia to support.[32]

In Idaho, politics in mid-1864 wobbled between a major election fraud spilling over from 1863 and the move toward establishing the new territory that became Montana. In late 1863, U. S. Marshal Dolphus S. Payne, a Lincoln appointee, either forged an election report from the distant Fort Laramie area (then in Idaho, later in Wyoming Territory) or knowingly allowed a fraudulent report to be filed that added nearly all of its illegal five hundred votes behind Governor Wallace's candidacy for Idaho's first territorial delegate. Probably Wallace was not involved in the subterfuge, but the "Fort Laramie fraud" damaged his reputation, so much so that even the Republicans did not support him for reelection. Most of the damage from the ruse surfaced in spring and summer of 1864.[33]

At the same time, Idaho's political competitors were playing leapfrog with the possibility of organizing a new territory to the east. Republicans, including Wallace, favored Montana as a new territory because its existence would allow for Lincoln's appointments of new territorial officials, the addition of party loyalists to the governmental payroll, and the launching of the Republican Party in still another western area. Also, Democrats were the more numerous voters in the mining regions east of the Bitterroot Mountains, so Republicans were looking for ways to curb that growing strength. A new territory under the control of Lincoln's Republicans would help accomplish the goal. Democrats, on the other hand, were hesitant to back the new territory unless they could at least control the territorial legislature and Montana's first territorial delegate. These partisan competitions added to the continuing complications that convulsed the first eight months of Idaho's long territorial period.

Caleb Lyon, Lincoln's choice to succeed William H. Wallace, was an even heavier weight overbalancing Idaho's fragile political scales. Lyon could not reach out to fellow Republicans, let alone to opposing Democrats, of both Union and secessionist stripes. Moreover, the transplanted New Yorker was absent for much of his gubernatorial period, gone for seventeen of twenty-seven months. His replacement, Territorial Secretary and Acting Governor Clinton DeWitt Smith, proved inadequate as a stand-in, leading to additional chaos. Lyon's problems were two-fold. He served in a territorial system that rarely worked well, and not much at all without diligent, wise leadership. Lyon did not exhibit the latter. Lincoln's Republican appointees were superimposed on a Democratic majority in Idaho. Similar to governors Pickering to the west in Washington and Edgerton to the east in Montana, Lyon was a minority governor in an increasingly Democratic territory. Adding to that, Lyon personally was not up to the demanding task of working with partisans of another camp. The governor's opponents might correctly label him an alien carpetbagger out of touch with local politics, but probably more influential in his failures was his flawed personality. Lyon was blind to his cultural light-headedness in a physical, hands-on society, his seeming repugnance for a decidedly masculine community, and his inability to discern that compromise was necessary to successfully

Caleb Lyon was a curious Lincoln appointment as Idaho's second territorial governor. Often absent from the territory and unsuccessful in communicating with frontiersmen, Lyon led Idaho almost to the abyss of collapse. (Library of Congress, Prints & Photographic Division, LC-DIG-cwpbh-01858.)

lead Idaho. His absence during most of 1864 only augmented Idaho's problems.[34]

In Montana in 1864, Sidney Edgerton faced similar dilemmas. Although more in tune with Montana society than Lyon was with that of Idaho, Edgerton was tone-deaf on politics. Once he took up the governor's chair in July 1864, the political transplant from Ohio pushed for Union and Republican agendas alone, even though he could plainly see large numbers of Democrats already in the territory—and more coming every month. As we have seen, he played only partisan cards in that fall's election for territorial delegate, and Democrats gleefully trumped his Republican tricks—and won. Edgerton tried to champion Lincoln's causes in Montana, but he had so alienated the Democratic majority and even some fellow Republicans with his Radical emphases that he was climbing a steeper hill as the year wore on.[35]

• • •

If Lincoln's depressing memorandum written on 23 August represented the nadir of his reelection year, in the next two months three military events led to an amazing turn of direction. The tide had begun to turn, even before the gloomy memorandum day, when earlier in August David Farragut, the redoubtable Union admiral, stormed into Mobile Bay to go after the Confederates. Tying himself to the rigging of his ship, he yelled out—so the story goes—"Damn the torpedoes! Four bells ... full speed"—and won a remarkable battle against a southern flotilla.[36]

Even more significant was the terse telegram Gen. William Tecumseh Sherman hummed to Washington on 3 September. "Atlanta is ours, fairly won," the telegram read. Immediately the news flashed across the North. The Unionist and tireless commentator George Templeton Strong told his diary, "Glorious news this morning—Atlanta taken at last!!! ... If it be true, it is ... the greatest event of the war."[37] Observers in the South discerned a pattern after the Farragut and Sherman victories. The Richmond *Examiner* told its readers "The disaster of Atlanta ... [came] in the very nick of time [to] save the party of Lincoln from irretrievable ruin."[38]

But there was more soon to come. After Jubal Early had been chased out of the Washington, D. C., area in mid-July, he returned to the picturesque breadbasket of the South, the Shenandoah Valley of northern Virginia. In late June and early July, Early drove Union troops out of that food-producing wonderland and came back to protect the region. But the North had other ideas. Union leaders wanted the Shenandoah taken—and, if possible, destroyed. Its loss would be huge to the South.

The outcome in the Shenandoah helped shift directions in the war, made Gen. Phil Sheridan into a hero, and clearly helped Lincoln's campaign for reelection. Miffed that other generals had failed to root Early out of the Shenandoah, Grant put Sheridan in charge; he was to pursue and destroy Early's forces. After a series of punitive attacks, Sheridan had Early on his heels. But Early rallied his men and almost succeeded in turning the tide while Sheridan was in Washington for a meeting on war strategy. Returning to the field on 19 October and hearing of Early's possible successes, Sheridan dramatically rode to the front (his gallop has been immortalized in poetry and drama as "Sheridan's Ride"), shouting at his men, "God damn you, don't cheer me! If you love your country, come up to the front! ... Come up, God damn you! Come up." Seeing Sheridan dashing to the front and courageously exposing himself to enemy fire, his command rallied behind their leader, charged into Early's advancing lines, turned the tide, and virtually destroyed all of Early's forces.

Sheridan was even more destructive in the valley itself. His troops burned barns and crops, killed animals, and destroyed mills. Grant had ordered that the Shenandoah be turned "into a barren waste ... so that crows flying over it for the balance of the season will have to carry their provender with them."[39] Sheridan did exactly that, in so doing adding luster to his Union reputation and hatred among southerners. After hearing of Sheridan's earlier victories, Lincoln had telegraphed the general: "Have just heard of your great victory. God bless you all, officers and men." One month later, Lincoln wrote again to Sheridan thanking him for his "splendid work" and "for the month's operations in the Shenandoah Valley."[40]

The military victories of Farragut, Sherman, and Sheridan more than rehabilitated Lincoln's political prospects; they sent them soaring. Other events added to a redirection in Lincoln's reelection run. In late August the Democrats decided to nominate Gen. George McClellan, a dedicated

War Democrat, as the presidential candidate but on a peace platform. The Democratic strategy, half war and half peace, helped Lincoln since McClellan, wanting to support his loyal, valorous troops, could not run on a peace ticket and thereby undercut his party's stated platform. Once the Union victories had been won and were making headlines across the North and the Democrats' wobbly stances complicated their election campaign, Lincoln's spirits and prospects were resurrected.

Still, Lincoln, cautious as ever, wanted to take no chances. No U. S. president had been reelected since Andrew Jackson, thirty-two years before in 1832. Worried about the election outcome, the president moved to close other loopholes that might lead to defeat. He made sure that soldiers were allowed to vote—in their Civil War camps or at home while on leave. Lincoln wrote to General Sherman, asking but not requiring, that soldiers be allowed to return to Indiana and elsewhere to vote. "The bad effect upon the November election, and especially the giving the State Government to those who will oppose the war in every possible way, are too much to risk," the president told Sherman.[42]

Lincoln made another move to attempt to unify his own party. As Radical Republicans continued to register their distaste for conservative Montgomery Blair, Lincoln's postmaster general, and threatened to support John Frèmont as a splinter Republican candidate, Lincoln and the Radicals evidently reached an agreement. In September, Frèmont would retreat from his candidacy, and Lincoln would ask for Blair's resignation. Lincoln tried to soften his request to Blair by hinting at the political needs of the time: "you very well know that this proceeds from no dissatisfaction of mine with you personally or officially. Your uniform kindness has been unsurpassed by that of any friend." Blair, responding the same day, sent in his resignation, indicating that it was "advisable for the public interests that I should do so." A split among the Republicans was avoided, and a renewed unity prevailed.

In the weeks immediately before the November election the Republicans blasted the Democrats as "traitorous" disunionists. In these charges, Republicans chose to overlook that many Democrats supported the Union even while castigating Lincoln's policies: the draft, emancipation, suppression of newspapers, and suspension of writs of habeas corpus. Indeed, the political playing field for many northern Democrats had notably narrowed. Their political careers would be effectively shut down if they could not become and remain loyal Unionists. What remained were the possibilities of severely criticizing the incumbent for what they considered his unconstitutional actions and his clear infringement on citizens' rights and freedoms.

But the carping Democrats found too little traction in these criticisms to upset Lincoln. The possible outcome of the November vote became clearer as state elections took place in October. Indiana, Ohio, and Pennsylvania were crucial northern states, and all went for Lincoln's Union Party in October. The soldier vote helped considerably in these states, although it was not the deciding factor. Seeing these encouraging results, some optimistic Republicans enthusiastically predicted a strong Union victory the next month. Lincoln was more cautious, estimating in mid-October that he might have only one hundred twenty to McClellan's one hundred fourteen electoral votes. Lincoln put the California and Oregon vote, and that of the brand new state of Nevada, in his column—in fact, all Union states west of the Mississippi save for Missouri.[43]

Even though Lincoln apprehensively approached the reelection vote of 8 November, he need not have done so. Trends and events were moving positively in his direction, as the votes reported on 8-9 November made clear. Only three states—Kentucky, New Jersey, and Delaware—went for McClellan. Lincoln received 2,213,665 popular votes to McClellan's 1,802, 237, with the president's electoral win——two hundred twelve to twenty-one—even more impressive. Despite the criticisms Lincoln had received, he won a larger percentage of the vote than in 1860. A large majority of the soldiers also voted for their commander-in-chief, and the Union sentiments of the Republicans clearly appealed to northern voters and also to Border State voters in such states as Maryland and Missouri. Perhaps voters wanted Lincoln the Unionist back in the White House for four more years rather than a questionable Democratic candidate who favored continued war but whose party spoke of compromise and peace.[44]

In the press of events and the blizzard of telegrams arriving at his desk, the busy president found time to write to his old friend Anson Henry the day after his election victory. "With returns and States of which we are confident, the election of the President is considered certain," Lincoln informed Dr. Henry.[45] Lincoln had promised his surveyor-general of Washington Territory that he would send news of the electoral outcome as soon as it was known. This missive, written during such a busy time for the president, provided still another sign of Lincoln's ongoing links with friends and political acquaintances in the faraway Oregon Country.

Several other significances emerged from Lincoln's victory in November 1854. In addition to those previously mentioned, a vote for Lincoln meant a country on the road to general emancipation, which would come slightly more than a year later with the passage of the 13th Amendment in December 1865. Lincoln's victory also indicated the clear arrival of the Republican Party. In 1860 he had received less than 40 percent of the popular vote, but he gained 55 percent four years later. Lincoln's win also signaled that the Civil War would be pushed to the finish, without a compromise of an early peace allowing for the retention of slavery or a broken Union. With Lincoln at the patronage helm for four more years his political colleagues and friends could expect additional appointments, especially out in the western territories. Finally, Lincoln's reelection revealed that a majority Americans had come to trust and perhaps admire the tall, gaunt railsplitter from Illinois. He had become Father Abraham, the man they wanted to keep in the White House. Long Old Abe a little longer.

• • •

"GLORY TO GOD! LINCOLN ELECTED," the *Oregonian* headline rang out. Four days after the 1864 election, the telegraph connecting Oregon to the East now repaired, the leading Republican newspaper in the state could trumpet Lincoln's reelection. Although only partial results from the East Coast were available, the *Oregonian* reporter could rhapsodize, "It is as we expected, to be sure. We knew it in advance, but we did not know so certainly as to prevent our hearts from now exulting at the result. ... All is well!"[46]

Not all Oregonians were as enthusiastic about Lincoln's reelection as the Portland journalist. Just fifty miles down the Willamette Valley, in Salem, rumors of a political revolt threatened that community, enough so to bring out law enforcement officers and to encourage political leaders to remind citizens of the need for law and order. And though

Lincoln would also win in Oregon, some parts of the state illustrated their persisting ties to the Democrats by voting for General McClellan. Support for the Democrats remained strong, too, in other parts of the Oregon Country even though residents of those territories could not vote in the presidential election. Even if only Oregon residents could vote in the November election, many others in the Far Corner without ballots in the national election nonetheless became involved in the lively politics that swirled around the reelection contest.

The leading authority on Oregon Country politics in the Civil War era provides a valuable one-sentence précis of cross-continental politics in the early 1860s but one that is also useful for understanding events of 1864. What historian Robert W. Johannsen writes about the Washington Territory in 1860-61 was true for the Oregon Country at the time of Lincoln's run for a second term: "The political events in this frontier area during the months of the secession crisis recapitulated, on a small scale, the national situation."[47] The events and issues that challenged Lincoln's national campaign were remarkably similar to those that confronted voters in Oregon and the nearby territories in 1864.

Pro-Union sentiments still united many Oregon voters in the early fall of 1864, but divisions were also evident. As they had nationally, Unionist Democrats in Oregon had few options open to them as opponents of Lincoln's Union Republican Party. So they saved their sharpest weapons of criticism for Lincoln's handling of controversial issues—for instance, emancipation, confiscation acts, the draft, suspension of the writ of habeas corpus, and free speech and press rights. For these opponents, Lincoln's federal government had so expanded and its acts had become so arbitrary that their rights were being trampled upon—if not entirely curtailed.

Senior Senator James Nesmith represented this Democratic position. Although he backed Lincoln's Unionism, he was harshly critical of the president's handling of other issues. In October 1864 Lincoln's friend at Ft. Vancouver, Simeon Francis, sent the president a letter enclosing a Nesmith letter "published in the leading Copperhead sheet of Oregon … with the view of affecting our Presidential election." Francis urged Lincoln "to examine" the Nesmith letter since it backed McClellan for president and criticized Lincoln's Emancipation Proclamation.[48] Nesmith epitomized those who criticized Lincoln's decisions as prima facie evidence of his tyrannical tendencies. After McClellan was nominated and the election of 1864 approached, many Oregon Democrats praised "Little Mac's" patriotism, courage, and balance. Like their national counterparts, they had difficulty with McClellan's unwillingness to accept the peace plank adopted by his party, but better to support him than Old Abe, who was undermining their personal rights and freedoms.

A major difference separated Lincoln's ties to Oregon leading up to the elections in 1860 and then in 1864. His close friends and acquaintances—Dr. Henry, Edward Baker, Simeon Francis, and David Logan—were either all gone from the state in 1864 or not in a position to help Lincoln. Henry and Francis were serving as Lincoln's appointees in Washington Territory, Baker was dead, and Logan was curiously off scene, largely because of his controversial ins and outs in Oregon politics. No person emerged to general Lincoln's campaign in Oregon 1864 as Baker and Henry had done so well four years earlier.

Other political shifts and continuities in Oregon undoubtedly influenced the outcome of the reelection bid in the state. Although John McBride had been defeated in his second run for Congress and his replacement, James H. D. Henderson, had not yet taken office, George H. Williams had been elected to the U.S. Senate in September 1864 and was already making his presence known in the state. A. C. Gibbs remained in the governor's chair and continued his strong support for Lincoln's war policies. Most important of all, the Unionists dominated Oregon politics, a sure sign that Lincoln's reelection would come about.

As the *Oregonian* reporter had noted, many in the state thought Lincoln's success was assured before the ballots were cast on 8 November. Although Lincoln's margin of victory in Oregon was modest, its extent was reassuring nonetheless. Lincoln won the popular vote by 9,888 to McClellan's 8,457, a margin of 1,432 compared to that of 270 in 1860. But Henderson had defeated the Democrat Kelly by twice that margin in the congressional race the previous June. Those figures are misleading, however, since Lincoln totaled 1,129 more than Henderson, and McClellan topped Kelly's total by 2,461.

The most significant change taking place in Oregon's political landscape was the swelling number of voters moving into hitherto sparsely settled eastern Oregon. And the Democrats were the primary beneficiary of the change. Although new counties were organized in eastern Oregon and named Union and Grant, it was the Democrats who garnered most of the newcomers' votes. East of the Cascades in June, 3,291 had voted, but the following November, 4,560 cast their ballots. Had the left wing of Price's Army invaded the mining towns and mountain areas of eastern Oregon?[49] This mythical contingent of Copperheads became the Unionists' major bogeyman throughout the Oregon Country and other parts of the American West in the later years of the Civil War era.

There were clear challenges for Unionists in some of the out-of-the-way areas east of the mountains. One family later recalled when their father was in the mining boomtown of Auburn during Lincoln's reelection, southern sympathizers, said to be from "the left wing of Price's army," made clear they would brook no *viva voce* voting (verbally stating one's preference at the voting booth rather than voting by secret ballot) for Lincoln and his Union Party. If the father spoke for Lincoln, he "was courting trouble"; indeed voting "for Lincoln … would mean a fight." But the sturdy Union man appeared at the voting site and stated firmly, "I cast my vote for Abraham Lincoln." An eerie and tense silence ran through the crowd—and the voter walked away. "Immediately thereafter a whole group of Union men walked past the window and voted for Lincoln."[50]

Perhaps even more revealing evidence for understanding Lincoln's reelection victory in Oregon came in a letter from Judge Matthew Deady to his old friend Democratic Senator Nesmith. Three days after the election, Deady told Nesmith, "I took no part in the election of consequence, but voted for Lincoln. This change of Presidents every four years, to make a new deal of the offices, is the curse of the country, and was much the cause of our present troubles, as all other things combined." "I have no very exalted … opinion of Mac at best. He is neither one thing or the other," Deady added. On the other hand, he considered Lincoln "a pure man, means well and is gifted with as much good common sense and sagacity as often falls to the lot of men, particularly Presidents."[51]

Deady's decision to vote for Lincoln signaled a major turn in the judge's political journey. Just a few short years earlier, Deady was a leading spokesman for allowing slavery in Oregon and a strong supporter of everything Democratic, including Joseph Lane, Asahel Bush, and the Salem Clique. Now he was voting for an antislavery president who had announced the Emancipation Proclamation and was pushing for a constitutional amendment to end all slavery in the U. S. And, surprisingly, Deady was telling Nesmith of his support for Lincoln when Nesmith had recently announced he would vote for McClellan and that Lincoln must be retired from office because of the Emancipation Proclamation. A remarkable letter indicating one facet of the realignment of parties transpiring in Oregon.

In a larger sense Deady may serve as an illuminating figure for many more Oregonians. In 1860 Lincoln gained but 36 percent of the vote, and the combined Democratic factions supporting Breckinridge and Lane totaled 62 percent. Now, four years later, the Union Republicans in Oregon, with Lincoln at their head, had won 53.9 percent of the vote. Why the shift? What had moved Oregonians from the Democratic to the Republican camp? Two answers seem apparent. First, and more significant, the Union cause. As was true nationally, it was difficult for Democrats not to favor the Union. They might hate abolition, the draft, and Lincoln's controversial acts, but they could not abandon the Union. Second, the swing toward Lincoln. Despite their discontents, many Union Democrats and Radical Republicans preferred Lincoln to secession, peace, and other compromises. And they had come to trust Lincoln. Old Abe seemed a man of balance and common sense. For Judge Deady, "the people are the authors of most of Mr. Lincoln's mistakes (if they be mistakes), and as usual now seek to hold him alone responsible for them."[52] Quite possibly Deady represented the views of many who had not been Republicans in 1860 and had not voted for Lincoln, but now in 1864 the need to be a Union supporter and the draw of Lincoln as man and leader had brought them into his camp.

Residents of Washington, Idaho, and Montana might not be able to vote in Lincoln's bid for reelection, but they often disclosed their political sentiments in the closing months of 1864. Unfortunately, all three territories were badly divided politically. Lincoln's three appointed governors—Pickering in Washington, Lyon in Idaho, and Edgerton in Montana—were, at worst, incompetent (Lyon) or so partisan they were unable to rule well (Pickering and Edgerton). Complicating matters were the incoming tens of thousands of newcomers whose politics was more Democratic than Republican. When given an opportunity to vote for territorial delegates to Congress—the clearest indicator of political leanings in a territory—all three territories voted in Democrats in 1863-64.[53] That meant Republican-appointed governors would have to compete with elected delegates for leadership in all three territories.

The Republicans were also badly divided between more conservative-to-moderate figures like Lincoln and those closer to the Radicals, such as Pickering and Edgerton. These intraparty squabbles not only undercut Republican strength, they opened the way for Democratic victories.

For example, in Washington Alfred R. Elder, Lincoln's acquaintance and a man the president had appointed Indian agent in the territory, wrote on 24 October to warn Lincoln of "a viper warmed into life" in the territory's political hierarchy. Elder was speaking of Territorial Secretary Elwood Evans, another of Lincoln's appointees. Evans, in a surprising act of disloyalty, had hired Urban E. Hicks, the editor of the *Washington Democrat* and an opponent of Lincoln's administration, as one of the territorial printers. Although these men were supposed to be Republicans, they were "a disgrace to our Territory and to the Government." They should be cashiered, Elder asserted, and replaced with Arthur A. Denney, whose father in Illinois had been an acquaintance of Lincoln and Elder.[54] Two months later Pickering sent a similar telegram to Lincoln, telling him "Pray remove Secy Evans immediately. Appoint John [A. A.?] Denny by telegraph thereby save public printing from your bitter enemies." But even after Dr. Henry added to these criticisms of Evans, Lincoln chose to retain him.[55] Lincoln knew all about Evans's actions. He had written Secretary of State William Seward earlier in the year, stating that Evans "has gone wholly over to the enemy, using the patronage to establish and uphold a paper to oppose & embarrass the Administration."[56]

In Idaho similar divisions rent the Republican Party, divisions widened by the incompetence of Governor Lyon. Divided over whether the territorial capital would remain in Lewiston or move to Boise, the Radical-conservative split among the Republicans opened the door for Democratic advancement. Although William H. Wallace remained a stable, loyal supporter of Lincoln, he was not able to win reelection as territorial delegate and was replaced by Democrat E. D. Holbrook. In their intense bickering the Republicans had aided the Democrats. Something of a conservative, Governor Lyon was absent for most of 1864, seemed unable to work with other Republicans, and gradually shifted toward the Democrats. Overall, with the loss of Wallace, the inadequacy of Lyon, and the growing strength of the Democrats, Lincoln's support in Idaho was middling at best. (Eventually, Senator Nesmith of Oregon entered Idaho politics when he helped block the re-appointment efforts of Wallace and Lyon.)[57]

The same problems beset Montana in the closing months of 1864. In the newest of the territories in the Oregon Country, Governor Edgerton and his nephew Wilbur Fisk Sanders had failed to gather much support for their Radical Republican agendas. In the final months of 1864, just weeks after Sanders lost to Democrat Samuel McLean in the initial election for Montana's territorial delegate, support for Lincoln was as shaky as in adjacent Idaho.

• • •

Lincoln, tied up with a pressing Civil War and numbing administrative duties, had little time for the territories of the Oregon Country. Perhaps he realized how much still needed to be done in getting them on the road to stability—and perhaps statehood—but he hoped things were headed in that direction. He hinted at these conclusions in his annual message to Congress in early December. "Idaho and Montana, by reason of their great distance and the interruption of communication with them by Indian hostilities, have been only partially organized; but it is understood that these difficulties are about to disappear, which will permit their governments, like those of the others, to go into speedy and full operation."[58] That was only part of the story, one smoothed over for public consumption. A private and more realistic examination would have admitted that Lincoln's appointees and his fellow Republicans would have to administrate more wisely and get along better with one another if Lincoln's connections with the territories of the Oregon Country were to go more smoothly in 1865.

Chapter 6: Lincoln and the Oregon Country: 1865 and Beyond

D r. Anson G. Henry's itchy feet of ambition were burning again. He had worked energetically to get his good friend Abraham Lincoln reelected in 1864. That had occurred. Now, his own ambitions were pushing to the forefront. He had been surveyor-general in Washington Territory for nearly three and a half years. That position had been satisfying, but now it was time to move up. To achieve that dream, he had to make another time-consuming and sometimes dangerous trip to Washington, D. C. There, he would see his good friend Mr. Lincoln and plead his case. In the next few weeks, Lincoln's closest personal link with the Oregon Country would be disconnected and rearranged, with the indefatigable political doctor now at the president's back door.

Indeed, in the five months following Lincoln's reelection in November 1864, his connections with the Oregon Country nearly disappeared. Both ends of the linkage seemed burdened with too many changes. Lincoln's heavy duties of keeping the Union ship afloat and bringing the ruinous war to a close sidelined nearly all other pressing obligations. He had little or no time for the West and Pacific Northwest, including Oregon and the territories. At the western end, Lincoln's appointed governors—Pickering, Lyon, and Edgerton—were, as we have seen, all struggling in territories where Democratic majorities, including thousands of Copperheads, were opposing their Republican policies. Lincoln's political friends were also off-scene—Baker dead, David Logan nowhere to be found, and Simeon Francis strangely silent and uncommunicative. Would Lincoln's ties to the Oregon Country virtually fall apart and disappear?

• • •

The ambitious Dr. Henry did not want the Lincoln connections to fall away. He desired, in fact, to close the gap between himself and Lincoln. He wanted more than he currently had. After loyally serving Lincoln in Washington Territory and pushing for the president's reelection, Henry thought he deserved advancement. For a dozen years he had pushed for Whig and Republican interests through support of partisan and patronage decisions in the Oregon Country; now, the good doctor headed to the nation's capital to cultivate more diligently his own political garden. That meant getting to his friend in the White House, as Henry had in 1863, to urge patronage decisions on the president, including a new plum for himself. Who could know the disappointments and tragedies that lay in wait for both the political doctor and the man in the White House?

Henry secured a leave in December 1864, headed for San Francisco, and made for Washington, D.C., where he arrived early the next February. As he embarked for California, he reiterated his dream in the

Dr. Anson G. Henry was a lifelong friend of Abraham and Mary Lincoln. He became Lincoln's strongest, most enduring political link to the Oregon Country in the 1850s and 1860s. Lincoln appointed him surveyor-general of Washington Territory. Henry's life ended tragically a few weeks after Lincoln's assassination. (Oregon Historical Society Research Library, image 9152.)

first of a set of revealing letters to his supportive wife, Eliza. "I have no misgivings about being able to accomplish all I hoped for when I left home," he wrote. In a second letter sent days later from San Francisco, Henry was more specific—and yet mysterious. "I feel very confident of realizing all *reasonable* expectations in regard to matters in Washington Territory." He was sure, he told Eliza, that he could "secure the mission to Honolulu," but he still hoped for "the Miracle we talked of." Was Henry expecting a cabinet position or, less ambitiously, to be named the bureau chief, for example, of Indian affairs? Most certainly he wanted a westerner—or two—to be high up in Lincoln's cabinet or among his chief advisors.[1]

Early in February Dr. Henry was in Washington, D.C., "flourishing largely on Mrs. Lincoln's capital." He had been recognized in Washington, albeit rather awkwardly, as Mary Lincoln's escort, and he was becoming well acquainted with the new senator from Oregon, George H. Williams. But he had been unable to talk with the president, and acrimonious divisions over patronage between Henry and Governor Pickering and others in Washington Territory were coming to the fore—even in Washington, D.C.[2]

Henry's ambitions had crystallized. "I now think I shall be Commissioner of Indian Affairs," he told his wife. He was convinced that he could reform the Indian service by hiring devoutly religious Indian agents committed to "the great work of Christianizing & civilizing the Indians." On this issue Senator Williams and he were "on the best of terms," and he expected support from other westerners in his run for the commissioner's position. A few days later and just five days after Lincoln's second inaugural, Henry, accompanied by a group of western friends, got to see the president. His western supporters, with Senator Williams leading the way, told Lincoln, "We have unanimously agreed upon Dr. Henry for either the Land or Indian Bureaus, and would regard it as a special favor to the Pacific Coast" to have Henry appointed. Then they went on to endorse the doctor's "honesty/competency." The president replied that praise was unneeded "for he had known … [Henry] long and well." Others, lining up to champion Henry, informed the president that they wanted Henry in a new position. But Lincoln did not make a decision.[3]

Four days later, with the backing of Noah Brooks, a California journalist and good friend of Lincoln, Henry was again in the president's chambers. Now he let it be known he "would *like* to remain in Washington." After Henry presented his interests and his promise "to promote the welfare and prosperity of the Government," Lincoln replied, "the thing that troubles me most is that I dislike the idea of removing Mr. Dole [commissioner of the Indian bureau] who has been a faithful and devoted personal and political friend." The Pacific Coast Republicans wondered, as Henry told the president, if they were being left out at the top of Lincoln's advisors. "It does look a little that way," Lincoln admitted.[4] Again, Lincoln did not act, less than a month before Lee's surrender to Grant at Appomattox on 9 April. Disappointed and more than a little frustrated with the inactivity, Henry decided to visit recently conquered Richmond, where Lincoln had just been, for a quick trip—and perhaps to get away from the pressures he felt. Tragedy struck like lightning while Henry was in Virginia, when John Wilkes Booth shot Lincoln at Ford's Theater on the evening of 14 April.

• • •

The horrific news of Lincoln's assassination flashed across the entire country in a few hours after his death on Saturday morning 15 April. The tragic report out of Washington was all the more shocking because six days earlier the long Civil War had all but ended. As journalist Noah Brooks wrote later, "No living man ever dreamed that it was possible that the intense joy of the nation over the recent happy deliverance from war could be so soon turned to grief more intense and bitter than the nation ever before had known."[5] The euphoria over the joyful victory vanished, like an unexpected heat wave evaporating snow.

By spring 1865 the recent transcontinental telegraph connected into the Oregon Country allowed the sensational news of Lincoln's assassination and death to flash into the region hours after the horrendous event more than three thousand miles away. The dramatic message set off traumatic reverberations that convulsed the Pacific Northwest. When the telegraphed news reached Portland just after noon on Saturday 15 April, the staff of the *Oregonian* quickly prepared an "extra" that hit the streets later in the afternoon. When fuller details out of Washington,

In his last picture, Abraham Lincoln's face exhibits the toll of the heavy, taxing burdens he carried during a long, bitter Civil War. His assassination on 14 April 1865, just five days after Robert E. Lee's surrender at Appomattox, tragically illustrated the high and low points for Unionists in the final days of the war. (Library of Congress, Prints & Photographic Division, LC-USZ62-8812.)

D.C., were available (Secretary of War Edwin M. Stanton closely shepherded what went out on the wire), the *Oregonian* prepared a much more extensive story.

Not surprisingly, the tone and content of the newspaper stories were remarkably similar to those of other American stories about Lincoln. The *Oregonian*, thoroughly Republican and a stout Lincoln supporter, found little difficulty in lionizing his superb leadership and saluting his sterling character. In an editorial "The Great Atrocity," the paper described Lincoln as a "pure, large-hearted, generous man," "one of the noble men and great souls of the earth," magnifying the tragedy of his removal from the presidency. Then, the reporter went on to suggest that the assassination was the likely result of the "fiendish spirit of murder which has been sedulously propagated and inflamed by the disloyal men and disloyal press of the North"; these fomenters deserved the "fullest retribution."

The *Oregonian* pushed farther in its criticism than many other Oregon Country newspapers. After summarizing the details of the assassination and the simultaneous attack on Secretary of State William Seward, the Portland newspaper provided a lively account of the destruction of five "Secesh" newspapers in California, suggesting, by withholding any criticism of these actions, that the "cleaning out" of these "anti-Administration" papers was not such a bad thing. Still, the *Oregonian* hoped, "all party rancor will be forgotten, as no right thinking man can hear of Mr. Lincoln's death without accepting it as a national calamity."[6]

Other newspapers in the Pacific Northwest, receiving the sorrowful news in the next week or two, exhibited similar but also slightly different reactions. The 20 April issue of the weekly *Seattle Gazette* devoted its front page headlines to the Union-Republican nomination for a territorial delegate; the story of Lincoln's assassination in "The Deed of Horror" was relegated to the second page. Unfortunately, the reporter's blowsy style obscured and thereby blunted his clear support for Lincoln. He thought "most probably"that the assassination was "the result of a deeply laid plot, the off-spring of secession malevolence and blind fury at seeing their fall certain." But unlike the *Oregonian* reporter, the Seattle journalist castigated the attacks on California newspapers as the evil deeds of a "mob of misguided men."[7] One day later the *Walla Walla Statesman*, a moderate Democratic weekly, declared, "there can be none among the ranks of honorable men who would sympathize with the assassin." But, the paper asserted, neither should one, violently, seek to wreck revenge on the murder(s). "The hour is a dark one," the editor concluded, but he also promised "there will yet be brighter pages written."[8]

The leading newspapers in Idaho and Montana published similar sentiments on Lincoln's assassination. The Republican *Idaho Statesman* reported that "the terrible news fell like a pall on this [Boise] community," but, the editor added, "be it to the credit of our political opponents that the good men and sensible portion of them seem to grieve and deprecate the foul deed with more bitterness than we did." The Democratic *Idaho World* of Idaho City, which bitterly opposed the politics of the *Statesman* on other issues, agreed with it on the foulness of Lincoln's assassination. "The deed was an act abhorrent to human nature and one which all men and all parties must condemn and denounce." These nonpartisan views found an echo in the strongly Republican *Montana Post* of Virginia City. Its editorial, "The Dark Day," avowed that "all feeling of party division, all sentiments of political difference, must be swallowed up and lost in the consternation and grief that this news will produce throughout the civilized world." But the editor was willing to point a finger of guilt, too: The "Rebellion" (secession) led to this—now "finished in cowardly assassination."[9]

• • •

These deeply tinged emotional words resembled the expressions of most newspapers across the United States, especially those published outside the South. But beneath the seeming bipartisan, accepting surface were there more complex feelings and attitudes? In their more personal and private sentiments and actions were residents of the Oregon Country truly as approving and magnanimous as the newspaper accounts suggested? Some scattered evidence indicates that more complex, less unified reactions to the Lincoln assassination existed in the Pacific Northwest.[10]

Even though Major General Irvin McDowell, commander of the Department of the Pacific, issued an order to arrest anyone exulting over the assassination, a few residents of the Oregon Country tested that order. McDowell had also ordered the suppressing of any newspaper that published similar sentiments.[11] An account by a volunteer soldier stationed at Fort Vancouver illuminates one such incident. He wrote in his diary, "A Soldier is in the chokebox for saying that 'Lincoln ought to have been shot 4 years ago.'" One month later the diarist added, "The Soldier that rejoiced over the death of the President is sentenced to ten years hard labor and a ball & chain, rather expensive rejoiceing to that 'blue' coat."[12]

Sometimes Republicans attacked Democrats they considered so anti-Lincoln as to be guilty of supporting the assassination. Such a charge was leveled at Matthew P. Deady, a Democrat who had supported slavery before the Civil War and disagreed with several of Lincoln's White House decisions. But Deady's opponents refused to accept the possibility that Deady had changed his mind and become a supporter of the president. They were wrong. Deady wrote, "Although at first, I regarded Mr. Lincoln as a man borne to the pinnacle by the waves of political revolution and estimated him accordingly ..., I have come to look upon him and trust him, as a man of Providence as well as of the people."[13]

On one occasion in Montana, the celebration of Lincoln's assassination resulted from actions that a young participant rued many years later. When news of Lincoln's death reached Virginia City, Montana, in April 1865, thirteen-year-old Mary Sheehan (Ronan) and her young friends dramatically demonstrated their families' pro-South and anti-Lincoln perspectives. As Mary recalled many years later, the "Southern girls, by far the majority, picked up their ankle-length skirts to their knees and jigged and hippity-hopped around and around the room. They cheered the downfall of that great, good, simple man whom they had been taught to regard as the archenemy of the South." As an adult Ronan confessed that it "pained" her "to recall what we did when we were told of Lincoln's death."[14]

• • •

Coming to the fore alongside these more isolated and clandestine supports for Lincoln's assassination was a much more widespread and long-lasting movement. The first glimpses of the "Lincoln myth" were emerging. As one scholar has noted, in the weeks and months immediately following Lincoln's death his "apotheosis" began.[15] A number of needs and cultural traditions converged to formulate and launch the persisting image of Lincoln as the near-perfect Christian martyr, blameless and sacrificed.

A major impetus in the formulation of the Lincoln myth was the universal, timeless human need for heroes and heroines. Americans exhibit this need. We rallied around George Washington as the leader of the American Revolution and prime Founding Father. Much later, many Americans embraced Franklin Delano Roosevelt as the savior from the Great Depression and a victorious leader in the Allied triumph in World War II. And even later the aura of a romantic Camelot helped launch a John F. Kennedy myth. Quite naturally, Lincoln became the hero of the Civil War era, remembered as commander-in-chief, as the savior of the Union, as the Great Emancipator, and as generous, warm-hearted resident of the White House.

Residents of the Oregon Country participated in the origins of the Lincoln myth and thus illustrated what recent historians have described as the shaping impact of memory in our views of the past. For Radical Republicans that meant forgetting about Lincoln's slowness in moving toward Emancipation and his hesitancy to launch a "hard" war against the South. For War Democrats that meant deemphasizing their discontents with Lincoln's Emancipation, his suppression of newspapers, the draft, and other measures they considered as snatching away their personal freedoms. For others, that meant they could overlook any of Lincoln's human weaknesses in order to salute only his giant achievements and his seemingly pure character. Like a surviving spouse recalling and trying to remember a less-than-perfect mate, the Lincoln mythmakers filtered out any limitations, thus ensuring a "memory" that portrayed him as a man of largely saintly qualities.

The contributions in the Oregon Country to the Lincoln apotheosis appeared in private and public mediums. George Himes, an early newspaperman and a later giant in historical circles in the Pacific Northwest, privately recorded his initial reactions to Lincoln's assassination. He noted in his diary, soon after the news of the assassination arrived on 15 April, that a "deep feeling exists in the hearts of all true men." Four days later on the day of Lincoln's funeral, Himes thought, "all nature seemed to weep at a national loss." He then freighted Lincoln's memory with magnified meaning: "Alas! These are fearful times [.] I should not be surprised to see the rise and fall of the Roman Empire, reenacted in our once glorious and happy Republic."[16] A contemporary newspaper story substantiated Himes's interpretation when it stated: Lincoln's "death will be an era in our history, and is scarcely paralleled in that of the world." Lincoln's violent death, the journalist added, "will tend to embalm his memory in all hearts, and his name will be even more potent dead, than living."[17]

Lincoln's two long-time friends, Simeon Frances and Anson Henry, were also involved in shaping attitudes of the Oregon Country toward the post-assassination Lincoln. Francis wrote to an Illinois acquaintance shortly after Lincoln's death: "Time passes—but the dead Lincoln is always before me." And then he applied his gloss to the meaning of Lincoln's demise: "May God control the terrible event for the good of our nation. Surely our beloved has sat in dust and ashes for the great sin of slavery. Is it not enough, O God of our fathers! May Thy chastening turn to kindness and our nation be purified and again see prosperity as in days past."[18]

Dr. Henry's final days with Lincoln contained a double tragedy, including eventually his own. He was traveling in Richmond, Virginia when he heard of Lincoln's assassination, and rushed back to Washington, D.C. Seeing Lincoln lying "cold and still in the embrace of death," Henry wrote to his wife, caused a "fountain of tears" to break forth. "I wept like a child, refusing to be comforted."[19] Although Henry was greatly disappointed that Lincoln had not named him to a new and more important position, as he believed would happen, he could not criticize his deceased friend. Instead, he proved a devoted comforter to Mary Lincoln, settling some of her accounts and helping her move to Chicago. Then he boarded a steamer to return home. Ironically, as he transferred ships at Panama, his arch-enemy from the Washington Territory, Victor Smith, was assigned as his berth mate; regarding each other as vipers, he and Smith immediately importuned the purser to provide separate cabins. Then a greater tragedy overtook Dr. Henry. On 30 July, his overloaded steamer, the *Brother Jonathan*, en route to Olympia, struck uncharted rocks off the coast near the Oregon-California border and quickly sank. Dr. Henry's body was never recovered. Hearing of this "terrible news," Mary Lincoln wrote to Eliza Henry, "We have both been called upon to resign, to our Heavenly Father, two of the best men & the most devoted husbands, that two unhappy women, ever possessed."[20]

The religious sentiments that Mary Lincoln reiterated and that Simeon Francis expressed earlier became bedrock ingredients of the Lincoln myth. Lincoln's last days were quickly shrouded in Christian symbolism. Gen. Lee surrendered on Palm Sunday, Lincoln was assassinated on Good Friday, and the president died, yet was symbolically resurrected and personified as a Christian martyr, on Easter Sunday. Across the country, ministers in their Easter Sunday sermons made reference to—sometimes conjoined—the lives of Jesus Christ and Abraham Lincoln.

The process of Christianizing Lincoln also occurred in the Oregon Country. Some writers began to refer to the most important day on the

Christian calendar as "Black Easter" after Lincoln's assassination. Even before Lincoln's funeral took place, a service replicated in Portland, one journalist was linking Lincoln and Christ. "Good Friday, heretofore sacred to the memory and death and passion of our Savior," he wrote, "will henceforth bear upon the calendar the DEATH OF LINCOLN also." Later, Oregon's Senator George H. Williams added another facet of the religious image of Lincoln in stating, "There was an indescribable charm about the speeches of Lincoln. ... I should say that they occupy about the same relation to the oratorical world that 'Lead Kindly Light' and 'Abide With Me' do the hymnal world."[21]

Other similar sentiments appeared in Oregon Country newspapers. Both the *Seattle Gazette* and the Virginia City *Montana Post* published a poem that included these four lines:

Who trusts the strength, will with the burden grow
That GOD makes instruments to work his will,
If but that will we can arrive to know,
Nor tamper with the weights of good and ill.

Lincoln as a God-ordained instrument to bring forth freedom captured another poet's emotions:

Rest, noble martyr, rest in peace!
Rest with the true and brave,
Who, like thee, fell in Freedom's cause,
The nation's life to save.

• • •

Oh God, before whom we in tears
Our fallen chief deplore,
Grant that the cause for which he died
May live forevermore.[22]

These efforts to turn Lincoln into a Christ figure and to endow him with God-like qualities are the more remarkable because he never joined a church nor fully subscribed to orthodox Christian doctrine.

By mid-summer 1865, many of the ingredients of the mythic Lincoln were in place—in the Oregon Country as well as nationally. He was the Savior of the Union and the Great Emancipator. He was a man of unblemished character, magnanimous, kind, and bipartisan. He was a Godly man, with Christ-like ways. In the assassination aftermath, in the Easter services, in the Lincoln funeral services, and in the following summer's Fourth of July celebrations, Abraham Lincoln had become a martyr beyond all other men, only matched by George Washington in his service to God and country.

Present-day journalist Malcolm Gladwell, in his provocative volume *The Tipping Point* (2002), helps explain how Lincoln's reputation could almost overnight become something quite different. Seeing swift changes like these in terms similar to the spread of a communicable disease, Gladwell points to contagion, the large impact of small changes, and the rapid velocity of change leading to the explosion of diseases. In less than two years, Lincoln was transformed from a partisan presidential politician running for reelection to something of a demigod beyond all other humans. Several "infections" rapidly spread, quickly elevating Lincoln's memory and meaning. They were his assassination, the need to honor someone for bringing the bloody Civil War to an end, and the desire to find a symbol of magnanimity when fractious battles broke out between Congress and President Andrew Johnson, especially over Reconstruction policies.[23]

After the initial virus of Lincoln's myth spread so rapidly and thoroughly across the country, not much was added to this particularly positive image in the Oregon Country in the coming decades. Following the controversies over Reconstruction and President Andrew Johnson's inadequate leadership, when the Republican Party became more closely tied to leading American capitalists and less reformist as it had been in Lincoln's time, others wondered if he could not have avoided the rancor of Reconstruction and kept the Robber Barons from capturing the party. These wonderings added to Lincoln's expanding reputation, but generally, even though the Lincoln myth was in place and widely accepted, it was largely off stage, not much referred to (except in Fourth of July celebrations) or expanded.[24]

One of the reasons little was published about Lincoln early on in the Oregon Country is that after his death his close connections in the region provided no stories about those linkages. Baker and Dr. Henry, of course, were snatched away before they could tell about their Lincoln links. But

Logan turned sour and provided no information, and when Eliza Francis many years later was asked to speak of her remembrances of Abraham and Mary Lincoln, she refused to do so. She told William Herndon, in reply to his request for information, that her "intimacy with Mr & Mrs Lincoln was of so sacred a nature, that on no consideration would I be induced to open to public gaze, that which has been buried these many years. To me it would look like a breach of trust."[25] Her husband Simeon may have been of the same mind. Nor did Lincoln's appointees write about their ties to Lincoln. William H. Wallace, William Pickering, A. R. Elder, John R. McBride, Samuel Parks, and Sidney Edgerton all knew Lincoln, but they left nothing more substantial than a scattered page or two of passing reference to him.[26]

• • •

The first histories of the Oregon Country written after the end of the Civil War and before 1900 also overlooked Lincoln's influences in the region. Indeed, in the half century from Lincoln's first strong appearance in the Pacific Northwest in 1860 until the Lincoln Centennial in 1909 no historian provided more than brief reference to him. Newspapers furnished, in assassination and centennial references, more information on Lincoln than any other sources. The oversight among historians and other authors was surprising. H. H. Bancroft—or better yet, Francis Fuller Victor, since she did most of the research and writing—in his three huge books on the Oregon Country included almost nothing on Lincoln, even though those volumes on Oregon, Washington, Idaho, and Montana contained extended comments on military happenings and Indian affairs during the Civil War era. Nor did Elwood Evans deal with Lincoln, although his two-volume history of nearly fourteen hundred oversized pages about Oregon and Washington thoroughly covered events that involved Lincoln. Lincoln, revealingly, had also appointed Evans secretary in Washington Territory. These historians, as well as several others, focused on the local events in the Oregon Country, placing little emphasis on the cross-continental currents that also did much to shape politics in the faraway region.[27]

In other ways, however, the Oregon Country has revealed its links with Lincoln. Before the turn of the century, Oregon and the other territories becoming states were naming counties, towns, schools, streets, and other public places after Lincoln. All, eventually, had Lincoln counties, some had towns of Lincoln, and all had numerous Lincoln schools and streets. Even though historians might have been slow in dealing with Lincoln in the Oregon Country, by 1890 all four states of the region were busy naming parts and places after him.

The event that brought Lincoln back to center stage in the Oregon Country was the centennial of his birth in 1909; the events and newspaper stories were the most revealing sources of information about Oregon Country attitudes toward Lincoln until the bicentennial a century later. But the happenings and writings in 1909 spoke very little to the specific Lincoln links with the Pacific Northwest; that information would come later. Since Congress refused to appropriate funds to sponsor a Lincoln Centennial, state and local groups had to bear the brunt of organizing celebrations. In the first two weeks of February 1909, residents of the region were treated to many newspaper stories and community activities that linked them to the national, well-organized centennial of Lincoln's birth. For example, newspapers carried numerous stories about making Lincoln's homes and farms into historical sites. The same outlets published notices of Lincoln pennies being minted.

The content of a few of the journalistic endeavors provides a window into what residents of the Oregon Country were thinking about Lincoln early in the twentieth century. Nothing in the Northwest matched the special issue of the *Chicago Tribune*, which stretched out to 194 pages and weighed in at more than three pounds, but the Far Corner's newspapers did carry a surprising amount of Lincoln Centennial coverage. The Portland *Oregonian* and the Boise *Idaho Daily Statesman* provided particularly thorough coverage of the event. The Sunday, 7 February 1909 issue of the *Oregonian* devoted an entire section to the centennial, including numerous photos, selections from the writings of Lincoln biographer Ida M. Tarbell and Lincoln acquaintance Carl Schurz, as well as a reprint of the 17 April 1865 assassination issue. The *Idaho Statesman* carried a seven-part centennial series by journalist Frederick Trevor Hall reprinted from the *New York Times* depicting Lincoln as the Divine Average Man everyone could emulate.

The Lincoln of these centennial celebrations in the Pacific Northwest closely resembles the God-like figure that emerged soon after the 1865 assassination. An *Oregonian* reporter took on the large, perplexing questions facing centennial participants: how was it that—without pedigree, financial backing, education, or training in philosophy or the arts—Lincoln led so ably? What "made him precisely the man to steer the ship of state to a safe harbor"? The answer: "More adequately than any other person he incarnated the true nature of the common man." Lincoln could deal with and preside over the wide gamut of American men and women because he embodied the best of the human race, and they, seeing and understanding this integrated and balanced person, gave him their faith and trust. His beauty of character, the reporter noted in a then-familiar comparison, "grew to a beauty which has been compared to the lone excellence of the Man of Galilee."[28]

Five days later, on Lincoln's birthday, another reporter for the same newspaper added his gloss on Lincoln's meaning. We must celebrate Lincoln, he told his readers, because "[b]y honoring the memory of the dead we help to put their precepts in practice and, in some small degree, at least, form our little lives upon their great ones." An Idaho journalist tagged into a widely voiced conclusion about Lincoln when he noted that the Illinois politician was a self-made man whose life could be a model for others, especially for young Americans. A Montana writer put his point more succinctly: "While Abraham Lincoln is dead, the good that he did lives after him, not having been interred with his bones."[29]

Several of the centennial celebrations across the region followed the same programmatic format. They were a mix of speeches touting Lincoln, readings of his most famous orations and writings, patriotic songs, and remembrance stories, all punctuated with prayers and sometimes a hymn or two. In Boise, the memorialists of Lincoln added a parade that marched through the city's downtown and included soldiers, political leaders, and several service organizations. "Sincerity" reigned over a large Lincoln gathering in Portland. A crowd jammed into the Armory to hear a gaggle of speakers praising Lincoln. A follow-up banquet and further honorings of the late president came on the heels of the Armory doings. In Vancouver, Washington, the Lincoln Centennial celebrated at Providence Academy included recitations, songs by young students, and booths selling hand-made goods.[30]

These were Lincoln love feasts. Hardly a discouraging word surfaced in the gatherings or in newspaper accounts. Even if Lincoln served during extraordinary fractious times and was not, in all ways, bipartisan, the centennial celebrations chose to accentuate his winsome character, able leadership, and nonpartisan deeds. They loved Lincoln.

But there were a few hiccups nationally that spilled out into the Oregon Country. The responses in the Pacific Northwest to these upsets are revealing. When Jim Crow treatments of black Americans kept them from participating in some of the national gatherings praising Lincoln, they organized their own celebrations.[31] No such exclusions occurred in the Oregon Country. On one occasion an Idaho newspaper made sure its readers knew that racism was not occurring in Boise. A story headlined "No Color Line at Lincoln Exercises" reported a story at the Lincoln school in which Adolph, "one colored pupil in the class," and Louie, "the little Chinese scholar," played notable roles in the festivities. More importantly, the same newspaper, on its front page, extensively covered Senator William A. Borah's recent speech in New York City, praising his handling of the "problem of races." Borah told his audience that Americans needed to see what Lincoln had accomplished and move ahead with those principles. We have not yet done enough, Borah continued; we ought to revisit how much Lincoln accomplished by following the doctrine of equal rights in the Declaration of Independence.[32] Not many white Americans were willing to address the controversial question of race in 1909, but Borah courageously did and pointed to Lincoln as a model to follow. The subject of race would become increasingly important—and controversial—in later discussions, especially those leading up to and through the Lincoln Bicentennial.

• • •

The Lincoln Centennial did not include tracings of Lincoln's political links with the Oregon Country. In fact, even though a flood of new books treating Lincoln were published in the eastern U. S., none came from the Pacific Northwest. But soon after the celebrations closed, one book did open new avenues for examining the politics of the Far Corner. In his revised University of California dissertation appearing as *The Rise and Early History of Political Parties in Oregon 1843-1868* (1913), young historian Walter C. Woodward produced a cross-continental study that, for the first time, examined political trails from the East into the Oregon

Country.[33] The role of Abraham Lincoln is not central to Woodward's monograph, but he pioneered in demonstrating the northern, southern, and Washington, D.C., influences at work in shaping far-western politics, thus preparing the way for even more comprehensive stories.

In subsequent decades, historians began to trace political developments in the Pacific Northwest. Their emphases, however, were regional and local, with little attempt to demonstrate national influences on Oregon Country politics. The multivolume histories by *Oregonian* editor Harvey Scott and lawyer Charles H. Carey were thorough, fact-filled histories including much information on politics, political parties, and party leaders; but they did not find much place for Lincoln, and the authors seemed little interested in drawing strong, continuing lines between national and regional politics.[34]

An important breakthrough occurred in the 1950s in the publications of Robert W. Johannsen. A graduate of Reed College in Portland and a doctoral graduate of the University of Washington, Johannsen published a series of still-useful essays that eventuated in his first book, *Frontier Politics and the Sectional Conflict: The Pacific Northwest on the Eve of the Civil War* (1955), later retitled as *Frontier Politics on the Eve*

Historians were slow to trace Abraham Lincoln's political links to the Oregon Country. But in the twentieth century these three books became key sources for understanding the president's important connections to the Pacific Northwest. (Courtesy, Judith Radovsky.)

of the Civil War (1966).[35] Although these writings focused first—and largely—on the politics of Oregon and Washington, and primarily prior to 1863, they also pointed to the national political currents washing over and influencing the Pacific Northwest. Johannsen placed primary stress on the deeds of regional politicians and activists—for example, Joseph Lane, Isaac Ingalls Stevens, Matthew Deady, Asahel Bush, and James Nesmith—much more than on the shaping roles of Stephen A. Douglas and Abraham Lincoln. But, clearly, Johannsen led the way in establishing national-regional political configurations and prepared the paths for later writers wishing to examine Lincoln's role in these cross-continental political patterns.

In the next decades a few historians and other writers paid closer attention to the Oregon Country's ties to forces outside its region. From the 1960s to the 1990s up to two dozen books and essays traced the cross-country political connections between the national government, the nation's political parties, and the Pacific Northwest.[36] None of these historians centered on Abraham Lincoln, but they laid down the historiographical tracks that a half-dozen or more writers later traveled in displaying Lincoln's ties to the Far Corner.[37] By the year 2000, anyone wishing to consider Lincoln's impact on the Oregon Country had at hand more than a few books and essays on which to draw. This generation and more of late-twentieth-century scholars shed new light on the Oregon Country and Abraham Lincoln and their connections to Washington, D. C. Those illuminating scholarly works were important sources to draw on for the Lincoln Bicentennial in the Pacific Northwest.

The bicentennial celebrations, launched in 2009 and carried over into 2010, both built on and expanded recognition of Lincoln's roles in the Oregon Country. Idaho and Oregon, much more than Washington and Montana, emphasized Lincoln's influences in the Pacific Northwest, making that subject a central focus of their bicentennial plans.[38]

In Idaho, under the energetic leadership of David Leroy, the state put into play several programs during the Lincoln Bicentennial. Leroy not only led the Idaho committee but also chaired the organization of all state committee chairs. He also led the efforts to organize a Lincoln and Idaho traveling exhibit that circulated through many parts of the state. Leroy and his able colleagues on the state bicentennial committee, both academics and general Lincoln authorities, often opened these exhibit openings by speaking about Lincoln-Idaho connections as well as Lincoln's leadership roles. Leroy, guilty of a bit of hyperbole, asserted that "more than any other state, Idaho is related to Abraham Lincoln."[39] (Actually, Oregon, Missouri, and perhaps California had more contacts with Lincoln among the trans-Mississippi West states.)

Oregon's committee, like that in Idaho, was more lay-driven than an academic project of the state's colleges and universities. The Oregon committee, under the enthusiastic, skilled direction of Mike Burton, sent a group of Lincoln specialists to several parts of the state. A Lincoln presenter, two Lincoln scholars, a Lincoln troubadour, and a Lincoln novelist were the centerpieces of these presentations. Also of note, the Oregon Lincoln appearances dealt explicitly with Lincoln's connections with Oregon as well as his involvements with race and racial issues. These were emphases not much stressed in Oregon previous to this time and certainly not combined in a one-time presentation. The Lincoln Bicentennial in the Pacific Northwest profited from dozens of Lincoln books published nationally in 2009-2010, although none dealt specifically with Lincoln and the Pacific Northwest.[40]

The Lincoln Bicentennial meant that roughly a century and a half after Abraham Lincoln came on the scene in the Oregon Country in the election of 1860, his influence in the region was now clear, ubiquitous, and significant. For the first time, residents in the Pacific Northwest had abundant evidence that Lincoln had impacted—even shaped—the politics of the Far Corner.

•••

Abraham Lincoln's contacts with the Oregon Country linked a rising Illinois and national politician with the evolving Far Corner of the U.S. As Lincoln transitioned from an Illinois legislator to the U. S. Congress and beyond, he had to deal, even if obliquely, with an Oregon Country gradually becoming American, organizing its pre-territorial and territorial governments, and then its statehood. If Lincoln was slower than his long-time political competitor Stephen A. Douglas in looking west, he was eventually forced to face the Pacific Northwest.

First came Lincoln's rather evasive comments on the British-American competition in 1846 and other expansionistic moves of the mid-1840s. Like his fellow Whigs, and unlike Douglas's Democrats, Lincoln was not a strong advocate of the Manifest Destiny ideology. Next, in 1848, came his support in Congress for an Oregon Territory that would disallow slavery, a stance that exhibited Lincoln's hardening antislavery position. Then his rejection of offers to serve as secretary and then governor of the new Oregon Territory in 1849. During the 1850s Lincoln as a Whig and then a Republican convert stood solidly for the Wilmot Proviso disallowing the expansion of slavery into western territories. Oregon in 1848-49 and Washington in 1853 organized their territories on that principle rather than advocating the principle of popular sovereignty, which might have allowed slavery. In other words they stood with Lincoln and against the popular sovereignty that Douglas advocated in his controversial Kansas-Nebraska Act of 1854. Lincoln became a leading anti-Nebraska man in the mid-1850s, and most residents of the Oregon Country agreed with his no-extension principle. But in voting for a measure disallowing blacks into Oregon when writing their constitution in 1857, Oregonians went farther in that area than Lincoln had, though they replicated what had happened in his state. Illinois also had such a law.

All during the 1850s, but especially at the end of the decade, a handful of Lincoln's Illinois friends now living in Oregon wrote to him about the fiery politics of the region. David Logan and then Dr. Anson G. Henry, and finally Simeon Francis and Edward D. Baker, all Whigs and then Republicans (although there was some backsliding among them vis-à-vis popular sovereignty) apprised their friend Lincoln of the lively and contentious political competitions in Oregon. Baker's surprising election in 1860 to the U.S. Senate from Oregon was particularly pleasing to Lincoln.

The election of 1860 proved to be a key turning point in Lincoln's links with the Oregon Country. When the Democrats split into the Breckinridge and Douglas wings, Lincoln eased through to a very close victory in the Oregon presidential election, much closer than his win nationally over the divided Democrats. Even though Lincoln gained only 36 percent of the vote in Oregon, he won the election, allowing him to enter the White House and gain the patronage power of the presidency.

Lincoln had his largest impact on Oregon Country politics through his political appointments from 1861 to 1865. First in Washington

Territory, and then in the new territories of Idaho and Montana, Lincoln named his friends and political acquaintances to dozens of offices as governors, secretaries, justices, and other less powerful offices. (He was able to name a few officials too in the state of Oregon.) For the most part, Lincoln was a partisan Republican in these appointments, evidently agreeing with his friends Senator Baker, Dr. Henry, and editor Simeon Francis that loyal and supportive Republicans deserved these offices. Critics often disagreed, castigating Lincoln's appointments as "another lawyer from Illinois" or from "the Tribe of Abraham."

The outbreak of the Civil War, the massive influx of miners to the booming mining camps, and the ongoing controversies of Oregon Country politics added heavy loads to Lincoln's political duties. His continuing appointment of Republicans met with resistance in Washington, Idaho, and Montana, leading to conflicts too large and complicated to capture a war president's limited attention. But Lincoln's reelection in 1864, despite opposition from a somewhat reunited Democratic Party, indicated that his political policies and leadership gained increasing support in the only state in the Pacific Northwest. The three territories, with their recent development and heavy portion of miners, seemed less willing to follow Lincoln, often supporting Democratic candidates for territorial delegate and territorial legislatures.

Several of Lincoln's national political decisions won him support in the Oregon Country. Even though the Homestead Act and the Pacific Railroad Act, both passed in 1862 with Lincoln's support, did not impact the Pacific Northwest immediately, they were measures that won positive comments from the region's residents and political leaders. Lincoln's choices for Indian agents, often men who were politicians who knew little about Native Americans, stirred up more criticism than the legislative enactments.

Lincoln's assassination threw a dark blanket of grief over the Oregon Country. For most people in the region, intense partisanship lessened and then disappeared in the shock and bewilderment following the first assassination of a U. S. president. Although the Oregon Country seemed to lose much of its avowed connection to Lincoln in the following decades, Lincoln birthday celebrations each February, the naming of counties and towns, schools, and dozens of other places after him, as well as the outpouring of attention in the centennial birthday celebration in 1909, revealed how much the Pacific Northwest had embraced the Lincoln myth and accepted him as something of a demigod. Historians and other writers in the region were slow to treat Lincoln and his connections to the Oregon Country, but that oversight changed in the second half of the twentieth century. Several new books and essays clarified Lincoln's general ties to Oregon Country politics and began to trace his specific links with the region. The Lincoln Bicentennial of 2009-10 made even more explicit the high value Oregon Country residents placed on Lincoln as man and political leader.

Abraham Lincoln first looked west to the Pacific Northwest in the 1840s and 1850s. He forged important connections with the region in the politics of the early 1860s. But many decades passed before scholars and the lay public realized his indelible fingerprints on the region. At the beginning of the twenty-first century, more and more northwesterners were coming to realize that in several respects Abraham Lincoln could be considered a political founding father of the Oregon Country.

Bibliographical Essay

American historians have written more about Abraham Lincoln and the Civil War than about any other person or subject. It is estimated that nearly sixteen thousand books on Lincoln have been published and perhaps as many as sixty thousand on the American Civil War. But of these thousands of volumes, few deal even glancingly with Abraham Lincoln and the politics of the faraway Oregon Country during the Civil War era.

These oversights may result from three previous emphases. Military historians, for example, rarely deal with the Civil War impact on the Far Northwest because no major battles between northern and southern forces took place in the region. Concurrently, biographers of Abraham Lincoln, noting that he spent less than a month west of the Mississippi, overlook his palpable connections and influences on the region. Third, students of wars often play down the political, sociocultural, and economic shifts that frequently take place during prolonged military conflicts in favor of devoting more attention to battlefield strategy and tactics.

These trends in historical writing have kept specialists from examining the Oregon Country during the Civil War era. Until very recent years, most specialists on the Civil War focused on generals, battles, and other military matters to the exclusion of the other significant, shaping influences of politics, slavery and racism, Indian policies, and secessionist-Union conflicts. But the latter experiences are notably important for comprehending Abraham Lincoln and the impact of the Civil War on the Oregon Country. Readers need to know both the books and essays that discuss, separately, Lincoln and Oregon Country in the Civil War era as well as the very limited number of sources that examine Lincoln's links with the Far Corner. The following paragraphs point to, summarize, and sometimes evaluate these sources. Full citations of the sources appear in the appended bibliographical listing. I hope that this discussion of sources will encourage further research on Lincoln and the Oregon Country.

The thousands of books published on Abraham Lincoln include many very useful biographical studies. Hundreds of such life stories have been written, but this volume relies most heavily on a few recent books. Michael Burlingame's hefty two volumes, *Abraham Lincoln: A Life* (2008), totaling nearly two thousand pages, are particularly thorough and fact-filled. An even more extensive version of Burlingame's biography is online at Knox College Lincoln Studies Center, www.knox. edu/lincolnstudies. Richard Lawrence Miller's four-volume biography of Lincoln's prepresidential years, *Lincoln and His World* (2006, 2008, 2011, 2012), provides the most thorough account available of Lincoln's life before 1860-61. Ronald C. White, Jr.'s, very attractively written one-volume biography, *A. Lincoln: A Biography* (2009), has been especially helpful. So has David Herbert Donald's *Lincoln* (1995). Finally, Doris Kearns Goodwin provides a sparkling look at Lincoln, his cabinet members, and their families in her *Team of Rivals: The Political Genius of Abraham Lincoln* (2005).

Several other sources are valuable for the study of Lincoln. Particularly useful for examining his writings and speeches as well as his letters is Roy P. Basler, et al., eds., *The Collected Works of Abraham Lincoln*, 9 vols. (1953, 1955). This invaluable source is now fully online at http:// quod.libumich.edu/l/lincoln. Most letters to Lincoln remain unpublished, but those at the Library of Congress are digitally reproduced at http:// memory.loc.gov/ammem/alhtm/alhome.html. The fingertip availability of these major sources has markedly impacted Lincoln studies in recent years. The best of the reference volumes is Mark E. Neely, Jr.'s, *The Abraham Lincoln Encyclopedia* (1982), which now needs updating. Another invaluable source for tracing Lincoln's busy life is Earl Schenck Miers, ed., *Lincoln Day by Day: A Chronology 1809-1865* (1960, 1991).

Several books and essays treat Lincoln and major topics that affected the Oregon Country. The most thorough study of Lincoln and patronage, though now dated, is Harry J. Carman and Reinhard H. Luthin, *Lincoln and the Patronage* (1943). Particularly illuminating for an understanding of Lincoln and Republican thinking in the 1850s is Eric Foner, *Free Soil, Free Labor, and Free Men: The Ideology of the Republican Party before the Civil War* (1970). Don E. Fehrenbacher's *Prelude to Greatness: Lincoln in the 1850's* (1962) remains the best elucidation of that subject. On Lincoln and slavery, Eric Foner's Pulitzer Prize-winning study, *The Fiery Trial: Abraham Lincoln and American Slavery* (2010), is a work of first-rank importance. But see also Eugene H. Berwanger, *The Frontier Against Slavery* (1967; 2002), which includes a valuable chapter on slavery and race in early Oregon.

A handful of books and essays deal with Lincoln and the American West. The first to appear was a collection of essays edited by Ralph Y. McGinnis and Calvin N. Smith, *Abraham Lincoln and the Western Territories* (1994). Another more recent collection of essays with a long, interpretive introduction is Richard W. Etulain, ed., *Lincoln Looks West: From the Mississippi to the Pacific* (2010). The same author has contributed three essays: "Lincoln Looks West" (2009), "Abraham Lincoln: Political Founding Father of the American West" (2009), and "Lincoln and the Oregon Country" (2012). For Lincoln's role in the congressional debates over Oregon's territorial organization, one should consult Donald W. Riddle, *Congressman Abraham Lincoln* (1957). Michael S. Green expertly details Lincoln's ties to the 1850s West in his essay "Lincoln, the West, and the Antislavery Politics of the 1850s" (2010). Samuel E. Bell and James M. Smallwood discuss the early interpretations of Lincoln's connections to the West in their essay "The Pragmatic Lincoln: A Historiographical Assessment of His Western Policy" (1984).

For military matters, and additional treatment of Indian policies, Alvin Josephy, Jr's, *The Civil War in the American West* (1992) is by far the best study. Also consult Scott McArthur, *The Enemy Never Came: The Civil War in the Pacific Northwest* (2012). One should not overlook G. Thomas Edwards's unpublished dissertation, "The Department of the Pacific in the Civil War Years" (1963), which should be updated and published. The best study of Lincoln's Indian policies is David A. Nichols, *Lincoln and the Indians: Civil War Policy and Politics* (1978).

On Lincoln and the election of 1860, I have relied most heavily on Michael S. Green's superb work *Lincoln and the Election of 1860* (2011). On that subject I have also used Gary Ecelbarger, *The Great Comeback* (2008), and William C. Harris, *Lincoln's Rise to the Presidency* (2007). For Lincoln and the election of 1864, I used William Frank Zornow, *Lincoln and the Party Divided* (1954), Charles Bracelen Flood, *1864: Lincoln at the Gates of History* (2009), David E. Long, *The Jewel of Liberty* (1994), and John C. Waugh, *Reelecting Lincoln* (1997).

For general historical backgrounds of the Pacific Northwest, I have relied on four books. *Empire of the Columbia: A History of the Pacific Northwest* (2d ed., 1967) by Dorothy O. Johansen and Charles M. Gates remains the classic work. A newer work is Carlos A. Schwantes, *The Pacific Northwest: An Interpretive History* (1989). Pertinent chapters in Richard W. Etulain, *Beyond the Missouri: The Story of the American West* (2006), also provide a general overview of the mid-nineteenth-century Pacific Northwest. I am much indebted, too, to the insights of Earl Pomeroy in his interpretive overview *The Pacific Slope: A History of California, Oregon, Washington, Idaho, Utah, and Nevada* (1965, 2003).

Three books published nearly eighty years apart have been major sources in dealing with the early political history of the Oregon Country. Walter C. Woodward's *The Rise and Early History of Political Parties in Oregon, 1843-1868* (1913), a revised doctoral dissertation, is a pioneering but still valuable overview based chiefly on newspapers and research in a few manuscript collections. Much more useful is Robert W. Johannsen's *Frontier Politics and the Sectional Conflict: The Pacific Northwest on the Eve of the Civil War* (1955; reprinted as *Frontier Politics on the Eve of the Civil War*, 1966); it is probably the best study of the topic, but skewed somewhat by its Turnerian bias and the author's conviction that residents of the Oregon Country were largely "spectators of disunion." David Alan Johnson provides invaluable comparative perspectives on the territorial-to-statehood march of California, Oregon, and Nevada in his probing and analytical volume, *Founding the Far West: California, Oregon and Nevada, 1840-1890* (1992). Johnson's findings are richly expanded by his adept use of studies of republican ideology that appeared in the 1970s and 1980s.

Three other volumes provide useful overviews of western territorial politics. The classic in the field is Earl S. Pomeroy, *The Territories and the United States, 1861-1890: Studies in Colonial Administration* (1947). Also helpful is Jack Ericson Eblen, *The First and Second United States Empires: Governors and Territorial Government, 1764-1912* (1968). Still another important study is Kenneth N. Owens's dissertation, "Frontier Governors: A Study of the Territorial Executives in the History of Washington, Idaho, Montana, Wyoming, and Dakota Territories" (1959).

A clutch of other monographs and overviews are major sources of information on the political history of Oregon, Washington, Idaho, and Montana in the Civil War era. James E. Hendrickson's *Joe Lane of Oregon* (1967) remains a model monograph of thorough research, smooth writing, and sound conclusions. Robert E. Ficken's *Washington Territory* (2002) is a diligently researched and very informative overview but, unfortunately, a bit marred by its glib and sarcastic tone. Similar to Hendrickson's study of Lane, William L. Lang's treatment of William W. Miller utilizes the life of one northwesterner to illuminate his life and times. Lang's *Confederacy of Ambition: William Winlock Miller and the Making of Washington Territory* (1996) is an exemplary monograph of thorough research and appealing narrative. The best study of Idaho territorial politics is Ronald L. Limbaugh's revised dissertation *Rocky Mountain Carpetbaggers: Idaho's Territorial Governors 1863-1890* (1982). Equally valuable for Montana is Clark C. Spence's *Territorial Politics and Government in Montana 1864-89* (1975). Limbaugh and Spence remain the beginning places for the study of territorial Idaho and Montana.

Finally, three authors provide four very helpful books in tracing, over time, the shifting images of Lincoln in biographies and histories, novels and films, and other forms of popular culture. Sociologist Barry Schwartz, utilizing a more theoretical approach to focus on the differences between memory and history, treats the changing interpretations of Lincoln in two volumes: *Abraham Lincoln and the Forge of National Memory* (2000) and *Abraham Lincoln in the Post-Heroic Era* (2008). Jackie Hogan casts a wider net in examining the ways we have "sold" Lincoln in popular culture—from bobbleheads to tourist traps to a multitude of literary, historical, and cinematic representations—in her recent volume, *Lincoln, Inc.: Selling the Sixteenth President in Contemporary America* (2011). The most thorough—and traditional—study of the print, cinematic, and other interpretations of Lincoln is Merrill D. Peterson, *Lincoln in American Memory* (1994). I have relied heavily on Peterson's extraordinarily useful volume.

Abraham Lincoln and Oregon Country Politics in the Civil War Era: A Bibliography

Manuscripts

David W. Craig Papers, Oregon Historical Society.

Henry Cummins Papers, University of Oregon.

Matthew P. Deady Papers, Oregon Historical Society.

Winfield Scott Ebey Collection, University of Washington Library.

Edgerton Family Papers, Montana Historical Society.

Selucious Garfielde Papers, University of Washington Library.

Anson G. Henry Letters, Abraham Lincoln Presidential Library (transcript copies in the Oregon Historical Society).

George Himes Papers, Oregon Historical Society.

[George Himes] Scrap Books, Oregon Historical Society.

Idaho Territorial Papers 1863-1890, Idaho State Historical Society.

Journal of the Territorial Legislative Assembly, Washington State Archives.

Bion F. Kendall Papers, Oregon Historical Society.

Bion F. Kendall Papers, University of Washington Library.

Abraham Lincoln Papers, Library of Congress.

John McBride collection, Idaho State Historical Society.

William W. Miller Papers, University of Washington Library.

James W. Nesmith Papers, Oregon Historical Society.

William Pickering Papers, University of Washington Library.

William Pickering Papers, Washington State Library.

Harry E. Pratt Collection, Abraham Lincoln Presidential Library.

Victor Smith files, Washington State Archives.

Victor Smith files, Washington State Library.

Isaac I. Stevens Papers, University of Washington Library.

Samuel Thurston Papers, Washington State Library.

Surveyor General Papers, Washington State Archives.

William H. Wallace Papers, Idaho State Historical Society.
William H. Wallace Papers, University of Washington Library.
Washington Territorial Papers, University of Washington Library.

Newspapers

Anaconda (Montana) *Standard*
Boise *Idaho Daily Statesman*
The Idaho World
Montana Post
Olympia *Pioneer and Democrat*
Olympia *Puget Sound Courier*
Oregon City *Oregon Argus*
Oregon City *Oregon Spectator*
Portland *Daily Oregonian*
Portland *Weekly Oregonian*
Salem *Oregon Statesman*
Seattle Gazette
Steilacoom *Puget Sound Herald*
Walla Walla Statesman

Books

Arrington, Leonard J. *History of Idaho*. 2 vols. Moscow: University of Idaho Press, 1994.

Basler, Roy P., et al., eds. *The Collected Works of Abraham Lincoln*, 9 vols. New Brunswick, NJ: Rutgers University Press, 1953-55.

———. *The Collected Works of Abraham Lincoln, 2nd Supplement, 1848-1865*. New Brunswick, NJ: Rutgers University Press, 1990.

Beal, Merrill D., and Merle W. Wells. *History of Idaho*. 2 vols. New York: Lewis Historical Publishing Company, 1959.

Berwanger, Eugene H. *The Frontier Against Slavery: Western Anti-Negro Prejudice and the Slavery Extension Controversy*. 1967; Urbana: University of Illinois Press, 2002.

Blair, Harry C. *Dr. Anson Henry: Physician, Politician, Friend of Abraham Lincoln*. Portland: Binfords and Mort, 1950.

———, and Rebecca Tarshis. *Colonel Edward D. Baker: Lincoln's Constant Ally*. Portland: Oregon Historical Society, 1960.

Borchard, Gregory A. *Abraham Lincoln and Horace Greeley*. Carbondale: Southern Illinois University Press, 2011.

Boritt, Gabor S. *Lincoln and the Economics of the American Dream*. 1978; Urbana: University of Illinois Press, 1994.

Brazier, Don. *History of the Washington Legislature, 1854-1963*. Olympia: Washington State Senate, 2008.

Burlingame, Michael. *Abraham Lincoln: A Life*, 2 vols. Baltimore: The Johns Hopkins University Press, 2008.

———. *Abraham Lincoln and the Civil War*. Carbondale: Southern Illinois University Press, 2011.

Carey, Charles H. *A General History of Oregon Prior to 1861*. 2 vols. Portland: Metropolitan Press, 1935-36.

Carman, Harry J., and Reinhard H. Luthin. *Lincoln and the Patronage*. New York: Columbia University Press, 1943.

Curry, Leonard P. *Blueprint for Modern America: Non-Military Legislation of the First Civil War Congress*. Nashville, TN: Vanderbilt University Press, 1968.

Dirck, Brian. *Lincoln and the Constitution*. Carbondale: Southern Illinois University Press, 2012.

Donald, David Herbert. *Lincoln*. New York: Simon & Schuster, 1995.

Eblen, Jack Ericson. *The First and Second United States Empires: Governors and Territorial Government, 1784-1912*. Pittsburgh, PA: University of Pittsburgh Press, 1968.

Ecelbarger, Gary. *The Great Comeback: How Abraham Lincoln Beat the Odds to Win the 1860 Republican Nomination*. New York: St. Martin's Press, 2008.

Edwards, G. Thomas. "The Department of the Pacific in the Civil War Years." Ph.D. dissertation, University of Oregon, 1963.

Egerton, Douglas R. *Year of Meteors: Stephen A. Douglas, Abraham Lincoln, and the Election that Brought on the Civil War*. New York: Bloomsbury Press, 2010.

Etulain, Richard W. *Beyond the Missouri: From the Mississippi to the Pacific*. Albuquerque: University of New Mexico Press, 2006.

———, ed. *Lincoln Looks West: From the Mississippi to the Pacific*. Carbondale: Southern Illinois University Press, 2010.

Fehrenbacher, Don E. *Prelude to Greatness: Lincoln in the 1850's*. 1962; New York: McGraw-Hill Book Company, 1964.

Ficken, Robert E. *Washington Territory*. Pullman: Washington State University Press, 2002.

Fischer, LeRoy H., ed. *The Western States in the Civil War*. Manhattan, KS: Journal of the West, January 1975.

———, ed. *The Western Territories in the Civil War*. Manhattan, KS: Journal of the West, April 1977.

Fletcher, Randol B. *Hidden History of Civil War Oregon*. Charleston, SC: The History Press, 2011.

Flood, Charles Bracelen. *1864: Lincoln at the Gates of History.* 2009; New York: Simon & Schuster, 2010.

Foner, Eric. *The Fiery Trial: Abraham Lincoln and American Slavery.* New York: W. W. Norton and Company, 2010.

———. *Free Soil, Free Labor, Free Men: The Ideology of the Republican Party before the Civil War.* New York: Oxford University Press, 1970.

Goodwin, Doris Kearns. *Team of Rivals: The Political Genius of Abraham Lincoln.* New York: Simon & Schuster, 2005.

Hageman, Todd. "Lincoln and Oregon." Master's thesis, Eastern Illinois University, 1988.

Harris, William C. *Lincoln's Last Months.* Cambridge, MA: Belknap Press of Harvard University Press, 2004.

———. *Lincoln's Rise to the Presidency.* Lawrence: University Press of Kansas, 2007.

Hazen, David Wheeler. *Mr. Lincoln.* Portland: University of Portland, 1941. Chapter 4 "Lincoln and Old Oregon."

Hendrickson, James E. *Joe Lane of Oregon: Machine Politics and the Sectional Crisis, 1849-1861.* New Haven, CT: Yale University Press, 1967.

Hogan, Jackie. *Lincoln, Inc.: Selling the Sixteenth President in Contemporary America.* Lanham, MD: Rowman and Littlefield, 2011.

Holzer, Harold. *Lincoln at Cooper Union: The Speech that Made Abraham Lincoln President.* 2004; New York: Simon and Schuster, 2005.

———. *Lincoln President-Elect: Abraham Lincoln and the Great Secession Winter 1860-1861.* New York: Simon and Schuster, 2008.

Johannsen, Robert W. *Frontier Politics and the Sectional Conflict: The Pacific Northwest on the Eve of the Civil War.* Seattle: University of Washington Press, 1955. Reprinted as *Frontier Politics on the Eve of the Civil War,* 1966.

———. *Stephen A. Douglas.* New York: Oxford University Press, 1973.

———, ed. *The Frontier, the Union, and Stephen A. Douglas.* Urbana: University of Illinois Press, 1989.

Johansen, Dorothy O., and Charles M. Gates. *Empire of the Columbia: A History of the Pacific Northwest.* 2d ed. New York: Harper and Row, 1967.

Johnson, David Alan. *Founding the Far West: California, Oregon, and Nevada, 1840-1890.* Berkeley: University of California Press, 1992.

Josephy, Alvin M., Jr. *The Civil War in the American West.* New York: Alfred A. Knopf, 1992.

Lang, William L. *Confederacy of Ambition: William Winlock Miller and the Making of Washington Territory.* Seattle: University of Washington Press, 1996.

Limbaugh, Ronald L. *Rocky Mountain Carpetbaggers: Idaho's Territorial Governors 1863-1890*. Moscow: University of Idaho Press, 1982.

Long, David E. *The Jewel of Liberty: Abraham Lincoln's Re-election and the End of Slavery*. Mechanicsburg, PA: Stackpole Books, 1994.

McArthur, Scott. *The Enemy Never Came: The Civil War in the Pacific Northwest*. Caldwell, ID: Caxton Press, 2012.

McGinnis, Ralph Y., and Calvin N. Smith, eds. *Abraham Lincoln and the Western Territories*. Chicago: Nelson-Hall Publishers, 1994.

McPherson, James M. *Battle Cry of Freedom: The Civil War Era*. New York: Oxford University Press, 1988.

Matthews, Glenna. *The Golden State in the Civil War: Thomas Starr King, the Republican Party, and the Birth of Modern California*. Cambridge, England: Cambridge University Press, 2012.

Miers, Earl Schenck, ed. *Lincoln Day by Day: A Chronology 1809-1865*. 1960; Dayton, OH: Morningside House, 1991.

Miller, Richard Lawrence. *Lincoln and His World: The Early Years: Birth to Illinois Legislature*. Mechanicsburg, PA: Stackpole Books, 2006.

———. *Lincoln and His World: Prairie Politician 1834-1842*. Mechanicsburg, PA: Stackpole Books, 2008.

———. *Lincoln and His World: Volume 3, The Rise to National Prominence, 1843-1853*. Jefferson, NC: McFarland and Company, 2011.

———. *Lincoln and His World: Volume 4, The Path to the Presidency 1854-1860*. Jefferson, NC: McFarland and Company, 2012.

Neely, Mark E., Jr. *The Abraham Lincoln Encyclopedia*. New York: McGraw-Hill Book Company, 1982.

Nichols, David A. *Lincoln and the Indians: Civil War Policy and Politics*. Columbia: University of Missouri Press, 1978.

Owens, Kenneth N. "Frontier Governors: A Study of the Territorial Executives in the History of Washington, Idaho, Montana, Wyoming, and Dakota Territories." Ph.D. dissertation, University of Minnesota, 1959.

Peterson, Merrill D. *Lincoln in American Memory*. New York: Oxford University Press, 1994.

Pomeroy, Earl. *The Pacific Slope: A History of California, Oregon, Washington, Idaho, Utah, and Nevada*. 1965; Reno: University of Nevada Press, 2003.

———. *The Territories and the United States 1861-1890: Studies in Colonial Administration*. Philadelphia: University of Pennsylvania Press, 1947.

Richards, Kent D. *Isaac I. Stevens: Young Man in a Hurry*. 1979; Pullman: Washington State University Press, 1993.

Richardson, Heather Cox. *The Greatest Nation on Earth: Republican Economic Policies during the Civil War*. Cambridge, MA: Harvard University Press, 1997.

Riddle, Donald W. *Congressman Abraham Lincoln*. Urbana: University of Illinois Press, 1957.

Schwantes, Carlos A. *The Pacific Northwest: An Interpretive History*. Lincoln: University of Nebraska Press, 1989.

Schwartz, Barry. *Abraham Lincoln and the Forge of National Memory*. Chicago: University of Chicago Press, 2000.

———. *Abraham Lincoln in the Post-Heroic Era: History and Memory in Late Twentieth-Century America*. Chicago: University of Chicago Press, 2008.

Scott, Harvey W. *History of the Oregon Country*. 6 vols. Cambridge, MA: Riverside Press, 1924.

Shutes, Milton H. *Lincoln and California*. Stanford, CA: Stanford University Press, 1943.

Spence, Clark C. *Territorial Politics and Government in Montana 1864-89*. Urbana: University of Illinois Press, 1975.

Striner, Richard. *Lincoln and Race*. Carbondale: Southern Illinois University Press, 2012.

Waugh, John C. *Reelecting Lincoln: The Battle for the 1864 Presidency*. 1997; Cambridge, MA: Da Capo Press, 2001.

White, Ronald C., Jr. *A. Lincoln: A Biography*. New York: Random House, 2009.

Wilson, Douglas L., and Rodney O. Davis, eds. *Herndon's Informants: Letters, Interviews, and Statements about Abraham Lincoln*. Urbana: University of Illinois Press, 1998.

Winkle, Kenneth J. *Abraham and Mary Lincoln*. Carbondale: Southern Illinois University Press, 2011.

———. *The Young Eagle: The Rise of Abraham Lincoln*. Dallas, TX: Taylor Publishers, 2001.

Woodward, Walter C. *The Rise and Early History of Political Parties in Oregon, 1843-1868*. Portland: J. K. Gill, 1913.

Zornow, William Frank. *Lincoln and the Party Divided*. Norman: University of Oklahoma Press, 1954.

Essays

Alexander, Gerry L. "Abe Lincoln and the Pacific Northwest." *Columbia: The Magazine of Northwest History* 16 (Winter 2002-3): 3-6.

Bell, Samuel E., and James M. Smallwood. "The Pragmatic Lincoln: A Historiographical Assessment of His Western Policy." *Lincoln Herald* 86 (fall 1984): 134-42.

Bird, Annie Laurie. "Portrait of a Frontier Politician [Willam H. Wallace]: The Delegate from Washington Territory." *Idaho Yesterdays* 2 (fall 1958): 12-22.

Dickson, Edward A. "Lincoln and Baker: The Story of a Great Friendship." *Historical Society of Southern California Quarterly* 34 (September 1952): 229-42.

Edwards, G. Thomas. "Benjamin Stark, the U. S. Senate, and 1862 Membership Issues." *Oregon Historical Quarterly*, Part 1, 72 (December 1971): 315-58; Part 2, 73 (March 1972): 31-59.

————. "Holding the Far West for the Union: The Army in 1861." *Civil War History* 14 (December 1958): 307-24.

———— "Six Oregon Leaders and the Far-Reaching Impact of America's Civil War." *Oregon Historical Quarterly* 100 (spring 1999): 4-31.

Etulain, Richard W. "Abraham Lincoln Looks West." *Wild West* 21 (April 2009): 26-35.

————. "Abraham Lincoln: Political Founding Father of the American West." *Montana: The Magazine of Western History* 59 (summer 2009): 3-22.

————. "Abraham Lincoln and the Oregon Country." *Lincoln Lore* 1899 (spring 2012): 12-20.

————. "Lincoln's Links to a Distant Oregon." *Portland Oregonian*, 18 February 2008.

Fenton, William D. "Edward Dickinson Baker." *Quarterly of the Oregon Historical Society* 9 (1908): 1-23.

Floyd, Elbert F. "Insights into the Personal Friendship and Patronage of Abraham Lincoln and Anson Gordon Henry, M.D.: Letters for [sic] Dr. Henry to His Wife, Eliza." *Journal of the Illinois State Historical Society* 98 (winter 2005-6): 218-53.

Green, Michael S. "Lincoln, the West, and the Antislavery Politics of the 1850s," in Richard W. Etulain, ed. *Lincoln Looks West: From the Mississippi to the Pacific*. Carbondale: Southern Illinois University Press, 2010, 90-112.

Hazen, David Wheeler. "Lincoln and Old Oregon," *Mr. Lincoln*. Portland, OR: University of Portland, 1941, 54-67.

Johannsen, Robert W. "National Issues and Local Politics in Washington Territory, 1857-1861." *Pacific Northwest Quarterly* 42 (July 1951): 3-31.

————. "The Secession Crisis and the Frontier: Washington Territory, 1860-61." *Mississippi Valley Historical Review* 39 (December 1952): 415-40.

————."The Tribe of Abraham: Lincoln and the Washington Territory," in David H. Stratton, ed. *Washington Comes of Age: The State in the National Experience*. Pullman: Washington State University Press, 1992, 73-93.

Kelsey, Harry. "Abraham Lincoln and American Indian Policy." *Lincoln Herald* 77 (fall 1975): 139-48.

———. "William P. Dole and Mr. Lincoln's Indian Policy." *Journal of the West* 10 (July 1971): 484-92.

King, Jeffrey S. "'Do Not Execute Chief Pocatello': President Lincoln Acts to Save the Shoshoni Chief." *Utah Historical Quarterly* 53 (summer 1985): 237-47.

LaLande, Jeff. "'Dixie' of the Pacific Northwest: Southern Oregon's Civil War." *Oregon Historical Quarterly* 100 (spring 1999): 32-81.

Leroy, David H. "Lincoln and Idaho: A Rocky Mountain Legacy," in Frank J. Williams, et al., eds. *Abraham Lincoln: Sources and Style of Leadership*. Westport, CT: Greenwood Press, 1994, 143-62.

———. "Lincoln and Idaho: A Rocky Mountain Legacy." *Idaho Yesterdays* 42 (summer 1998): 8-25.

Limbaugh, Ronald H. "Territorial Elites and Political Power Struggles," in David H. Stratton and George A. Frykman, eds. *The Changing Pacific Northwest: Interpreting Its Past*. Pullman: Washington State University Press, 1988, 79-93.

McDonnell, Anne, ed. "Edgerton and Lincoln." *Montana: The Magazine of Western History* 1 (October 1950): 42-45.

McFarland, Carl. "Abraham Lincoln and Montana Territory." *Montana: The Magazine of Western History* 5 (October 1955): 42-47.

Mahoney, Barbara. "Oregon Democracy: Asahel Bush, Slavery, and the Statehood Debate." *Oregon Historical Quarterly* 110 (summer 2009): 202-22.

Miller, Paul I., ed. "Lincoln and the Governorship of Oregon." *Mississippi Valley Historical Review* 23 (December 1936): 391-94.

Nichols, David A. "Lincoln and the Indians," in Gabor S. Boritt and Norman O. Furniss, eds. *The Historian's Lincoln: Pseudohistory, Psychohistory, and History*. Urbana: University of Illinois Press, 1988, 149-69.

Owens, Patricia Ann. "Wyoming and Montana during the Lincoln Administration." *Lincoln Herald* 91 (summer 1989): 49-57.

Pomeroy, Earl. "Toward a Reorientation of Western History: Continuity and Environment." *Mississippi Valley Historical Review* 41 (March 1955): 579-600.

Pratt, Harry Edward. "Dr. Anson G. Henry, Lincoln's Physician and Friend." *Lincoln Herald* 45 (October 1943): 3-17; 45 (December 1943): 31-40.

———, ed. "22 Letters of David Logan, Pioneer Oregon Lawyer." *Oregon Historical Quarterly* 44 (September 1943): 254-85.

Ross, Earle D. "Lincoln and Agriculture." *Agricultural History* 3 (April 1929): 51-66.

Schapsmeier, Edward L., and Frederick H. Schapsmeier. "Lincoln and Douglas: Their Versions of the West." *Journal of the West* 7 (October 1968): 542-52.

Schmidt, Louis B. "Abraham Lincoln's New Deal for Agriculture." *Arizoniana* 3 (summer 1962): 9-16.

———. "Abraham Lincoln's New Deal for Industrial Education." *Arizoniana* 3 (spring 1962): 10-15.

———. "Abraham Lincoln's New Deal for the Argonauts." *Arizoniana* 3 (winter 1962): 25-35.

———. "Abraham Lincoln's New Deal for the Pioneer." *Arizoniana* 3 (fall 1962): 34-43.

Scott, Leslie M. "Oregon's Nomination of Lincoln." *Oregon Historical Quarterly* 17 (September 1916): 201-14.

Shutes, Milton H. "Colonel E. D. Baker." *Historical Society of Southern California Quarterly* 17 (December 1938): 303-24.

Tegeder, Vincent G. "Lincoln and the Territorial Patronage: The Ascendancy of the Radicals in the West." *Mississippi Valley Historical Review* 35 (June 1948): 77-90.

Temple, Wayne C. "Dr. Anson G. Henry: Personal Physician to the Lincolns." Lincoln Fellowship of Wisconsin, *Historical Bulletin* No. 43 (1988): 1-15.

Wells, Merle. "Idaho and the Civil War." *Rendezvous* 11 (fall l976): 9-26.

———. "Idaho's Centennial: How Idaho Was Created in 1863." *Idaho Yesterdays* 7 (spring 1963): 44-58.

Williams, George H. "Political History of Oregon from 1853 to 1865." *Oregon Historical Quarterly* 2 (March 1901): 1-35.

Wynne, Patricia Hochwalt. "Lincoln's Western Image in the 1860 Campaign." *Maryland Historical Magazine* 59 (June 1964): 165-81.

Zall, Paul M. "Dr. Anson G. Henry (1804-65): Lincoln's Junkyard Dog," in Richard W. Etulain, ed., *Lincoln Looks West: From the Mississippi to the Pacific*. Carbondale: Southern Illinois University Press, 2010, 174-88.

Notes

Chapter 1

1. These pages draw on, without merely repeating, Richard W. Etulain, ed., *Lincoln Looks West: From the Mississippi to the Pacific* (Carbondale: Southern Illinois University Press, 2010). A very abbreviated section of this study also appears in Etulain, "Lincoln and the Oregon Country," *Lincoln Lore* 1899 (spring 2012): 12-20.

2. This discussion owes much to three books. Published eighty years apart, these volumes add considerably to our understanding of Oregon and the region's connections to as well as differences from national happenings. See Walter C. Woodward, *The Rise and Early History of Political Parties in Oregon, 1843-1868* (Portland: J. K. Gill, 1913), most of which appeared serially in the *Oregon Historical Quarterly*, 1911-12; Robert W. Johannsen, *Frontier Politics and the Sectional Conflict: The Pacific Northwest on the Eve of the Civil War* (Seattle: University of Washington Press, 1955), which was reprinted later as *Frontier Politics on the Eve of the Civil War* (1966); and David Alan Johnson, *Founding the Far West: California, Oregon, and Nevada, 1840-1890* (Berkeley: University of California, 1992). I draw on the factual material contained in the first two books and am much indebted to the insights and interpretations in Johnson's superb volume. Little has been published about the Pacific Northwest in the Civil War era; it is a topic worthy of much additional attention.

3. Dozens of good biographies of Abraham Lincoln are available. I have relied most heavily on David Donald, *Lincoln* (New York: Simon & Schuster, 1995), Ronald C. White, Jr., *A. Lincoln: A Biography* (New York: Random House, 2009), and Michael Burlingame, *Abraham Lincoln: A Life,* 2 vols. (Baltimore: Johns Hopkins University Press, 2008). An even more extensive version of Burlingame's huge biography, with additional sources cited, is available online at the Knox College Lincoln Studies Center, www.knox. edu/lincolnstudies. For a very useful overview of Lincoln's pre-presidential career, see William C. Harris, *Lincoln's Rise to the Presidency* (Lawrence: University Press of Kansas, 2007). A near-exhaustive account of Lincoln's life before 1861 appears in Richard Lawrence Miller's four-volume biography: *Lincoln and His World* (Vols. 1 and 2: Mechanicsburg, PA: Stackpole Books, 2006, 2008; Vols. 3 and 4: Jefferson, NC: McFarland and Company, 2011, 2012). Robert Bray insightfully deals with the books Lincoln read, including those about the West, before and after 1860. See Bray, *Reading with Lincoln* (Carbondale: Southern Illinois University Press, 2010).

4. Lincoln's economic ideas are perceptively covered in Gabor S. Boritt, *Lincoln and the Economics of the American Dream* (1978; Urbana:

University of Illinois Press, 1994). For Lincoln's ties to Whig ideas, see Daniel Walker Howe, *What Hath God Wrought: The Transformation of America, 1815-1848* (New York: Oxford University Press, 2007).

5. The best source for understanding Douglas's leading role in the expansion into the American West is Robert W. Johannsen's thorough biography, *Stephen A. Douglas* (New York: Oxford University Press, 1973).

6. Earl Schenck Miers, *Lincoln Day by Day: A Chronology, 1809-1865* (1960; Dayton, OH: Morningside, 1991), 1: 8-9; February 1843, p. 200; 5 June 1845, p. 252.

7. Roy P. Basler et al., eds, *The Collected Works of Abraham Lincoln*, 9 vols. (New Brunswick, NJ: Rutgers University Press, 1951-1953), 1: 382 (hereafter CW).

8. Kenneth J. Winkle, *The Young Eagle: The Rise of Abraham Lincoln* (Dallas, TX: Taylor Trade, 2001), 202, 238.

9. Dorothy O. Johansen and Charles M. Gates, *Empire of the Columbia: A History of the Pacific Northwest*, 2d ed. (New York: Harper and Row, 1967), remains the most thorough history of the region, but see also Carlos A. Schwantes, *The Pacific Northwest: An Interpretive History* (Lincoln: University of Nebraska Press, 1989).

10. The numbers of emigrants coming up the Oregon Trail differ slightly in varied sources. See, for example, Earl Pomeroy, *The Pacific Slope: A History of California, Oregon, Washington, Idaho, Utah, and Nevada* (New York: Alfred A. Knopf, 1965), 31, and Johnson, *Founding the Far West*, 43.

11. Kent D. Richards, "Growth and Development of Government in the Far West: The Oregon Provisional Government, Jefferson Territory, Provisional and Territorial Nevada" (PhD dissertation, University of Wisconsin, 1966), Robert J. Loewenberg, "Creating a Provisional Government in Oregon: A Revision," *Pacific Northwest Quarterly* 68 (January 1977): 13-24, and Robert W. Johannsen, "Oregon Territory's Movement for Self-Government," *Pacific Historical Review* 26 (February 1957): 17-32.

12. Johansen and Gates, *Empire of the Columbia*, Chapters 12-14.

13. William G. Robbins, "Oregon Donation Land Act," *The Oregon Encyclopedia, www.oregonencyclopedia.org/entry.*

14. Quoted in Johnson, *Founding the Far West*, 42.

15. Burlingame, *Abraham Lincoln*, 1:284.

16. Earlier, historians argued that Lincoln lost Whig support and alienated most of the party in Illinois with his antiwar statements, but more recent historians have proven, with more convincing evidence, that most Illinois Whigs were not upset with Lincoln's antiwar statements. For two of these more recent interpretations, see Gabor S. Boritt, "A Question of Political Suicide? Lincoln's Opposition to the Mexican War," *Journal of the Illinois State Historical Society* 67 (February 1974): 79-100, and Mark Neely, Jr., "Lincoln and the Mexican War: An Argument by Analogy," *Civil War History* 24 (March 1978): 5-24.

17. Eric Foner, *The Fiery Trial: Abraham Lincoln and American Slavery* (New York: W. W. Norton, 2010), 50-62.

18. CW, 2: 22; Harris, *Lincoln's Rise to the Presidency*, 54.

19 . This discussion of the congressional handling of the Oregon territorial debates follows accounts in David Potter (with Don E. Fehrenbacher), *The Impending Crisis 1848-1861* (New York: Harper and Row, 1976), 63-67, Johannsen, *Stephen Douglas*, and Paul Findley, *A. Lincoln: The Crucible of Congress* (New York: Crown Publishers, 1979). CW, 1: 501.

20. Quoted in Donald W. Riddle, *Congressman Abraham Lincoln* (Urbana: University of Illinois Press, 1957), 82.

21. Riddle, *Congressman Abraham Lincoln*, 83; Findley, *A. Lincoln*, 142.

22. CW, 2:323, 1: 505.

23. Here is a clear-cut example of how historian Elliott West's concept of a Greater Reconstruction—calling for the simultaneous and interrelated study of western expansion and the Civil War—can illuminate the complexities of mid-nineteenth-century American history. For West's views on a Greater Reconstruction, see his essay "Reconstructing Race," *Western Historical Quarterly* 34 (spring 2003): 7-26, and West, *The Last Indian War: The Nez Perce Story* (New York: Oxford University Press, 2009), especially xvi-xix, 180, 318-19.

24. Two important sources for understanding the territorial history of the U. S., especially as related to the American West, are Earl Pomeroy, *The Territories and the United States 1861-1890* (Philadelphia: University of Pennsylvania Press, 1947), and Jack Ericson Eblen, *The First and Second United States Empires: Governors and Territorial Government, 1784-1912* (Pittsburgh, PA: University of Pittsburgh Press, 1968).

25. CW, 2:61. Riddle devotes a full chapter to Lincoln's wrestling with the two offers to lead the Oregon territory, *Congressman Abraham Lincoln*, 222-35. Albert J. Beveridge mistakenly concluded that Lincoln was never offered the position of territorial governor of Oregon because he could not locate those materials in the National Archives. See Beveridge, *Abraham Lincoln 1809-1858*, 4 vols. (Boston: Houghton Mifflin, 1928), 2: 195-96. Paul I. Miller, ed., "Lincoln and the Governorship of Oregon," *Mississippi Valley Historical Review* 23 (December 1936): 391-94.

26. Riddle, *Congressman Abraham Lincoln*, 227. Quite possibly Riddle misread Dr. Henry's letter as August 1849, or Henry may have misdated his letter as August when it should have been September 1849; it was in September that Lincoln responded publicly to the offer of the Oregon governorship.

27. Riddle, *Congressman Abraham Lincoln*, 228; CW, 2:65.

28. Michael Burlingame, ed., *An Oral History of Abraham Lincoln: John G. Nicolay's Interviews and Essays* (Carbondale: Southern Illinois University Press, 1996), 136.

29. CW, 2:66. Curiously, even though Lincoln had rejected the Oregon secretary position almost a month before, he received a letter from Secretary Clayton on 17 September asking him for his answer to the

secretaryship offer. Lincoln explained that he had answered Clayton much earlier; perhaps his answer had been lost. CW, 2:65.

30. William H. Herndon and Jesse W. Weik, *Herndon's Lincoln,* eds. Douglas Wilson and Rodney O. Davis (1889; Urbana: University of Illinois Press, 2006), 192-93; Douglas L. Wilson and Rodney O. Davis, eds., *Herndon's Informants: Letters, Interviews, and Statements about Abraham Lincoln* (Urbana: University of Illinois Press, 1998), 480.

31. "Capitol Pageant Review," paraphrased in "Lincoln and Oregon," Portland *Morning Oregonian,* 12 February 1936, cited in Burlingame, *An Oral History of Abraham Lincoln,* 136.

32. Walter B. Stevens, *A Reporter's Lincoln,* ed. Michael Burlingame (Lincoln: University of Nebraska Press, 1998), 157-58; Davis's article first appeared in the *St. Louis Globe-Democrat,* 7 March 1909, magazine section, 3.

33. CW, 2: 65; Burlingame, *An Oral History of Abraham Lincoln,* 15.

34. Ibid.

35. Isaac N. Arnold, *The Life of Abraham Lincoln* (1884; Lincoln: University of Nebraska Press, 1994), 81; Frances Fisher Browne repeats the same story, again without a source, in *The Every-Day Life of Abraham Lincoln* (1887; Lincoln: University of Nebraska Press, 1995), 198; Noah Brooks, *Lincoln and the Downfall of American Slavery* (New York: G. P. Putnam's Sons, 1894), 116. William D. Pederson, "Oregon's Loss, Democracy's Gain," *Oregon Quarterly* 88 (spring 2009): 50-51. Michael Burlingame reviews most of the information available on Lincoln's two decisions concerning Oregon in his *Abraham Lincoln: A Life,* 1: chapter 8, pp. 899-900, www.knox.edu/lincolnstudies. Richard Lawrence Miller provides another brief but helpful overview of Lincoln's rejections of the two offers to serve in Oregon in his thorough volume, *Lincoln and His World: Volume 3, The Rise to National Prominence, 1843-1853,* 239-41.

Chapter 2

1. Roy P. Basler et al., eds., *The Collected Works of Abraham Lincoln* (New Brunswick, NJ: Rutgers University Press, 1953-55): 3:339. Hereafter CW. William C. Harris provides a helpful, well-written overview of this period of Lincoln's career in his *Lincoln's Rise to the Presidency* (Lawrence: University Press of Kansas, 2007). I've also learned much from Richard Lawrence Miller's near-exhaustive volumes: *Lincoln and His World: Prairie Politician 1834-1842* (Mechanicsburg, PA: Stackpole Books, 2008) and *Lincoln and His World: Volume 3, The Rise to National Prominence, 1843-1853* (Jefferson, NC: McFarland and Company, 2011).

2. Ibid.

3. Anson G. Henry to Abraham Lincoln, 16 February 1859, Abraham Lincoln Papers, Manuscripts Division, Library of Congress (hereater ALP), available online at http://memory.loc.gov/ammem/alhtml/alhome.html. All citations to the ALP are from this online site.

4. Ibid.

5. CW, 3:512.

6. These paragraphs owe much to Don E. Fehrenbacher, *Prelude to Greatness: Lincoln in the 1850's* (1962; New York: Mc-Graw-Hill Book Company, 1964), and the superb brief overview in Michael S. Green, "Lincoln, the West, and the Antislavery Politics of the 1850s," in Richard W. Etulain, ed., *Lincoln Looks West: From the Mississippi to the Pacific* (Carbondale: Southern Illinois University Press, 2010), 90-112.

7. CW, 2: 228, 230.

8. CW, 2:275

9. The full Peoria speech appears in CW, 2: 247-83. For the most complete study of the Peoria presentation, see Lewis E. Lehrman, *Lincoln at Peoria: The Turning Point* (Mechanicsburg, PA: Stackpole Books, 2008). I have also learned much from Eric Foner, *Free Soil, Free Labor, Free Men: The Ideology of the Republican Party before the Civil War* (New York: Oxford University Press, 1970).

10. Allen C. Guelzo, *Lincoln and Douglas: The Debates that Defined America* (New York: Simon & Schuster, 2008).

11. Ibid., 191. CW, 3: 145, 146. Eric Foner, *The Fiery Trial: Abraham Lincoln and Slavery* (New York: W. W. Norton and Company, 2010), 107-8.

12. Harold Holzer, *Lincoln at Cooper Union: The Speech That Made Abraham Lincoln President* (2004; New York: Simon & Schuster Paperbacks, 2005).

13. CW, 3:550.

14. The following paragraphs are indebted to the general information included in Dorothy O. Johansen and Charles M. Gates, *Empire of the Columbia: A History of the Pacific Northwest*, 2d ed. (New York: Harper & Row, 1967), Chapters 15-16; and Carlos A. Schwantes, *The Pacific Northwest: An Interpretive History* (Lincoln: University of Nebraska Press, 1989), 95-111.

15. Earl S. Pomeroy, *The Territories and the United States 1861-1890: Studies in Colonial Administration* (Philadelphia: University of Pennsylvania Press, 1947), 73.

16. Joseph Lane's connections with Oregon are the subject of a fine biographical study, James E. Hendrickson, *Joe Lane of Oregon: Machine Politics and the Sectional Crisis, 1849-1861* (New Haven, CT: Yale University Press, 1967).

17. Hendrickson, *Joe Lane of Oregon*, 29.

18. Neither Matthew Deady nor Asahel Bush has been the subject of major studies; both deserve such treatments. On Deady, see Philip Henry Overmeyer, "The Oregon Justinian: A Life of Matthew Paul Deady" (master's thesis, University of Oregon, 1935), and Malcolm Clark, ed., *Pharisee Among the Philistines: The Diary of Judge Matthew P. Deady, 1871-1892* (Portland: Oregon Historical Society, 1975). On Bush, consult Robert W. Johannsen, *Frontier Politics on the Eve of the Civil War* (Seattle: University of Washington Press, 1955); Florence Walls, ed., "The Letters of Asahel Bush to Matthew P. Deady, 1851-1863," (BA thesis, Reed College, 1941); Barbara Mahoney, "Oregon Democracy: Asahel

Bush, Slavery, and the Statehood Debate," *Oregon Historical Quarterly* 110 (summer 2009): 202-27, and Mahoney, "Asahel Bush (1824-1913)," http://oregonencyclopedia.org/entry/view/bush_asahel.

19. William G. Robbins, *Oregon: This Storied Land* (Portland: Oregon Historical Society Press, 2005), 50-51. Anson G. Henry, *Rogue River War. Speech of Dr. A. G. Henry...Dec. 3d, 1855 ...* ([Oregon City]: Oregon Argus, [1855]).

20. Robert M. Utley, *The Indian Frontier of the American West 1846-1890* (Albuquerque: University of New Mexico Press, 1984), 53; Kent D. Richards, *Isaac I. Stevens: Young Man in a Hurry* (1979; Pullman: Washington State University Press, 1993).

21. The fullest account of the Oregon Constitutional Convention is Charles H. Carey, ed., *The Oregon Constitution and Proceedings and Debates of the Constitutional Convention of 1857* (Salem, OR: State Printing Department, 1926). See also, David Alan Johnson, *Founding the Far West: California, Oregon, and Nevada, 1840-1890* (Berkeley: University of California Press, 1992), 139-88, an excellent source to which I am much indebted for its information and insights on the Oregon Constitutional Convention.

22. Johnson provides a systematic chart listing valuable information on all 60 delegates to the Constitutional Convention in *Founding the Far West*, 358-61.

23. Eric Foner points out how the exclusion of free blacks in the proposed Oregon constitution upset some eastern Republicans in Congress and delayed a decision on Oregon statehood for several months. Lincoln's Illinois had such a law excluding blacks. See Foner, *Free Soil*, 288-90.

24. The following pages treating Lincoln's four friends in Oregon draw on Richard W. Etulain, "Lincoln's Links to a Distant Oregon," *Portland Oregonian*, 18 February 2008, and Etulain, "Abraham Lincoln: Political Founding Father of the American West," *Montana: The Magazine of Western History* 59 (summer 2009): 3-22.

25. The best sources on David Logan are Johnson, *Founding the Far West*, 167-72, 288-92; Harry E. Pratt, ed., "22 Letters of David Logan, Pioneer Oregon Lawyer," *Oregon Historical Quarterly* 44 (September 1943): 254-85; and the Harry E. Pratt Collection, Abraham Lincoln Presidential Library, Springfield, IL.

26. Pratt, "22 Letters of David Logan," 259, 260.

27. Ibid., 263.

28. David Johnson makes a strong case for accepting Deady's charges against Logan in *Founding the Far West*, 170-71.

29. Quoted in Pratt, "22 Letters of David Logan," 254.

30. Salem *Oregon Statesman*, 16 January 1855, quoted in Robert W. Johannsen, *The Frontier, the Union, and Stephen A. Douglas* (Urbana: University of Illinois Press, 1989), 24.

31. Pratt, "22 Letters of David Logan," 272.

32. Walter Carleton Woodward, *The Rise and Early History of Political Parties in Oregon, 1843-1868* (Portland: J. K. Gill Company, 1913), 156ff; Johannsen, *Frontier Politics*, 68-70 ff.

33. Woodward, *The Rise and Early History*, 156.

34. George H. Williams, "Political History of Oregon from 1853 to 1865," *Oregon Historical Quarterly* 2 (March 1901): 21; Hendrickson, *Joe Lane of Oregon*, 211.

35. Lincoln to Anson G. Henry, 4 July 1860, CW, 4: 81; Lincoln to Simeon Francis, 4 August 1860, Lincoln papers, Oregon Historical Society; CW, 4:90; Lincoln to Amory Holbrook, 27 August 1860, Holbrook Collection, Oregon Historical Society; CW, 4:101.

36. John T. Hanks to Abraham Lincoln, 22 July 1860, ALP; Lincoln to Hanks, 24 September 1860, CW, 4:120

37. The most useful sources on Dr. Anson G. Henry are Harry Edward Pratt, "Dr. Anson G. Henry, Lincoln's Physician and Friend," parts 1 and 2, *Lincoln Herald* 45 (October 1943): 3-17; 45 (December 1943): 31-40; and Paul M. Zall, "Dr. Anson G. Henry (1804-65): Lincoln's Junkyard Dog," in Etulain, *Lincoln Looks West*, 174-88.

38. Harry C. Blair, *Dr. Anson G. Henry: Physician, Politician, Friend of Abraham Lincoln* (Portland: Binfords and Mort, 1950), 5.

39. CW, 2: 78.

40. CW, 1: 228.

41. Paul Angle, *"Here I Have Lived": A History of Lincoln's Springfield* (1935; Chicago: Abraham Lincoln's Book Shop, 1971), 65.

42. CW, 1: 221, 228; CW, 2: 31, 46, 68-69; CW, 1: 93-94.

43. CW, 2: 78.

44. Elbert F. Floyd, "Insights in the Personal Friendship and Patronage of Abraham Lincoln and Anson Gordon Henry, M. D.: Letters for [sic] Dr. Henry to His Wife, Eliza," *Journal of the Illinois State Historical Society* 98 (winter 2005-6): 226-27.

45. Pratt, "Dr. Anson G. Henry," 1: 15.

46. *Oregon Statesman*, 4 October 1853, 18 July 1854; John E. Tysell, "Anson G. Henry—The Political Doctor," Eugene (Oregon) Roundtable presentation, 12 October 1971, A. G. Henry folder, Yamhill County Historical Society, Lafayette; Edward D. Baker to Anson G. Henry, 11 May 1853, Anson G. Henry Papers, folder 2, Abraham Lincoln Presidential Library, Springfield, IL (hereafter ALPL).

47. *Oregon Statesman*, 13, 20 June 1854.

48. Portland *Weekly Oregonian*, 17 February 1855.

49. *Oregon Statesman*, 20 October 1855; Anson G. Henry, *Rogue River War*.

50. For example, see Stephen Dow Beckham, *Requiem for a People: The Rogue Indians and the Frontiersmen* (Norman: University of Oklahoma Press, 1971), and E. A. Schwartz, *The Rogue River Indian War and Its Aftermath, 1850-1980* (Norman: University of Oklahoma Press, 1997).

51. Edward D. Baker to Anson G. Henry, 15 December 1859, Henry Papers, ALPL: Kay Atwood, *Chaining Oregon: Surveying the Public Lands of the Pacific Northwest, 1851-55* (Blacksburg, VA: McDonald and Woodward Publishing Company, 2008), 137, 150.
52. Henry to Baker, 1857, and Baker to Henry, 18 September 1857, Henry Papers, ALPL; Harry C. Blair and Rebecca Tarshis, *Colonel Edward D. Baker: Lincoln's Constant Ally* (Portland: Oregon Historical Society, 1960), 92-93.
53. Henry to Lincoln, 16 February 1859, ALP.
54. Michael Burlingame, *Abraham Lincoln: A Life*, 2 vols. (Baltimore: Johns Hopkins University Press, 2008), 1:95; Douglas A. Wilson and Rodney O. Davis, eds., *Herndon's Informants: Letters, Interviews, and Statements about Abraham Lincoln* (Urbana: University of Illinois Press, 1998), 431; Albert J. Beveridge, *Abraham Lincoln 1809-1858*, 4 vols. (Boston: Houghton Mifflin Company, 1928), 1: 212.
55. Kenneth J. Winkle, *The Young Eagle: The Rise of Abraham Lincoln* (Dallas: Taylor Trade Publishing, 2001), 115; Richard Lawrence Miller, *Lincoln and His World: Prairie Politician 1834-1842* (Mechanicsburg, PA: Stackpole Books, 2008), 116.
56. Miller, *Lincoln and His World*, 184, 516-27.
57. CW, 1: 206; Miller, ibid, 375.
58. CW, 1: 291-97, 299-302.
59. Miller, *Lincoln and His World*, 156; Wilson and Davis, *Herndon's Informants*, 446; Burlingame, *Abraham Lincoln*, 194, 803.
60. CW, 1: 61, 64, 65, 67.
61. *Illinois Journal*, 16 October 1850; *Oregon Spectator*, 10 April 1851.
62. Simeon Francis to Anson G. Henry, 14 July 1855, Anson G. Henry Collection, folder 2, ALPL.
63. Simeon Francis to Abraham Lincoln, 29 October 1859, ALP.
64. Simeon Francis to Abraham Lincoln, 26 February 1859, ALP; Paul M. Zall, "Simeon Francis, 1796-1872," unpublished essay in the possession of the author.
65. Blair and Tarshis, *The Life of Colonel Edward D. Baker*; Gayle Anderson Braden, "The Public Career of Edward Dickinson Baker," Ph.D. dissertation, Vanderbilt University, 1960; Richard W. Etulain, "Edward Baker (1811-1861)," http://oregonencyclopedia.org/entry/view/baker_edward.
66. William H. Herndon, "Analysis of the Character of Abraham Lincoln," *Abraham Lincoln Quarterly* 1 (December 1941): 436, as quoted in Miller, *Lincoln and His World*, 164.
67. Blair and Tarshis, *Colonel Edward Baker*, 28, 29.
68. Burlingame, *Abraham Lincoln*, 1:213. Burlingame may be a bit too harsh in adding: "In many ways, he [Baker] seemed a perpetual adolescent" (214).
69. Ibid., 214.

70. E. R. Kennedy overstates Baker's role in his book *The Contest for California in 1861: How Colonel E. D. Baker Saved the Pacific States to the Union* (Boston: Houghton Mifflin Company, 1912). The most recent study of California during the Civil War era includes illuminating comments on Baker's years there; see Glenna Matthews, *The Golden State in the Civil War: Thomas Starr King, the Republican Party, and the Birth of Modern California* (Cambridge, England: Cambridge University Press, 2012).

71. E. Kimbark MacColl (with Harry H. Stein), *Merchants, Money, and Power: The Portland Establishment 1843-1913* (Portland: Georgian Press, 1988), 93-95.

72. Johannsen, *Frontier Politics*, 115-18; David W. Hazen, [article on Baker], Portland *Oregonian*, 12 February 1939.

73. Edward D. Baker to Anson G. Henry, 15 December 1859, Anson Henry Collection, folder 2, ALPL.

74. George M. Himes, "David Watson Craig," *Oregon Historical Quarterly* 18 (June 1917): 140-43; *Oregon Statesman*, 19 December 1916.

75. *David Newsom: The Western Observer 1805-1882* (Portland: Oregon Historical Society, 1972), 2, 6, 8-9; Alfred R. Elder to Abraham Lincoln 13 November 1860, ALP; CW, 6:208-9.; Milton H. Shutes, *Lincoln and California* (Stanford, CA: Stanford University Press, 1943), 218.

76. See, for example, Holbrook's letters to Lincoln: 2 October 1860, 20 June 1861, 11 July 1861, 13 June 1863, ALP.

Chapter 3

1. Roy P. Basler, et al., eds., *The Collected Works of Abraham Lincoln*, 9 vols. (New Brunswick, NJ: Rutgers University Press, 1953-55), 4:45. Hereafter CW.

2. Several significant studies of the election of 1860 have been published. In this chapter, for national political trends I have relied most heavily on Michael S. Green's very helpful study, *Lincoln and the Election of 1860* (Carbondale: Southern Illinois University Press, 2011). See also Gary Ecelbarger, *The Great Comeback: How Abraham Lincoln Beat the Odds to Win the 1860 Republican Nomination* (New York: St. Martin's Press, 2008), Douglas R. Egerton, *Year of Meteors: Stephen Douglas, Abraham Lincoln, and the Election that Brought on the Civil War* (New York: Bloomsbury Press, 2010), pertinent chapters in Michael Burlingame, *Abraham Lincoln: A Life*, 2 vols. (Baltimore: The Johns Hopkins University Press, 2008), and William C. Harris, *Lincoln's Rise to the Presidency* (Lawrence: University Press of Kansas, 2007). The three best sources on Oregon Country politics in 1860 are Walter C. Woodward, *The Rise and Early History of Political Parties in Oregon 1843-1868* (Portland: J. K. Gill, 1913), Robert W. Johannsen, *Frontier Politics on the Eve of the Civil War* (Seattle: University of Washington Press, 1955), and James E. Hendrickson, *Joe Lane of Oregon: Machine Politics and the Sectional Crisis, 1849-1861* (New Haven: Yale University Press, 1967).

3. For general backgrounds leading to the election of 1860, I have relied on James M. McPherson, *Battle Cry of Freedom: The Civil War Era* (New York: Oxford University Press, 1988).

4. Woodward, *The Rise and Early History*, 166-88.

5. Oregon City *Oregon Argus*, 11 February 1860.

6. Harold Holzer, *Lincoln at Cooper Union: The Speech that Made Abraham Lincoln President* (New York: Simon & Schuster, 2004).

7. CW, 3:555.

8. Richard J. Carwardine, *Lincoln: Profiles in Power* (London: Pearson Longman, 2003), chapter 3.

9. CW, 4:48-49. See Gary Ecelbarger, *The Great Comeback*, 182, 206n10, for an explanation of the banner wording.

10. For a valuable discussion of some of these terms used in describing Lincoln, see Patricia Hochwalt Wynne, "Lincoln's Western Image in the 1860 Campaign," *Maryland Historical Magazine* 59 (June 1964): 165-81.

11. Doris Kearns Goodwin, *Team of Rivals: The Political Genius of Abraham Lincoln* (New York: Simon & Schuster, 2005), 254.

12. Johannsen, *Frontier Politics*, 113; nearly a century ago Leslie M. Scott in his essay "Oregon's Nomination of Lincoln," *Oregon Historical Quarterly* 17 (September 1916): 201-24, advanced the mistaken notion that Oregon's switch to Lincoln won his nomination in Chicago. Unfortunately, too many Oregon aficionados have followed this false conclusion.

13. Hendrickson, *Joe Lane of Oregon*, 177-104, quote on p. 186.

14. Ibid., 223-30.

15. Kent Richards, "Isaac Ingalls Stevens," http://www.oregonencyclopedia. org/entry/view/stevens_isaac_ingalls/; Kent D. Richards, *Isaac I. Stevens: Young Man in a Hurry* (1979; Pullman: Washington State University, 1993).

16. Joseph Lane to William W. Miller, 15 February 1859, Miller Papers, University of Washington, Seattle; William L. Lang, *Confederacy of Ambition: William Winlock Miller and the Making of Washington Territory* (Seattle: University of Washington Press, 1996), 126.

17. Robert E. Ficken, *Washington Territory* (Pullman: Washington State University, 2002), 50; Roy Lokken, "The Martial Law Controversy in Washington Territory, 1856," *Pacific Northwest Quarterly* 43 (April 1952): 91-119.

18. Elwood Evans, *History of the Pacific Northwest: Oregon and Washington* 2 vols. (Portland: North Pacific History Company, 1889), 1: 511; Robert W. Johannsen, "National Issues and Local Politics in Washington Territory, 1857-1861," *Pacific Northwest Quarterly* 42 (July 1951): 3-31, quote on p. 12.

19. Anson G. Henry to Abraham Lincoln, 16 February 1859, 17 July 1859, Abraham Lincoln Papers, Library of Congress (ALP).

20. Harry C. Blair and Rebecca Tarshis, *Lincoln's Constant Ally: The Life of Colonel Edward D. Baker* (Portland: Oregon Historical Society, 1960),

105; Leonard L. Richards, *The California Gold Rush and the Coming of the Civil War* (New York: Alfred A. Knopf, 2007), 216; Glenna Matthews, *The Golden State in the Civil War: Thomas Starr King, the Republican Party, and the Birth of Modern California* (Cambridge, England: Cambridge University Press, 2012).

21. Simeon Francis to Abraham Lincoln, 26 December 1859, ALP.
22. David Alan Johnson, *Founding the Far West: California, Oregon, and Nevada, 1840-1890* (Berkeley: University of California Press, 1992), 281-82.
23. CW, 4: 82, 81.
24. Lincoln to Simeon Francis, 4 August 1860, CW, 4: 90.
25. Edward Baker to Lincoln, 1 August 1860, ALP.
26. Anson G. Henry to Lincoln, 16 September 1860, ALP.
27. Edward Baker to Lincoln, 2 October 1860, ALP.
28. Amory Holbrook to Lincoln, 2 October 1860, ALP.
29. Anson G. Henry to Lincoln, 3 October 1860, ALP.
30. Blair and Tarshis, *Lincoln's Constant Ally*, 129.
31. *New York Times*, 11 October 1860.
32. Portland *Oregonian*, 3, 14, March 1860.
33. Johannsen, *Frontier Politics*, 117, 123.
34. Oregon City *Oregon Argus*, 10 November 1860.
35. Milton H. Shutes, "Colonel E. D. Baker," California Historical Society *Quarterly* 17 (December 1938): 316.
36. Alfred R. Elder to Lincoln, 13 November 1860, ALP.
37. Simeon Francis to Lincoln, 23 November 1860, ALP.
38. Jon Grinspan, "'Young Men for War': The Wide Awakes and Lincoln's 1860 Presidential Campaign," *Journal of American History* 96 (November 2009): 357-78; Eugene City *People's Press*, 24 November 1860.
39. Richard W. Etulain, "Abraham Lincoln: Political Founding Father of the American West," *Montana: The Magazine of Western History* 59 (summer 2009): 3-22. Some historians and political scientists, looking at western American voting patterns over time, have posited an independent, maverick-like voting pattern starting from the mid-nineteenth century forward. For a brief overview of this perspective, see Paul Kleppner, "Voters and Parties in the Western States, 1876-1900," *Western Historical Quarterly* 14 (January 1983): 49-68, and Kleppner, "Politics without Parties: The Western States, 1900-1984," in Gerald D. Nash and Richard W. Etulain, eds., *The Twentieth-Century West: Historical Interpretations* (Albuquerque: University of New Mexico Press, 1989), 295-338. For an alternative view stressing political continuities rather than discontinuities between East and West, see Earl Pomeroy, *The Pacific Slope: A History of California, Oregon, Washington, Idaho, Utah, and Nevada* (1965; Reno: University of Nevada Press, 2003).

Chapter 4

1. The most thorough study of Lincoln's appointments, political and diplomatic, is Harry J. Carman and Reinhard H. Luthin, *Lincoln and Patronage* (New York: Columbia University Press, 1943). For memoranda concerning Lincoln's possible appointments in the Oregon Country, see Roy P. Basler, et al., eds., *The Collected Works of Abraham Lincoln*, 9 vols. (New Brunswick, NJ: Rutgers University Press, 1953-55): 4: 304-9, 406-7; 5: 163. Hereafter CW.

2. Robert W. Johannsen discusses lists that Edward Baker, Anson Henry, and Simeon Francis compiled, in conjunction with William Henson Wallace (whom Lincoln later named Washington territorial governor), but provides no sources for those lists. See, Johannsen, "The Tribe of Abraham: Lincoln and the Washington Territory," in Richard W. Etulain, ed., *Lincoln Looks West: From the Mississippi to the Pacific* (Carbondale: Southern Illinois University Press, 201), 153-73.

3. The best accounts of Oregon politics in the 1861-64 period are Walter C. Woodward, *The Rise and Early History of Political Parties in Oregon, 1843-1868* (Portland: J. K. Gill Company, 1913), 189-225; Robert W. Johannsen, *Frontier Politics on the Eve of the Civil War* (Seattle: University of Washington Press, 1955), 191-219; and David Alan Johnson, *Founding the Far West: California, Oregon, and Nevada, 1840-1890* (Berkeley: University of California Press, 1992), 280-312.

4. On the controversies surrounding Stark and his abbreviated, contentious months in the Senate, see the extensive account in G. Thomas Edwards, "Benjamin Stark, the U. S. Senate, and 1862 Membership Issues," Part 1, *Oregon Historical Quarterly* 72 (December 1971): 315-38; Part 2, 73 (March 1972): 31-59.

5. Anson G. Henry to Lincoln, 17 October 1862, ALP. The Lincoln letter of March 1862, to which Henry refers, has not been located.

6. Addison C. Gibbs to Lincoln, 12 September 1862, ALP.

7. Holbrook's letters became increasingly critical of Lincoln's patronage decisions in Oregon and Washington. Lincoln ceased answering the letters when they descended into shrill animosity. See, for example, Holbrook to Lincoln 20 June 1861, 11 July 1861, and 13 June 1863, ALP.

8. Quoted in Robert W. Johannsen, *Frontier Politics*, 206, 208.

9. Matthew Deady to Joseph Watts, 20 January 1862, Deady Papers, quoted in Johnson, *Founding the Far West*, 452.

10. Johannsen, "The Secession Crisis and the Frontier: Washington Territory, 1860-61," *Mississippi Valley Historical Review* 39 (December 1952): 415-40; Johanssen, "The Tribe of Abraham."

11. Johannsen, "The Secession Crisis"; Robert E. Ficken, *Washington Territory* (Pullman: Washington State University Press, 2002), 62.

12. It is difficult to sort out what really happened because newspapers and political leaders were extremely partisan and critical of one another. Johannsen and Ficken are more inclined to accept criticisms of Lincoln and his appointees than the present account.

13. Anson Henry to "My dear Genl" [Sen. Edward Baker?], 30 October 1861, B. F. Kendall Papers, University of Washington. This letter, if to Baker, was written after his death in the Battle of Ball's Bluff, sad news that Dr. Henry had not yet received.

14. Anson Henry to Abraham Lincoln, 3 February 1862, ALP. Henry may have had a run-in with Turney, but evidence about their relationship is limited and vague.

15. Willis A. Katz, "Benjamin F. Kendall, Territorial Politician," *Pacific Northwest Quarterly* 49 (January 1958): 29-39; "News Department," *Washington Historical Quarterly* 10 (July 1919): 236.

16. CW, 4: 389; "Letter of General Winfield Scott in favor of B. F. Kendall," 27 May 1861, Bion F. Kendall Papers, University of Washington.

17. Anson G. Henry to B. F. Kendall, 29 September 1861, B. F. Kendall Papers, University of Washington; Ficken, *Washington Territory*, 65-66.

18. Anson G. Henry to "My Dear Genl "[Edward D. Baker?], 30 October 1861.

19. Anson G. Henry to Abraham Lincoln, 3 February 1862, ALP; William L. Lang, *Confederacy of Ambition: William Winlock Miller and the Making of Washington Territory* (Seattle: University of Washington Press, 1996), 144.

20. Paul J. Martin, *Port Angeles Washington: A History*, 2 vols. (1983; Port Angeles: Peninsula Publishing, 2005), 1: 13-29, 205-13.

21. "National Register of Historical Places—Inventory—Nomination Form," 1969; C. Milbrun Boundy, University of Washington, "Custom House dispute, Rise and fall of 2nd National City," undated; Patricia Campbell, "The Victor Smith Saga" and "Chapter 19: End of the line for Victor Smith," unidentified essays, all in Victor Smith files, Washington State Library and Washington State Archives, Olympia. The most extensive source on Victor Smith is Norman R. Smith, "Victory (Biography of Victor Smith)," an unpublished book-length manuscript in the Washington State Library, MSS 066. Unfortunately, the author, the son of Victor Smith, is so positive about his father and so critical of "the copperhead clique" that he is an unbalanced source. Dr. Henry, Norman Smith asserts, was unfitted to serve as surveyor-general, driven only "to find fault with and to discredit Victor Smith so as to cast discredit upon the administration of Mr. Chase as Secretary of Treasury" (p. 32).

22. Henry to J. M. Edmunds, commissioner of federal lands, 12 November 1863, Surveyor General Papers, RG 108, Washington State Archives, Olympia; Henry to Wallace, 6 December 1863, Wallace Papers, University of Washington; William Pickering to Fred A. Wilson, 19, 21 December 1863, Pickering Papers, University of Washington; William Pickering to Abraham Lincoln, 20 February 1864, ALP.

23. CW, 6: 202; Michael Burlingame, *Abraham Lincoln: A Life*, 2 vols. (Baltimore: The Johns Hopkins University Press, 2008), 2:621-22; Marian Parks, "A Man for His Season: Victor Smith 1826-1865" (master's thesis, Claremont Graduate School, 1981).

24. Johannsen, "Spectators of Disunion: The Pacific Northwest and the Civil War," in Johannsen, *The Frontier, the Union, and Stephen A. Douglas* (Urbana: University of Illinois Press, 1989), 58-74.

25. Ficken, *Washington Territory*, 74-75.

26. Ronald H. Limbaugh, *Rocky Mountain Carpetbaggers: Idaho's Territorial Governors 1863-1890* (Moscow: University of Idaho Press, 1982), 13-24; Carlos A. Schwantes, *In Mountain Shadows: A History of Idaho* (Lincoln: University of Nebraska Press, 1991), 49-53.

27. Merle Wells, "Idaho's Centennial: How Idaho Was Created in 1863," *Idaho Yesterdays* 7 (spring 1963): 44-58; Merrill D. Beal and Merle W. Wells, *History of Idaho*, 2 vols. (New York: Lewis Historical Publishing Company, 1959), 1: 329-37.

28. "Original Slate of Territorial Officers 1863," Idaho State Historical Society, *Reference Series*, No. 370, 12 July 1966.

29. Merle Wells, "Idaho and the Civil War," *Rendezvous* 11 (fall 1976): 13; Annie Laurie Bird, "Portrait of a Frontier Politician [William H. Wallace]: The Delegate from Washington Territory," *Idaho Yesterdays* 2 (fall 1958): 12-22.

30. Ronald H. Limbaugh, "The Carpetbag Image: Idaho Governors in Myth and Reality," *Pacific Northwest Quarterly* 60 (April 1969): 77-83; Leonard J. Arrington, *History of Idaho*, 2 vols. (Moscow: University of Idaho Press, 1994), 1: chapter 10.

31. William H. Wallace to Le [Mrs. Wallace], 6 March 1864, Wallace Collection, Idaho State Historical Society.

32. CW, 7: 163-64.

33. Elmo R. Richardson, "Caleb Lyon: A Personal Fragment," *Idaho Yesterdays* 1 (winter 1957-58): 2-6; Kenneth N. Owens, "Frontier Governors: A Study of the Territorial Executives in the History of Washington, Idaho, Montana, Wyoming and Dakota Territories" (Ph.D. dissertation, University of Minnesota, 1959).

34. Limbaugh, *Rocky Mountain Carpetbaggers*, 28.

35. Clark C. Spence, *Territorial Politics and Government in Montana 1864-89* (Urbana: University of Illinois Press, 1975); Michael P. Malone, et al., *Montana: A History of Two Centuries* (Seattle: University of Washington Press, 1976), chapter 5.

36. Anne McDonnell, ed., "Edgerton and Lincoln," *Montana: The Magazine of Western History* 1 (October 1951): 42-45.

37. R. E. Albright, "The American Civil War as a Factor in Montana Territorial Politics," *Pacific Historical Review* 6 (March 1937): 36-46; Robert G. Athearn, "Civil War Days in Montana," *Pacific Historical Review* 29 (February 1960): 19-33, Edgerton quote on p. 21.

38. Robert L. Housman, "The First Territorial Legislature in Montana," *Pacific Historical Review* 4 (December 1935): 376-85.

39. Spence, *Territorial Politics and Government in Montana*, chapter 2.

40. The two best sources on Lincoln and the congressional legislation dealing with the American West and the Oregon Country are Heather Cox

Richardson, *The Greatest Nation of the Earth: Republican Economic Policies during the Civil War* (Cambridge, MA: Harvard University Press, 1997), and Leonard P. Curry, *Blueprint for Modern America: Nonmilitary Legislation of the First Civil War* (Nashville, TN: Vanderbilt University Press, 1968).

41. Gabor S. Boritt, *Lincoln and the Economics of the American Dream* (1978; Urbana: University of Illinois Press, 1994), chapters 14 and 15.

42. The most thorough study of this subject is David A. Nichols, *Lincoln and the Indians: Civil War Policy and Politics* (Columbia: University of Missouri Press, 1978).

43. For a brief but helpful discussion of Lincoln and Indians, see William C. Harris, *Lincoln's Last Months* (Cambridge, MA: Harvard University Press, 2004), 168-75.

44. CW, 7: 112-13; 8: 322. Dr. Anson G. Henry to Abraham Lincoln, 3 February 1862, ALP.

45. Abraham Lincoln to William P. Dole [ca 11] June 1861, CW, 4: 403-4; Henry to Lincoln, ibid.

46. Ficken, *Washington Territory*, 65-68; CW, 7: 284-85.

47. Francis Paul Prucha, *The Great Father: The United States Government and the American Indians*, 2 vols (Lincoln: University of Nebraska Press, 1984), 1: 468.

48. Mark E. Neely, Jr., "Pale-faced People and Their Red Brethren," *Lincoln Lore* 1686 (August 1978): 2.

49. Alvin M. Josephy, Jr., *The Civil War in the American West* (New York: Alfred A. Knopf, 1992).

50. Anson G. Henry to Abraham Lincoln, 21 June 1861, Henry Collection, SC 683, ALPL.

51. Leonard L. Richards, *California Gold Rush and the Coming of the Civil War* (New York: Alfred A. Knopf, 2007), 226, 228; Joseph Ellison, "Designs for a Pacific Republic, 1843-1862," *Oregon Historical Quarterly* 31 (December 1930): 319-42.

52. Johannsen, "The Secession Crisis and the Frontier," 42-44; James E. Hendrickson, *Joe Lane of Oregon: Machine Politics and the Sectional Crisis, 1849-1861* (New Haven: Yale University Press, 1967), 248-49.

53. Jeff LaLande, "'Dixie' of the Pacific Northwest: Southern Oregon's Civil War," *Oregon Historical Quarterly* 100 (spring 1999): 32-81, quotes on pp. 44, 51; G. Thomas Edwards, "Six Oregon Leaders and the Far-Reaching Impact of America's Civil War," *Oregon Historical Quarterly* 100 (spring 1999): 4-31.

54. O. W. Frost, *Joaquin Miller* (New York: Twayne Publishers, 1967), 31, 32.

55. LaLande, "Dixie," 56.

56. Johannsen, "Spectators of Disunion," 63.

57. Limbaugh, *Rocky Mountain Carpetbaggers*, 20.

58. Ronald H. Limbaugh, "Idaho Territory" in Ralph Y. McGinnis and Calvin N. Smith, eds., *Abraham Lincoln and the Western Territories* (Chicago: Nelson-Hall Publishers, 1994), 138-58, quote on p. 139.

59. Governor Caleb Lyon to Secretary of State William H. Seward, 10 August 1864, quoted in Merle Wells, "Idaho and the Civil War," 20.

60. Quoted in K. Ross Toole, *Montana: An Uncommon Land* (Norman: University of Oklahoma Press, 1949), 98-99. For opposing views on the strength of pro-Confederate support in the Montana Territory, consult James L. Thane, Jr., "The Myth of Confederate Sentiment," *Montana: The Magazine of Western History* 17 (April 1967): 14-19, and the opposite and more convincing position in Stanley R. Davison and Dale Tash, "Confederate Backwash in Montana Territory," *Montana: The Magazine of Western History* 17 (October 1967): 50-58.

61. Spence, *Territorial Politics and Government in Montana*, 24.

62. The best overview of these topics is Josephy, *The Civil War in the American West*. I have relied heavily on this source for the discussion of military affairs in the Pacific Northwest in the Civil War years. See also Scott McArthur, *The Enemy Never Came: The Civil War in the Pacific Northwest* (Caldwell, ID: Caxton Press, 2012).

63. Eric Foner, *Free Soil, Free Labor, Free Men: The Ideology of the Republican Party before the Civil War* (New York: Oxford University Press, 1970).

64. G. Thomas Edwards, "Holding the Far West for the Union: The Army in 1861," *Civil War History* 14 (December 1958): 307-24; Josephy, *The Civil War in the American West*, 236-38.

65. Whiteaker quote in Johannsen, *Frontier Politics*, 207; Johannsen, "John Whiteaker, Governor of Oregon, 1858-1862," *Reed College Bulletin* 16 (January 1948): 63-87.

66. G. Thomas Edwards, "The Department of the Pacific in the Civil War Years," (Ph.D. dissertation, University of Oregon, 1963), 133.

67. Harry C. Blair and Rebecca Tarshis, *Lincoln's Constant Ally: Colonel Edward D. Baker* (Portland: Oregon Historical Society, 1960), 125.

68. Alvin M. Josephy, Jr., *The Nez Perce Indians and the Opening of the Northwest* (1965; Boston: Houghton Mifflin Company, 1997), 415 ff.

69. Josephy, *Civil War in the American West*, 251-59; Gregory F. Michno, *Encyclopedia of Indian Wars: Western Battles and Skirmishes, 1850-1890* (Missoula, MT: Mountain Press Publishing Company, 2003), 110-11.

Chapter 5

1. Roy P. Basler, et al., eds. *The Collected Works of Abraham Lincoln*, 9 vols. (New Brunswick, NJ: Rutgers University Press, 1953-55), 7:514.

2. David E. Long, *The Jewel of Liberty: Abraham Lincoln's Re-election and the End of Slavery* (1994; Mechanicsburg PA: Stackpole Books, 2008), xvii.

3. I have found three books particularly helpful for studying the election year of 1864 and have relied on them for general backgrounds in this chapter. Besides the Long volume (in previous note), see John C. Waugh, *Reelecting Lincoln: The Battle for the 1864 Presidency* (1997; New York: Da Capo Press, 2001), and Charles Bracelen Flood, *1864: Lincoln at the Gates of History* (New York: Simon & Schuster, 2009).

4. Robert W. Johannsen, "Spectators of Disunion: The Pacific Northwest and the Civil War," *Pacific Northwest Quarterly* 44 (July 1953): 106-14, reprinted in Johannsen, *The Frontier, the Union, and Stephen A. Douglas* (Urbana: University of Illinois Press, 1989), 58-74. In part, Johannsen's rather narrow and truncated view derived from his primary focus on the years immediately surrounding the outbreak of the Civil War. Chronologically, Johannsen rarely pushed his major examinations of the Pacific Northwest beyond 1862, thus omitting regional reactions through the last years of the war.

5. The classic corrective to Turnerians' overemphasis on the frontier and inadequate stress on eastern influences is Earl Pomeroy, "Toward a Reorientation of Western History: Continuity and Environment," *Mississippi Valley Historical Review* 41 (March 1955): 579-600.

6. David Alan Johnson, *Founding the Far West: California, Oregon, and Nevada, 1840-1890* (Berkeley: University of California Press, 1992), 284.

7. The best general study of Lincoln and civil rights is Mark E. Neely, Jr., *The Fate of Liberty: Abraham Lincoln and Civil Liberties* (New York: Oxford University Press, 1991). On suppressions of Oregon newspapers, see Robert S. Harper, *Lincoln and the Press* (New York: Mc-Graw Hill Book Company, 1951), 232-33.

8. Walter C. Woodward, *The Rise and Early History of Political Parties in Oregon, 1843-1868* (Portland: J. K. Gill Company, 1913), 221-25; Robert Treat Platt, "Oregon and Its Share in the Civil War," *Oregon Historical Quarterly* 4 (June 1903): 108.

9. Robert E. Ficken, *Washington Territory* (Pullman: Washington State University, 2002), 62-78.

10. Leonard J. Arrington, *History of Idaho*, 2 vols. (Moscow: University of Idaho Press, 1994), 1:217; David H. Leroy, "Lincoln and Idaho: A Rocky Mountain Legacy," in Frank J. Williams, et al., eds. *Abraham Lincoln: Sources and Styles of Leadership* (Westport: CT: Greenwood Press, 1994), 143-62.

11. William B. Daniels to William H. Wallace, 2 March 1864, Wallace Papers, Idaho State Historical Society; Ronald H. Limbaugh, "Territorial Elites and Political Power Struggles," in David H. Stratton and George A. Frykman, eds., *The Changing Pacific Northwest: Interpreting Its Past* (Pullman: Washington State University Press, 1988), 79-93, 167-69.

12. Carlos A. Schwantes, *In Mountain Shadows: A History of Idaho* (Lincoln: University of Nebraska Press, 1991), 63-71.

13. Harry W. Fritz, "Montana Territory," in Ralph Y. McGinnis and Calvin N. Smith, eds., *Abraham Lincoln and the Western Territories* (Chicago: Nelson-Hall Publishers, 1994), 164-65.

14. Clark C. Spence, *Territorial Politics and Government in Montana 1864-89* (Urbana: University of Illinois Press, 1975), 31.

15. CW, 7: 122, 228.

16. Gabor S. Boritt, *Lincoln and the Economics of the American Dream* (1978; Urbana: University of Illinois Press, 1994); Heather Cox

Richardson, *The Greatest Nation of the Earth: Republican Economic Policies during the Civil War* (Cambridge, MA: Harvard University Press, 1997), 202, 207.

17. CW, 7: 112-13.

18. CW, 7: 284.

19. Alvin M. Josephy, Jr. *The Nez Perce Indians and the Opening of the Northwest* (1965; Boston: Houghton Mifflin Company, 1997), 415-32.

20. Bruce Catton, *A Stillness at Appomattox* (1953; New York: Washington Square Press, 1958), chapters 2-3.

21. Ronald C. White, Jr., *A. Lincoln: A Biography* (New York: Random House, 2009), 630-32; Catton, *ibid.*

22. Waugh, *Reelecting Lincoln*, 268.

23. William Frank Zornow, *Lincoln and the Party Divided* (Norman: University of Oklahoma Press, 1954).

24. Flood, *1864: Lincoln at the Gates of History*, 261.

25. Henry J. Raymond to Abraham Lincoln, 22 August 1864, ALP.

26. Addison C. Gibbs to Abraham Lincoln, 24 September 1863, ALP.

27. Anson G. Henry to Abraham Lincoln, 18 November 1863, ALP.

28. Woodward, *The Rise and Early History of Political Parties in* Oregon, 228-32.

29. E. Kimbark MacColl, *Merchants, Money, and Power: The Portland Establishment, 1843-1913* (Portland, OR: Georgian Press, 1988), 97; Johnson, *Founding the Far West*, 293; George H. Williams, "Political History of Oregon from 1853 to 1865." *Oregon Historical Quarterly* 2 (March 1901): 1-35.

30. Limbaugh, "Territorial Elites and Political Power Struggles," and Robert W. Johannsen, "The Tribe of Abraham and the Washington Territory," in David H. Stratton, ed., *Washington Comes of Age: The State in the National Experience* (Pullman: Washington State University Press, 1992), 73-93.

31. Simeon Francis to William Pickering, 21 October 1864, in Frank A. Kittredge, et al., "Washington Territory in the War between the States," *Washington Historical Quarterly* 2 (October 1907): 38-39.

32. Don Brazier, *History of the Washington Legislature, 1854-1963* (Olympia: Washington State Senate, 2008), 14.

33. Ronald H. Limbaugh, "The Carpetbag Image: Idaho Governors in Myth and Reality," *Pacific Northwest Quarterly* 60 (April 1969): 78; Merle Wells, "Idaho and the Civil War," *Rendezvous* 11 (fall 1976): 9-26.

34. Wells, ibid; Limbaugh, *Rocky Mountain Carpetbaggers*, chapters 2-3: Arrington, *History of Idaho*, 1: 209-30.

35. Spence, *Territorial Politics and Government in Montana*, 23-24, 30-31, 34; James L. Thane, Jr., "An Ohio Abolitionist in the Far West: Sidney Edgerton and the Opening of Montana, 1863-1866," *Pacific Northwest Quarterly* 67 (October 1976): 151-62.

36. Quoted in Waugh, *Reelecting Lincoln*, 295.

37. George Templeton Strong, *Diary of the Civil War 1860-1865*, ed. Allan Nevins (New York: Macmillan Company, 1962), 3 September 1864, pp. 480-81, quoted in Long, *The Jewel of Liberty*, 211.

38. Long, ibid.

39. Long, ibid., 213.

40. CW, 8: 13, 74.

41. CW, 8:11.

42. CW, 8:18.

43. Zornow, *Lincoln and the Party Divided*, 190-95; CW, 8:46.

44. Michael Burlingame, *Abraham Lincoln: A Life*, 2 vols. (Baltimore: The Johns Hopkins University Press, 2008), 719-30.

45. CW, 8:98.

46. *Oregonian*, 12 November 1864, p. 2.

47. Johannsen, "The Secession Crisis and the Frontier," *Mississippi Valley Historical Review* 39 (December 1952): 415-40, reprinted in Johannsen, *The Frontier, the Union, and Stephen A. Douglas*, 51.

48. Simeon Francis to Abraham Lincoln, 24 October 1864, ALP. Interestingly, at the same time other leading Union Democrats considered Nesmith a loyal supporter of Lincoln because he was a Unionist. See John W. Forney to Lincoln, 24 October 1864, ALP.

49. Charles H. Carey, *A General History of Oregon Prior to 1861*, 2 vols. (Portland: Metropolitan Press, 1936), 2: 784.

50. Fred Lockley, *Conversations with Pioneer Men* (Eugene: One Horse Press, 1966), 251, 252.

51. Matthew Deady to James Nesmith, 12 November 1864, Nesmith Papers, Oregon Historical Society.

52. Ibid.

53. Earl Pomeroy, *The Pacific Slope: A History of California, Oregon, Washington, Idaho, Utah, and Nevada* (1965; Seattle: University of Washington Press, 1973), 148-49.

54. Alfred A. Elder to Abraham Lincoln, 24 October 1864, ALP.

55. William Pickering to Abraham Lincoln, 27 December 1864, ALP.

56. CW, 7: 188; William L. Lang, *Confederacy of Ambition: William Winlock Miller and the Making of Washington Territory* (Seattle: University of Washington Press, 1996), 150-51.

57. Wells, "Idaho and the Civil War," 19, 21, 22-23, 25.

58. CW, 8: 145.

Chapter 6

1. Anson G. Henry to "My Dear Wife," 18, 28 December 1864, Anson G. Henry Collection, SC 683, Abraham Lincoln Presidential Library (ALPL), Springfield, Illinois. Transcriptions of many of Henry's letters are also on file at the Oregon Historical Society, Anson G. Henry Collection, 638. Selections from several of the letters appear in Elbert F. Floyd, "Insights into the Personal Friendship and Patronage of Abraham Lincoln and Anson

Gordon Henry, M. D.: Letters for [sic] Dr. Henry to His Wife, Eliza," *Journal of the Illinois State Historical Society* 98 (winter 2005-6): 218-53.

2. Henry to My Dear Wife, 8 Feby 1865, ALPL. The conflicts over patronage seem to have occurred when Henry was willing to accept into the Republican fold Democrats who would support Lincoln, whereas Pickering, Illinoisian A. R. Elder (a Lincoln-appointed Indian agent in Washington Territory), and Calvin Hale wanted only pure Republicans in their band. Seeing the irony of the divisive Republican squabbling over patronage, the Democratic *Walla Walla Statesman* chortled "Father Abraham is besieged by thousands of Pickerings and Henrys from all quarters of the country." (Robert E. Ficken, *Washington Territory* [Pullman: Washington State University Press, 2002], 77).

3. Henry to My Dear Wife, 9 March 1865, ALPL

4. Henry to My Dear Wife, 13 March 1865, ALPL

5. P. J. Staudenraus, ed., *Mr. Lincoln's Washington: Selections from the Writings of Noah Brooks Civil War Correspondent* (South Brunswick, NJ: A. S. Barnes and Company, 1967), 442.

6. "The Great Atrocity" essay was penned by Harvey W. Scott, his "first regular contribution to *The Oregonian*," in a long, distinguished career including editorship of that newspaper for many years (Harvey W. Scott, *History of the Oregon Country* 6 vols. [Cambridge, MA: The Riverside Press, 1924, 1: 6]. Portland *Daily Oregonian*, 17 April, 1865. This "assassination" issue was reprinted on 7 February 1909 as part of the Lincoln Centennial. The details of Lincoln's assassination and its reception in the state of Oregon are chronicled in Leone Cass Baer, "How the News of Lincoln's Death Was Received in Portland," *Oregonian*, 7 February 1909.

7. *Seattle Gazette*, 20 April 1865.

8. *Walla Walla Statesman*, 21 April 1865.

9. *The Idaho Tri-Weekly Statesman*, 29 April 1865; *The Idaho World*, 29 April 1865; the *Montana Post*, 29 April 1865.

10. Some of the negativity toward Lincoln is covered in "Bitter Feeling in Idaho Then," *Idaho Daily Statesman*, 12 February 1909. See also "When Lincoln Was Shot," 9 September 1901, unidentified clipping, Scrapbook 38, p. 84, Oregon Historical Society. Controversies over reactions to Lincoln's assassination lasted into the decade following his death. In 1876, an Idaho candidate for office, S. S. Fenn, accused of celebrating Lincoln's death in 1865, took his case to court to clear his name. See Territorial Journals, Diaries, Memoirs 1860-1890, Box 60, Ms2-106, Idaho Historical Society, and Merrill D. Beal and Merle W. Wells, *History of Idaho*, 2 vols. (New York: Lewis Historical Publishing Company, 1959), 1: 452.

11. Robert S. Harper, *Lincoln and the Press* (New York: McGraw-Hill Book Company, 1951), 350.

12. Herbert B. Nelson and Preston E. Onstad, eds., *A Webfoot Volunteer: The Diary of William M. Hilleary 1864-1866* (Corvallis: Oregon State

University Press, 1965), 57, 65. On occasion, Lincoln supporters became their own judge and jury in handling pro-assassination outbursts. When one "drunken secessionist" in southern Oregon demonstrated the "feelings of a wicked and depraved heart" via a "full-throated rebel yell," "a good Union man" belted him off the sidewalk. (Jeff LaLande, "'Dixie' of the Pacific Northwest: Southern Oregon's Civil War," *Oregon Historical Quarterly* 100 [spring 1999]: 64.)

13. Matthew P. Deady to John McCracken and others, 22 April 1865, Deady Papers, Oregon Historical Society; Eugene H. Berwanger, *The West and Reconstruction* (Urbana: University of Illinois Press, 1981), 34-38.

14. Mary Ronan, *Girl from the Gulches: The Story of Mary Ronan. As told to Margaret Ronan.* Ed. Ellen Baumler. (Helena: Montana Historical Society Press, 2003), 47, 48. I am indebted to Ken Egan for this citation.

15. The best study of the development of the Lincoln myth and the literary, historical, and popular cultural treatments of the president over time is Merrill D. Peterson, *Lincoln in American Memory* (New York: Oxford University Press, 1994). For the perspectives of a sociologist, much more theoretical in nature, consult Barry Schwartz, *Abraham Lincoln and the Forge of National Memory* (Chicago: University of Chicago Press, 2000), and Schwartz, *Abraham Lincoln in the Post-Heroic Era: History and Memory in Late Twentieth-Century America* (Chicago: University of Chicago Press, 2008). The most recent such study, also from a sociologist, is Jackie Hogan, *Lincoln, Inc.: Selling the Sixteenth President in Contemporary America* (Lanham, MD: Rowman & Littlefield, 2011).

16. George Himes diary, George Himes Papers, 1462, Oregon Historical Society (OHS).

17. Undated [ca. April 1865] newspaper clipping, Scrapbook 112, p. 137, OHS.

18. Simeon Francis letter, 24 May 1865, quoted in Harriet Ramsey Taylor, "Simeon Francis," *Transactions of the Illinois State Historical Society* (Springfield: Illinois State Historical Society, 1907), 329-31.

19. Anson Henry to his wife, 19 April 1865, quoted in Harry E. Pratt, "Dr. Anson G. Henry: Lincoln's Physician and Friend," Part 2, *Lincoln Herald* 45 (December 1943): 38.

20. Mary Lincoln to Eliza Henry, 31 August 1865, quoted in Pratt, "Dr. Anson G. Henry," 38, 39.

21. Undated clipping, Scrapbook 112, p. 137, OHS; George Williams, undated clipping, Scrapbook 50, p. 6, OHS; *Oregonian*, 18 April 1965.

22. *Montana Post*, 1 July 1865, and *Seattle Gazette*, 12 August 1865; *Montana Post*, 8 July 1865.

23. Malcolm Gladwell, *The Tipping Point: How Little Things Can Make a Big Difference* (Boston: Little, Brown and Company, 2000).

24. A major exception to this off-scene treatment of Lincoln came in 1886 in Oregon when stout, aging Republicans William L. ("Billy") Adams and Leander Holmes engaged in an extended, contentious argument

about Oregon's role in Lincoln's nomination of 1860. For this intriguing exchange in the *Oregonian*, see the issues dated 28 March, 11 April, 18 April, 9 May, 16 May 1886.

25. Mrs. Simeon Francis to William H. Herndon, 10 August 1887, in Douglas L. Wilson and Rodney O. Davis, eds. *Herndon's Informants: Letters, Interviews, and Statements about Abraham Lincoln* (Urbana: University of Illinois Press, 1998), 624.

26. Four brief exceptions should be noted: Anne McDonnell, ed., "Edgerton and Lincoln," *Montana: The Magazine of Western History* 1 (October 1950): 42-45; John R. McBride, "Idaho Pioneer Reminiscences," unpublished manuscript, Idaho Historical Society, n.d; George H. Williams, "Lincoln and Grant," *Sunday Oregonian*, 2 June 1895, and "Lincoln as Williams Knew Him," 15 February 1909, unidentified clipping, Scrapbook 50, pp. 5-6, OHS.

27. Hubert Howe Bancroft, *History of Oregon* 2 vols. (San Francisco: The History Company, 1886, 1888); Bancroft, *History of Washington, Idaho, and Montana 1845-1889* (San Francisco: The History Company, 1890). These three books are volumes 29, 30, 31 of *The Works of Hubert Howe Bancroft*. [Elwood Evans, et al.] *History of the Pacific Northwest: Oregon and Washington*, 2 vols. (Portland: North Pacific History Company, 1889).

28. *Oregonian*, 7 February 1909.

29. *Oregonian*, 12 February 1909; *Idaho Daily Statesman*, 1, 7, 8 February 1909; *Anaconda Standard*, 9 February 1909. For a helpful overview of the Lincoln Centennial, see Peterson, *Lincoln in American Memory*, 175-94, which I draw on heavily here. Grand Army of the Republic, *Observance of the Centennial Anniversary of the Birth of Abraham Lincoln February Twelfth, 1909* (New York: J. J. Little & Eves, 1910), provides brief comments on observances in Oregon, Montana, and Washington, but Idaho is missing.

30. *Idaho Daily Statesman*, 12 February 1903; *Oregonian*, 13, 7 February 1909.

31. Peterson, *Lincoln in American Memory*, 183.

32. *Idaho Daily Statesman*, 12 February 1909.

33. (Portland, OR: J. K. Gill Company, 1913).

34. Harvey W. Scott, *History of the Oregon Country*, 6 vols. (Cambridge, MA: Riverside Press, 1924); Charles H. Carey, *A General History of Oregon Prior to 1861*, 2 vols. (Portland: Metropolitan Press, 1935-36). An exception to this general oversight of Lincoln and the Oregon Country was in the work of *Oregonian* reporter David W. Hazen. His newspaper essays and his relatively unknown volume sketched in some of the details of Lincoln's bonds to the Pacific Northwest. See Hazen, *Mr. Lincoln* (Portland: University of Portland, 1941), especially Chapter 4 "Lincoln and Old Oregon."

35. (Seattle: University of Washington Press, 1955).

36. The most important books studying the 1850s and 1860s in Oregon were James E. Hendrickson, *Joe Lane of Oregon: Machine Politics and the Sectional Crisis, 1849-1861* (New Haven: Yale University Press, 1967), and David Alan Johnson, *Founding the Far West: California, Oregon, and Nevada, 1840-1890* (Berkeley: University of California Press, 1992); in Idaho, Ronald H. Limbaugh, *Rocky Mountain Carpetbaggers: Idaho's Territorial Governors 1863-1890* (Moscow: University of Idaho Press, 1982); in Montana, Clark C. Spence, *Territorial Politics and Government in Montana 1864-89* (Urbana: University of Illinois Press, 1975); and in Washington, Kent D. Richards, *Isaac I. Stevens: Young Man in a Hurry* (1979; Pullman: Washington State University Press, 1993), William L. Lang, *Confederacy of Ambition: William Winlock Miller and the Making of Washington Territory* (Seattle: University of Washington Press, 1996), and Ficken, *Washington Territory*.

37. Among these early essays emphasizing Lincoln's links with the Oregon Country are Robert W. Johannsen, "The Tribe of Abraham: Lincoln and the Washington Territory," in David H. Stratton, ed., *Washington Comes of Age: The State in the National Experience* (Pullman: Washington State University Press, 1992), 73-93; David H. Leroy, "Lincoln and Idaho: A Rocky Mountain Legacy," in Frank J. Williams et al., *Abraham Lincoln: Sources and Style of Leadership* (Westport, CT: Greenwood Press, 1994), 143-62; H. D. Smiley, "Washington Territory," Ronald H. Limbaugh, "Idaho Territory," Harry W. Fritz, "Montana Territory," all in Ralph Y. McGinnis and Calvin N. Smith, eds., *Abraham Lincoln and the Western Territories* (Chicago: Nelson-Hall Publishers, 1994), 127-68; and Richard W. Etulain, "Abraham Lincoln: Political Founding Father of the American West," *Montana: The Magazine of the American West* 59 (summer 2009): 3-22.

38. Although there were some Lincoln Bicenntenial emphases in Montana and Washington, neither state organized a state-based committee for the celebration. Abraham Lincoln Bicentennial Commission, *Final Report to Congress and the American People,* April 2010. www.abrahamlincoln200. org.

39. http://lincolnbicentennial.idaho.gov. See also David H. Leroy, "Lincoln and Idaho," and Leroy, "Lincoln and Idaho: A Rocky Mountain Legacy," *Idaho Yesterdays* 42 (summer 1998): 8-25.

40. One volume provided the first thorough overview of Lincoln's relationships with the trans-Mississippi American West: Richard W. Etulain, ed., *Lincoln Looks West: From the Mississippi to the Pacific* (Carbondale: Southern Illinois University Press, 2010).

Index

Boldface numbers indicate an extended treatment of a subject.

About the Author

Richard W. Etulain grew up on a sheep ranch in eastern Washington and graduated with high honors in 1960 from Northwest Nazarene College (now University) in Nampa, Idaho. He earned a master's degree (1962) in American Literature and a PhD (1966) in American history and literature at the University of Oregon. He taught at NNC (1966-1968), Idaho State University (1970-1979), and the University of New Mexico (1979-2001).

He has authored or edited more than fifty books. The best known of these volumes are *Conversations with Wallace Stegner on Western History and Literature* (1983, 1996); *The American West: A Twentieth-Century History* (with Michael P. Malone, 1989, 2007); *Re-imagining the Modern American West: A Century of Fiction, History, and Art* (1996); and *Beyond the Missouri: The Story of the American West* (2006). His most recent works are *Lincoln Looks West: From the Mississippi to the Pacific* (2010) and *Seeking First the Kingdom: Northwest Nazarene University, A Centennial History* (2012).

His writings have won several awards, and he was elected as president of both the Western Literature and Western History associations. In 2000, Northwest Nazarene awarded him an honorary Doctorate of Humane Letters.

He is currently at work on other studies of Abraham Lincoln and the American West and a biography of the Old West woman Calamity Jane (Martha Canary).